self-portrait of a family

Self-Portrait of a Family

Letters by Jessie, Dorothy Lee, Claude and David Bernard

WITH COMMENTARY BY

Jessie Bernard

BEACON PRESS : BOSTON

The quotation by Sally Quinn on page 254 is reprinted
from her article "Old Pals, New Pals, The Generation
Gap," *The Washington Post,* June 5, 1976, reprinted by
permission of The Washington Post.

Library of Congress Cataloging in Publication Data

   Bernard, Jessie Shirley, 1903–
   Self-portrait of a family.
   Includes bibliographical references.
   1. Bernard, Jessie Shirley, 1903–
   2. Sociologists–Biography. 3. Mothers–Biography.
   4. Single-parent family–United States–Case
   studies. 5. Mother and child. I. Title.
   HM22.U6B472 1978   301.42'7   77–88361
   ISBN 0–8070–3798–2

contents

Preface   vii

Before the Letters Began: A Family Album   xvii

Part I   Dorothy Lee and I   1

   Autobiographical Introduction   3
   Chapter One   Report from Graz to Geneva   9
   Chapter Two   Hard Issues, Soft Answers   20
   Chapter Three   Odyssey   56
   Chapter Four   A Losing Battle   90

Part II   Claude and I   127

   Autobiographical Introduction   129
   Chapter Five   Handyman, Assistant, Surrogate   134
   Chapter Six   Hard Issues, Hard Answers   148
   Chapter Seven   Two Major Decisions   171

Part III   David and I   207

   Autobiographical Introduction   209

Chapter Eight   Family and Friends   215
Chapter Nine   Lengthening Tether   232
Chapter Ten   Will the Real David Please Stand Up?   243
Chapter Eleven   Girls and Jobs   259

Part IV   Home and Career   269

Chapter Twelve   Woman's Work   271
Chapter Thirteen   What is Mother Doing?   283
Chapter Fourteen   The Other Child   296
Chapter Fifteen   Reprise   304

Notes   324

preface

As an expression of their esteem and in recognition of her contribution to the advancement of sociology and of her dedication to the Profession and to this Society, her colleagues present Jessie Bernard with the 1971 Merit Award of the Eastern Sociological Society, April 24, 1971.

The District of Columbia Sociological Association presents the Stewart A. Rice Award to Jessie Bernard, scholar, teacher, sociologist, feminist, social critic, for constantly directing the attention of sociologists to public issues, her outstanding contributions to the study of the family and the status of women, and the advancement of the discipline and profession of sociology. Presented at the 23rd annual meeting of the Society in Washington, D.C., March 1, 1974.

The Kurt Lewin Award is granted by the Society for the Psychological Study of Social Issues to Jessie Bernard, 1976, for furthering in her work, as did Kurt Lewin, the development and integration of psychological research and social action, September 8, 1976.

Jessie Bernard, long dedicated to and successful in advancing equality of races and sexes—her writings have been reprinted again and again—they are indispensable to her students and colleagues—her

*honors are many—we add to them now hoping that some day her
honors may equal her merits (Northwestern University, June 18,
1977).*

*It is particularly fitting that Hood—a woman's college—honor
Jessie Bernard. For seven decades she has personified the ideals of
this college, achieving high excellence in writing, in research, and in
public service. She is widely recognized as one of the outstanding
voices in sociology today, as a researcher, a writer, and a feminist
. . . . (Hood College, May 28, 1977).*

I am proud to be the woman who won these, and other accolades.[1] I
would like to believe she deserved them all. As well as all the term
papers and seminar reports and even the doctoral dissertation[2] written about her and her work. But she is not the woman this book is
about. She does appear from time to time—often to explain why she
cannot see a child off to boarding school or meet a returning child's
plane or attend a parents' day event—but only incidentally. This
book is about the mother of those children. And the children
themselves.[3]

In 1972, in what now seems to me a fit of bad manners, I declined an invitation to participate in a conference sponsored by the
New York Academy of Sciences on the grounds that the title—
"Successful Women in the Sciences"—had an "I-made-it-why-can't-
you?" overtone. It was not, as the editor of the volume later
published as *Women and Success* said, that I was "reluctant . . . to
be considered successful," a fact which she interpreted as a "pathetic
revelation" of the fear of success which Matina Horner had revealed
to us as characteristic of women. What deterred me was not fear of
success. It was, as I had said in my refusal, that I found myself
"somehow or other turned off by the aura of elitism" in the title.
If the conference could concentrate on the factors or forces that
made for success among women I would be delighted to participate.
I was later rebuked by my feminist consoeurs who did attend and
I have since regretted the decision myself. But that is a different
story.

Its relevance here is that the idea of the conference began to work
on my unconscious. And when I saw the published papers I was
fascinated, especially by the autobiographies of the twelve success-

ful women included among them. There was an architect, a crys-
tallographer, a mathematician, an electrical engineer, a physicist,
an educator, a horticulturist, a pediatrician, a meteorologist, a physician and public health educator, a chemist and "eco-freak," and a
consumer specialist. The stories of their professional careers were
interesting enough; but the occasional glimpses of their lives as wives
and mothers were even more so. They were, in varying degrees,
engrossing. It occurred to me then that my own life might have been
just as interesting to others as these were to me. A seed was planted
which broke the soil of my resistant unconscious and eventuated
finally in the present book.

Only it was not as a successful professional woman that my own
life seemed to me to warrant recounting. Professional success had
been the least interesting part of my life. Further, my professional
life had been well documented in reviews and critiques over many
years. As contributor, furthermore, to the literature of the revivi-
fied women's movement of the late '60s and early '70s, my life,
along with the lives of dozens of other women would, in due course,
come in eventually for its share of attention. Rather, I would examine my life as a professional women in relation to her children.

The idea became increasingly appealing to me. Especially since
there were—in drawers, trunks, files—a whole cache of letters—some
twenty years of them—between my three children and me—waiting
to serve as a resource. For although neither the children nor I had
kept diaries we had written letters. And kept them. I, theirs; they,
mine. Letters to and from boarding school, college, camp, Honolulu,
Tokyo, Hong Kong, Seoul, Saigon, Stresa, Paris, London, Innsbruck,
North Africa, Limoges, Graz, the USSR. . . . Why a family as peripatetic as ours had kept all those letters I do not know. Perhaps as
physical symbols of family relations? If not exactly as a security
blanket, perhaps still not so far removed from that? Some one had
written that letter. Someone had been *thinking* about them. Someone was *sharing*. Problems, joys, anxieties, pleasures. Lives. So to the
astonished people who raise this question I can only say I just do
not know. But there they were. Waiting to be collated, read, organized, interpreted, invested with meaning.

I was the more challenged because of the remarkable things the
young women historians were doing with nineteenth-century letters

to and from women. They were recreating the experiences of those women and revealing a whole new dimension of life in those days. If, using letters to and from people they never knew, they could produce such interesting results, why couldn't I, using letters to and from people I knew well, do the same? The seed took hold.

But I was not at all sure how to cultivate that seed. I did not know how to handle letters. They are versatile as a medium, but not at all easy to work with. The earliest novels in the English language were in the form of letters; so also were some of Paul's great sermons. Letters have been the foundation for the work of scholars in history, literature, belle lettres, sociology. Important scientific work has been presented in the form of letters to editors of scientific journals. But they are, I was to find, easier to write than to interpret. Before the scholar lies a file of letters, carefully classified by the skillful archivist. Somewhere in those letters there is a book. Or several possible books. It is up to the scholar or researcher to find the best—in the sense of most authentic, least biased, most informative, and, I would add, most sympathetic—book embedded in the raw data.

Since I was so inexperienced in this genre,[4] true to my academic last, I went to the Library of Congress to search for a model and, like a bulldozer digging its way through the earth, I worked my way through the card catalog searching for a pattern to follow. Among letters from mothers and letters from daughters, to sons, to children. They varied widely.

The earliest, from a son to his mother, was dated 1471. John Paston, two weeks after the battle of Barnet, wrote to his mother: "See that my horses are taken care of; and, oh, yes, have my shirts, three long gowns, two doublets, and a jacket sent to me; take care of the 'writings and stuff' on my desk but don't let anyone look at the writings. And please send money."[5] What mother of a son cannot resonate to that letter? Or, take Henry VII in 1547, age forty, writing to tell his mother, Margaret, age fifty-four, that he appreciated her advice about making sure to settle his title to the French holdings but he didn't think it a good idea yet because it would surely involve force.[6] Or, on the mother's side, Catherine of Aragon's letter to her fifteen-year-old daughter in 1531, addressed simply, "Daughter." The queen was glad to hear from the child, especially when the letters showed that she was "well amended." It was good

she was going to Master Fetherstone for Latin because now she
would learn "to write right." She would also like to see her "own
inditing" after Master Fetherstone had gone over it, for it would be
a great comfort to her to see her keep up her Latin and fair writing
and all.[7] What parent of a boarding-school child has not written a
letter pretty much like that? Then, more soberly, Mary, Queen of
Scots, to her son, James VI of Scotland, when he was fifteen, in
1582. She had not heard from him for thirteen years, nor he from
her. Her extreme indisposition during the winter had now caused
her to entreat the Queen of England, her good sister, to permit her
to send an emissary to visit him. She is therefore warning him about
it.[8] Or, in 1638, Henrietta Maria (1601-1661), wife of Charles I of
England, to her son, eight, who was to become Charles II. She did
not like to have to begin her letter by chiding him, but she must because she had heard that he would not take his physic. She hoped
it was only that day and that tomorrow he would take it or otherwise she would have to come herself and make him take it, for it
was for his health. She had given orders to be informed about his
behavior and she hoped she would not have to go to the pains of
doing it herself.[9] Or the redoubtable Abigail Adams to son John
Quincy, age ten, in 1778 in Paris. He was now old enough to improve under the advantages Paris offered if he would but properly
attend to them. They were talents put into his hands for which an
account would be required and he should see to it that he doubled
their number. Still, great learning and superior abilities would be
of little value and small estimation unless virtue, honor, truth, and
integrity were added to them. He was to obey his father as he valued
the happiness of his mother as well as for his own welfare. He was to
write her about his voyage, his situation, and everything entertaining
he could recall.[10] Or the Baroness Bunsen (1791-1876) to her
youngest child, Mathilda, ten in 1853, from Windsor Castle. Mathilda
was to learn to draw for her own pleasure. The baroness hoped she
was taking pains with her reading aloud. She was to try to perfect
and polish herself till she was as "the polished corners of the temple"
described in the Psalms. Such polish rendered the marble corners
beautiful to look at without losing the power of supporting the
building.[11] Or Mrs. Nathaniel Hawthorne to Julian, nine, in Liver-
pool, from Lisbon, in 1855. Julian's letter was delightful, well ex-

pressed, and spelt pretty well. When he saw any spots on his clothes he was to be sure to ask someone to wash them off for him.[12] Or Clara Schumann, to her son Felix. She was glad, now that he was six, that he had a violin; how many notes could he play; she hoped he had a bag for it because a violin was not a toy; her "dear little fiddler" was to be industrious and obedient. When her dear little fiddler was twelve, the tone changed. She had heard that he was thinking of becoming a violinist. She had to impress on him that he should consider this only if he were a genius, for his gifts were not such as would carry him to the summit of art. As the son of Robert Schumann he would be invidiously compared to his father. He had other talents. . . .[13] He became a lawyer.

There were letters consisting of moral and ethical homilies and advice to sons not to marry beneath them. There was Lady Wortley Montagu telling her daughter how to rear her grandchild, and references to mother-daughter relations in other letters, as in Mary Wollstonecraft's to Imlay. Some were filled with gossip and news; some were essays describing travels, some were moral tracts, some were more or less like diaries or journals. There was Madame Montez reassuring her daughter about the liaison her husband had arranged for her; such relations were quite de rigeur. And Madame Savigny—nine volumes!—surely the very paragon of a mother writing to a daughter. They had had time in those days and everything seemed worth writing about. More recently there were letters from a businesswoman to her daughter instructing her how to make good on the job, using market terms to bring home her message: be sure to package your product right and if there is no market for what you have to offer in the way of skills, find out what the market wants and offer that.

There were anthologies of letters from all kinds of people—belletrists, scientists, scholars, what-have-you—to their mothers, each surprisingly different from the writer's public image. Henry James, for example, addressing his letters to "Dear Mammy." But all, at the same time, recognizably the same as their public image. Mark Twain, for instance, trying—too hard—to be funny even behind the scenes. Queens and empresses, businesswomen and actresses, chatelaines and novelists all in their own way writing to their children. Most either themselves colorful persons or placed in colorful positions. No drab characters. No colorless women. No academic women. No professors. And few, as I recall, solo mothers.

The letters were fun to read and they helped me procrastinate in a virtuous frame of mind. I was learning from them. But I had finally to concede that they offered me no model to follow. I did not find one that fit exactly the letters I was to be dealing with. I was going to have to create my own, to find my own way. I was not to know until the book was finished what it was going to turn out to be or what it was to prove to be about.

Although I had found no ready-made model that fit precisely the letters I was to be dealing with, I knew I did not want it to be of the genre that played up the amusing aspects of parent-child relations. Not the cheaper-by-the-dozen, the please-don't-eat-the-daisies, the eight-is-enough, the little-monsters-but-I-love-them genre, though I was to find enough letters to serve as a nucleus for such an approach. For emotion recollected in tranquility can turn into humor as well as into poetry. But I could not see family relationships as humorous or amusing. Mine or anyone else's. They were too power-ful—tragic in the dictionary sense of dealing with terrible things—to deal with frivolously.

I knew that the format of the book could not—should not—be a how-to-do-it one. For I knew that I had never known the best way to be a mother. Or the best way to combine career and mothering. And the letters did, indeed, prove to be filled with self-doubt. I knew I could not teach other women how to do it. All I could hope to do was present an "ungeneralizable" story of one—extremely fallible—mother and her children.

Nor did autobiography seem to me to be the appropriate format. The idea was not new.[14] But I had always resisted it, for it was clear to me if not to others that autobiography was not my genre. Further-more, the letters to and from my children encompassed only part of my life. Not everything was included. And in this book only what the letters dealt with would be relevant. The book to be quarried was mainly in the letters, rather than in my memories or professional records.

But parent-child correspondence was, I knew, especially vulnerable to dullness. Neither party could reveal the underlying stresses in-volved in the relationship. Both had to maintain a delicate balance, as Edward Albee had made so dramatically clear. And a parent could share her interests only at the expense of boring the child beyond measure. So what was left? A host of trivia and banalities. I knew from my reading that a set of exchanges might lead up to a dramatic climax, but the reader would look in vain, as in a play or novel, for a meaningful denouement. Instead, the correspondence would continue as though nothing had happened. What had that been all about? the reader would want to know. What had it meant? It was often hard to tell. Even now, looking back after many years when the significance of events in the letters I was to deal with should have made itself clear, it is still hard to tell. Life, somehow or other, went on. Ups, downs, and all. In drama there is a climax, a denouement, and a resolution. Not so in families. Nor, I knew, had the letters been written with literary pretensions. They would not prove to be literary in either conception or execution. They had not been written for a public, for posterity, for publication. There had been no reading public in the backs of our minds as we had sat down to write. Surely not in the minds of the children and, as surely, not in mine. If I had had posterity in mind I would have been at pains to present a more flattering picture than the one I expected to find in the letters. In some cases I knew the medium itself had been the message. It wouldn't make much difference what the contents of the letters were. It was the idea that counted. The idea that someone was paying attention.[15]

One of the great classics in my own discipline, sociology—*The Polish Peasant in Europe and America*[16]—was based on letters. And a distinguished social psychologist, Gordon W. Allport, had once said that "dyadic relationships tapped by letters constitute a neglected chapter in social psychology."[17] More to the point and especially relevant for the letters I was to be dealing with, "the possibility of using exchanges of letters . . . as a means of studying . . . the parent-child bond" especially "seems almost overlooked by social psychologists."[18] Here, then, was my charter. This obiter dictum spelled out the nature of the book I was to look for.

In preparing this book, I have received assistance from many sources. I am grateful to Mr. Ronald Filipelli, archivist at Pattee Library, Pennsylvania State University, for his perceptive help in dealing with the Bernard archival materials and to his assistant, Mr.

Charles Mann. I am also appreciative of Ms. Raphaela Best's help in getting materials typed.

Since I had lived a long time—some thirty-eight years, in fact—before my first child was born, there was a considerable amount of life and living that has to be given at least a bow in order to see the context in which the letters were written. So, before the letters themselves are presented, a brief glance at their background.

before the letters began: a family album

The paternal and maternal ancestry of the children who wrote these letters came from two totally different worlds. On their father's side, that of eastern Kentucky, and on their mother's, Transylvania in eastern Europe.[1] The genealogical background on both sides remains too vague to reconstruct either one. But my mind has nevertheless sometimes played with the contrast. What would a confrontation between these forebears have been like? What if they had known that in the middle of the twentieth century their family lines would converge in the lives of the children as portrayed in these letters? I am not imaginatively equal to the task of exploring the question and all the possible answers to it. But it has intrigued me.

I sometimes playfully reconstruct an imaginary confrontation between two of the children's ancestors, Hiram Hamilton on their father's side and Bettsy Kanter on their mother's. Hiram Hamilton, of the Kentucky Bernards,[2] was their grandfather on their father's side. Or, perhaps it would be more psychologically accurate to think of him as really a great-grandfather for there was, in effect, a generation missing between the children and Hiram Hamilton's son, Luther Lee, their father, who was in his sixty-first year when the first child, Dorothy Lee,[3] was born and in his seventieth when David, the last one, was. This genealogical hiatus explains the improbable fact that the children had a grandfather who had fought in the 13th Kentucky cavalry in the Civil War. On the Union side, it might be added, and a brave thing it must have been in Kentucky. Bettsy Kanter, as the 1900 U.S. census for Minneapolis listed her, was the children's indomitable great-grandmother on their mother's side. As a young widow in the 1880s she had left her three grown sons in Europe to come to America with her only daughter, the children's grandmother, Bessie.[4] Bettsy was a living presence in my home when I was a child. It was she, in fact, not my mother, who ran the household. At least from where I sat she seemed to be the boss of everything.[5] I have a feeling that Hiram Hamilton and Bettsy Kanter would have understood one another. Both had participated in great historical treks, he from Kentucky to Texas and she from eastern Europe to America, both in the 1880s. Both had been pioneers, both had had to confront frontier challenges. Both strong characters, as I see them. There was a considerable amount of American history encapsulated in the confluence of these two lines.

I have not infrequently searched the hearts and minds of the children for clues of any impact of this ancestry on them. I must confess I find none.[6] Neither Hiram Hamilton nor Bettsy Kanter nor anything they represented was present in the lives of the children who wrote the letters. So far as they were concerned Hiram Hamilton and Bettsy Kanter were "spurlos versunken," as we had learned to say in World War I. No trace of them left in the children's twentieth-century lives. They seemed almost rootless, completely the product of a single generation. The tiny unit we formed was the only matrix in their lives. No grandparents. Uncles and cousins only on their mother's side; only an aunt on their father's. And, for the most part, all so far removed as to be for all intents and purposes, nonexistent. And, because the children came so late in my own life, even my own childhood was remote from their lives.

There was a university, if not in the back yard of my home at least not too distant, and my sister had pioneered the way for me.[7] So, although my parents thought a business college would be much more suitable for a girl there was no serious objection when, not quite seventeen, I entered the University of Minnesota, January 1920. I had great teachers.[8] One of them, L. L. Bernard, enthralled me—literally held me in thrall[9]—from the moment when, at the suggestion of my freshman English instructor, I had visited his class. He seemed to have all the answers a seventeen-year-old could ask for, nor was I the only one who felt this way about him. I became his scholarship assistant, first as an undergraduate and then as a graduate student.

The distance between a mentor-student relationship—flattering as it is on both sides—and bona fide courtship is not great. LLB, as he was known, read poetry and wrote sonnets to me. The sweep of his mind was breathtaking to an acolyte. And it was exciting to be part of the whole intellectual enterprise in which he was engaged[10] and in which he encouraged me to participate. But when the subject of marriage was broached I protested that I could not entertain it. I could not marry him. My parents would object on the grounds of the age difference—more than twenty-one years—and on the basis of religious faith. I could not do such a thing to them. It would wound them too deeply. But, in time, I did. I was twenty-two and one year into a doctoral program. The marriage constituted the first great separation trauma of my life.[11] Family ties were severed, painfully.

Eleven years later, an angry and hostile woman, I left LLB for reasons not relevant here. My flight from marriage constituted a kind of emancipation from his spell and having children became the price I put on my returning. I was in Washington, earning $2,600 in those Depression years, as much as the men I associated with. My name was attached to the work I did when it was published. I was in a position to make my own terms. Why did I impose those conditions?

Why people have or do not have children and why they have as many or as few as they do are questions that have preoccupied social scientists for a long time and still do. Attempts to answer them have constituted a considerable segment of demographic, economic, psychological, and sociological research, much of which implies that rational decisions are involved. In my case I think the desire for children was unrelated to commonly invoked factors—economics, war, social pressures, or Freudian ideology. We had lived in relative affluence during the depression; there had been no economic need to postpone babies. A tenured professor with a $5,000 salary was positively wealthy in those days. He was far too old to be threatened by the draft. There were no pressures on me from friends or family to have children. Nor did I have to prove my femaleness. If anything, the pressures were the other way. In the 1930s, in fact—I can't remember precisely when—I had even written a paper, never submitted anywhere for publication, explaining why I was not going to have children. The reasons given were all properly sociological, standard for the time. I said, LLB had too much to offer through his own work to devote time to fatherhood. (A young scholar, searching the Bernard archives, says it does not sound like me nor seem to reflect my mentality but LLB's.[12] She may be right.)

From time to time while I was carrying my first child I wrote letters to the unborn infant. In one of them, written about two months before the birth was due, I wrote:

. . . all through your life you will be ten to fifteen years younger than you should have been if we had been able to make up our minds earlier to have you. It took us a long

time to make the decision. Your father was reluctant
to bring a child into this kind of world. He felt that in this
day and age parents had so little chance against the outside world of commercialized amusements, propaganda,
and other forces competing for the mind and attention of
children. Parents must necessarily stand . . . for the hard
things of life. The outside forces are interested only in
exploiting the child; they care nothing for his character and
integrity. That is why parents feel they are their enemies.

When I was in a position to counter these apprehensions I
did. I made my return to the marriage contingent on having children.[13]
I think some mutant of the "togetherness" idea may
have had something to do with the terms I laid down.
"Togetherness" in a manner of speaking, that is. I think
now—I did not at the time—that I was seeking "separation-
proof" ties to replace the lost ones. To create a nexus, to
reweave a social fabric. Whatever the reason, having children had become important to me. Then necessary. LLB
wanted me back enough to make the concession acceptable, for concession it was.
On my side the bargain was to prove a good one. The
children may—as both their letters and mine so clearly
show—have caused anxiety, but they brought me also
much happiness.[14] Despite the touched-up phoniness of
the posed picture of January 1941—it was taken for a
college yearbook and this was the way the college wanted
its faculty to look—there is no hiding its radiance. I was
then three months pregnant and inscribed on the back
were these words: "To my beloved child, for a wedding
present. Taken when I was carrying you. Your loving
mother."
The letters to this unborn child began three months
later. They were paeans of joy to the child,[15] who was
due to arrive late in July of that year. Almost embarrass-
ingly ecstatic, they are filled with the dreams I had for
this much-wanted child. But misgivings as well. All the

beauty of spring, but also concern for the babies in Europe born to hunger. A little humor from time to time, as when I described the graduation exercises: "Since I last wrote you I have attended baccalaureate and commencement exercises, hiding you under the voluminous folds of your father's doctor's gown. I am sure no one who did not know you were there could have guessed. Those academic gowns are very fine maternity dresses. As I told one of my colleagues, I could have carried five children without showing it. . . . Everyone was solicitous for you, but neither of us minded it too much, I guess." But mainly expressions of loving anticipation.

The young women in the school—Lindenwood College— where I was then teaching had been lovingly concerned about my welfare all that spring. They had monitored my activities with anxiety. Wasn't I wearing too high heels? Wasn't I running up and down the stairs too fast? Especially at my age—almost thirty-eight? Wasn't the commuting from the city by bus really too strenuous? The answers to all these questions were, doubtless, yes. But there seemed to be no way to brake my pace. I was in a hurry. Gestation took too long.[16]

Planned originally for late May in order to make my return to teaching in the fall more feasible, Dorothy Lee missed the mark by about two months and was born July 23, 1941. The first letter to my first child after she was born reported to her all the events of her birth and the first month of her life. They made "the earlier letters I wrote you in the spring seem rather remote and academic." Now that I was so completely absorbed in her physical care, "the more abstract values in your development are crowded out."

In the fall, Dorothy Lee and I moved out to St. Charles, where the college was located, to spare ourselves the commuting. Three months later there was a solemn letter beginning "My dear little girl, We have just heard the President of the United States ask the Congress to pass a resolution stating that a state of war has existed between the United States and the empire of Japan." And the next week a similar letter from her father. They adumbrated the weight of war and the fear of war that was to hang over a whole generation. Four years later, just before Hiroshima, my second child was born and five years after that, at the time of the Korean military "action," the third.

This, in brief, is the family and historical background of the four authors of these letters.

part I

Dorothy Lee and I

autobiographical introduction

Although the death of the children's father in January 1951 spelled the end of my marriage, it did not yet mark the beginning of my single parenthood. That came two and a half years later. During that brief interval of time there was Ezra who, for all intents and purposes, became the children's father.

It was Ezra who built the work bench in the basement where he and Claude happily hammered and nailed and planed and sawed. He had a true master craftsman's respect for tools, a visceral feel for good workmanship. His hands reacted to wood and metal as a musician's might to a piano, with an artist's kinesthesia. He taught my first son, Claude, the sensuous pleasure of handling good tools skillfully. As surrogate father he attended the father-daughter events that peppered the calendar of Dorothy Lee's scout troop, Sunday School class, PTA events. She was the only one of the three children who had really known their father. She saw Ezra as an interloper. She rejected him, but she was too drawn to him to escape a fundamental ambivalence. She needed him. And punished him for it. He understood. He accepted her punishment. Ezra gave my infant son his only physical experience

with an adult male. He tossed the infant high overhead to
his gurgling, half-frightened delight, gently fed him a
bottle, to his secure contentment. David was always to
feel a filial warmth for the only man who had ever fath-
ered him.

It was Ezra who drove us over the lovely hills and dales
of central Pennsylvania in all seasons. To ten-year-old
Dorothy Lee at camp, for example, I wrote: "It was a
lovely ride and we all enjoyed it, including David, who
helped Ezra drive." It was Ezra who spelled me off in
reading: "In the evening Ezra came over and read Pooh to
Claudie, practically laughing his head off." We all loved
him, each in our own way, even Dorothy Lee.

A quarter of a century later during a visit to David, he
asked about Ezra and me. What was it like in those distant
days? This is what I put on paper for him:

How did I love Ezra? I couldn't count the ways. Not
exactly in the ways Elizabeth Browning loved Robert,
ways I do not understand even to this day, but in more
earthy ways. First of all, in the delight of his vivid way of
expressing himself. "That's a long way to go to fetch an
answer" was the way he once put it to Claude's offering
some outrageous answer to a question. "I found myself
looking at the mothers rather than the students" was the
way he expressed his recognition of the male fortyish
blahs. (He was forty-three when I first knew him.) Stanley
Burnshaw, then of Dryden Press, was as entranced as I was
with his manner of expression and urged him to write.
Put it down. Give me a book. A quite impossible chore for
Ezra. In a letter, yes. But alone, faced with a blank sheet
of paper, he became matter-of-fact and the poetry, the
fun, the energy, the humor evaporated. Only a special few
of us knew the funny, unexpected flashes of insight; only a
small group of intimates evoked them from him.

And he was handsome! The very prototype of every "tall,
dark, and handsome" hero in romantic literature. With the
Byronic intensity that writers endowed such heroes with

but more controlled. Controlled but still burning bright
like the tiger in the night. For there *was,* as it turned out, a
tiger behind that controlled intensity. Such tight control
that only alcohol could relax it. I did not know the dimensions or the costs of that control. If I had, I would
never have tampered with it.

The offer that brought us to the University had been
negotiated by your father. He had been forced into unwill-
ing retirement and was casting about for another position.
At the professional meetings that year he mentioned his
search to Ezra. As it turned out, Ezra had been a long-time
admirer and the idea of getting both of us for his department—he had recently become the chairman—appealed
to him. Your father came as lecturer and I as assistant
professor.

I had thought him attractive from the beginning. And I
was grateful. He was offering us a life line, your father from
his distress and me from having to temper that distress.
He was appreciative of your father at a time when he
needed such appreciation. He coddled him academically.
Whatever he wanted to teach or whenever, the arrangements were made to comply. Even when your father was so
obviously dying, Ezra came by to help him get to class, to
go to meetings.

He was appreciative of me, too, He shot me up the academic ladder to the top in record time. Even before we
became lovers. And during the last three bedridden months
of your father's life he came by every day to pay his respects and ask what he could do. For your father, for me,
for the children. How could a woman not love such a man?

When I read this to David a slightly quizzical look came
over his face. This was, of course, only a rough draft. Because, well, you know, it's awfully sentimental. All those
references. To the Brownings? And Blake's tiger in the
night? Byronic heroes? A slight note of incredulity in his
voice. A question in his almost-embarrassed eyes.

David, David. Of course it's sentimental. People do feel

like that. And not only Victorian poets. Just ordinary people do too. Like Ezra and me. This is the way we felt. That is the way it was.

After LLB's death Ezra continued to drop by every day to see what needed doing. And it was my response to his concern that broke the control. He violated every canon that had held his life together, that had made it possible for him to rise from a blue-collar background to university professor and then to dean. His drinking grew.

The community viewed it all more or less indulgently at first. There was little pressure from Gown; just be discreet was all our professional peers asked of us. Don't make us have to take notice. Town was less permissive. It frowned. Gown could take the recklessness in stride; it could look the other way. Town could not deal with it. And neither could Gown when alcohol triggered a crisis—a public incident that could not be ignored.

The relationship reached an impasse. It became apparent that it could not continue in its equivocal form. He could not forsake the woman he still felt responsible for. So the time finally came for the decision that would either end the relationship or make the new family official. The costs of a decision on the side of the new family would be shatteringly high for him. Enormous agony was involved.

To take myself away from the scene so that he could work it out by himself, I applied for a sabbatical leave. The project I submitted was wholly legitimate. The ostensible, official, manifest purpose was: to study postwar trends in sociological research in Europe and the newly burgeoning research centers then in process of development. It was not without relevance and intrinsic interest. Sociology in Europe was having a rebirth after the collapse of Nazism. A social science that had buttressed racism, that had denuded the universities of their brightest stars, was now being replaced by a social science with a wholly different orientation. A former refugee, once a participant in that renaissance, later told what was happening:

> What took place under the eyes of the fascinated observer was the transformation of an elitist academy into an instrument of higher learning at the service of a modern mass society. These upheavals . . . also destroyed the old ideology. . . . The critical tradition of the intellectual left, exemplified not only by Marx and his successors, but even more by the members of the Frankfurt School of social thought, such as Walter Benjamin, Theodor Adorno, and Max Horkheimer, were incorporated in the mainstream.[1]

German scholars who had spent the Hitler years in the United States were returning to rebuild the great center at Frankfurt. René Koenig at Cologne was introducing the newer American research techniques there. In addition, Oslo was doing interesting work, as were London and Paris. My sabbatical proposal was simply to observe what was happening. I was not even to be required to write a report. There was to be little academic payoff. The payoff was to be psychological.

We settled in Graz, Austria, centrally located and one of the cheapest places in Europe at the time. So it was on the sunny flagstone terrace of a house on a hill overlooking the lovely hills and valleys of the Austrian landscape that I waited in the early autumn days for the letter from Ezra bearing the message. Letters came. But not the message. When it did come, the decision was no. He was not to join us. He was not to become part of our family. There were to be just the four of us: one parent—a mother two generations removed from her children—a daughter, two sons. It was to take a considerable amount of "psychological work" to come to terms with that stark fact. Thus, although on my professional vita the year 1953–1954 shows up as a sabbatical year spent studying the reestablishment and resuscitation of sociological research in postwar Europe, in my life as a woman it was a final apprenticeship year for solo motherhood.[2]

After the first knee-jerk reaction to Ezra's message—a trip to and around Spain with a friend—I settled down to the psychological work called for in learning how to live with the decision—how, that is, to be a solo mother.

chapter one

reports from
graz to geneva

Dorothy Lee was barely twelve when I left her in Ostende
in charge of the boys while I was off to Liège to give a
paper at the meeting of the International Sociological
Association. When I told my European and British colleagues at the conference that I had left my three children,
the oldest only twelve, alone for a week, they were aghast.
You Americans! How strange it was that Americans as children were so much more mature than European children
while as adults they were so much less mature. . . .

I had, of course, made all the arrangements for the children at the pension and planned for bus tours to Dunkirk
and other points of interest. True, I had qualms. But, as I
so often reminded them, before and after, I could not
afford to have children who could not look after themselves. They had to be more responsible than children
whose mothers did not work. Dorothy Lee made no protest at the time. Later, though, she felt it had been too
heavy a responsibility to have placed on her.

We had had a pleasant vacation at Ostende, already recovered enough to present a lovely surface and hide the
ugly debris of war. The children had enjoyed the beaches
but now we were on our way to Geneva where Dorothy

Lee was to spend the year at the International School. It did not occur to me then, as it does now, that it must have been pretty traumatic for her to be left for so long a time, at least until Christmas, so soon after being left with the boys at Ostende. However, I experienced my chronic qualms, for I wrote to her every day, beginning at once. The ties had to be kept close. I wrote about David, about the train, the scenery, the weather, the other passengers, the food, about anything at all to show that we still thought of her. The first letter, reporting the trip from Geneva to Graz, was prototypical of the dozens that were to follow.

                              Salzburg, September 11, 1953
Dear Dorothy Lee,
   Believe it or not, after a very bad beginning, which you saw, we had a good day Wednesday. We went into the dining car soon after we got on the train and filled David up, so that he soon fell asleep and slept most of the way to Zurich. In fact, we had to wake him up when we arrived. It was a beautiful trip. Zurich is wonderful, more like Basle than like Geneva. We found a room in a very nice hotel—Simplon—and went out for a little walk down to the lake. All the way down David wanted me to buy him a watch and all the way back he complained that he hadn't had enough time to play. After supper we went back to the hotel and got to bed fairly early. Yesterday we got up early enough to catch the 9:05 train to Innsbruck. . . . We had lunch on the train just after we left Buchs, but the food was not as good as in the Swiss diner. The scenery in Austria was beautiful, but it was so cloudy and rainy that we could hardly see it. We went through a lot of tunnels.
As usual, David became very boisterous as he became more tired and we had quite a time of it. He drove one man out of our compartment. The other occupant, a girl, was used to American children, being a nurse to an American family at Salzburg. She stuck it out to the bitter end. It was raining when we arrived here and I took the first hotel I could find, the Arleberghof. But I decided not to stay

there, but to make the final dash to Graz today. It is foolish to stay here in the rain. We leave at eleven this morning and arrive at Graz at 8:30 tonight. We are going second
class. I hope it is comfortable. We all miss you and send
you oceans of love.

Mother

The next day, two letters, continuing the saga. The trip
had been through beautiful country, but we had had no
seats; the only way second class was better than third was
that the corridor where we stood was a little less crowded.
Since, however, there was nothing we could do about it we
had just had to grin and bear it. No diner or even buffet, so
we bought food at the stations and from the vendor on the
train. We had arrived only forty-five minutes late, and
found a huge, musty room at Die Goldene Rose. The Benndorfs, who were to be our hosts for the year, were to come
to fetch us in the afternoon. Later the same day, I brought
the story up to date:

Dearest daughter,
    . . . I am writing again to tell you that we are finally set-
tled here and that we have a lovely large room, big as our
living room at home, overlooking a garden. The boys seem
to love it and finally David has a place to play. The view
from the dining room is as beautiful as from our room.

Graz was a provincial capital, known I soon learned, for
its conservatism—there were hints about its Nazi sympathies before and during the war—and a preferred place for
retired generals and civil servants. Even the peasants who
went with the Benndorf estate in true feudal fashion still
looked back to the golden days of the Empire when everything was so much better, including the weather and the
behavior of children. In 1953, the city was bound in all
kinds of red tape; it was in the English sector of a still
divided country. It was still part of a defeated nation.

While there was some war damage, it was nothing like the miles of ruins we had seen in Germany.

The elegant Benndorf house where we were to live had been designed during the time of the Empire to be run by a large staff of servants; it had all the amenities, to be sure, but at a fearful cost in human labor. Hot water for the bath, yes. But a wood fire had to be built each time under the tank which supplied it. And who had the heart to add that chore to the household's load? Beautiful ceramic tile corner stoves in all the rooms, a delight to look at, an unending task to keep supplied with fuel. Laundry facilities in the basement so primitive that they called for a full day's work for a week's linen. Laundromats were just beginning to be introduced and people were only learning how to use them. Simple, plain fare for the table but even so calling for hours of time because the kitchen was so ill-equipped. On sunny days we could eat on the flagstone terrace; otherwise, in the great beamed dining room.

The cast of characters in the Benndorf establishment consisted of the Herr Doktor, Frau Benndorf, their two children—Bernhard and Barbara—Tante Frieda, and Gisela. The Herr Doktor was a gentleman and scholar of the old school, former librarian at the university, who had paid dearly for his anti-Nazi sentiments and activities under Hitler. A burnt-out case. No word of bitterness ever escaped his lips. He spent most of his time in his study, lined with books from floor to ceiling, which looked out over the gardens. Not, like Frau Benndorf, fluent in English, he left us to her care and kept his decorous, polished, aristocratic, but hospitable, distance. Frau Benndorf, also cultivated and well-traveled, had never dreamed as a girl that she would ever have to run a large household without a staff of servants. She had spent some time in England when she was young and had loved it. She had felt terribly cut off under the Hitler regime and was now voraciously curious about the outside world. She had promised us that German would be spoken in the house so we could all learn to speak and understand it. But she

was so eager to practice her own English that all too little
German was actually used. She expressed again and again
the gratitude mothers had felt when the Americans had
supplied warm snacks to school children in the bitter postwar years. Graz was in the British occupied zone; Vienna,
in the Russian sector. There was never any question where
her sympathies lay. Tante Frieda, an elderly relative whose
connection with the family was never quite clear to us,
was lively and alert, hoping she would live long enough to
go to the moon. Gisela, a twelve-year-old grandchild of
Tante Frieda, was as active and adventurous as any of the
other children in the neighborhood despite a slight crippling as a result of wartime polio. Bernhard and Barbara
were teenagers, as hard for their parents to understand as
teenagers anywhere. The usual scene: parents trying to
find out what was going on in their lives outside and the
children determined that they should not succeed. There
was little overt squabbling—usually in informal, family-
style, elliptical German which I could not understand—but
a sort of pervasive evasion. Fearful of their mother's discussions with me in a language they had not mastered,
they shied away from talking to me. My questions, motivated only by my own curiosity, were politely but defen-
sively answered so I never felt I knew anything about
them.[1]

Then, of course, there were the three of us. Claude, eight
years old, pupil in the neighborhood Volkschule, first grade
for reading, third grade for arithmetic. And David, three
years old, a reluctant nursery-schooler. And, though not
in the Benndorf household, there was Ralph Lewis, completely dedicated to his work at the local Amerika Haus.
He had contacts with the most interesting people in the
area, including writers, artists, newspaper people, and
brought into his program any fellow American he could
locate, including me. He supplied a good deal of our extra-
curricular recreation.

It may not be quite true of the almost daily letters I
wrote to Dorothy Lee that if you've seen one you've seen

them all. But they were pretty much of a piece. In addition to the hardy perennial parent-child topic—money—I chatted almost aimlessly about the boys, their clothes, what we were eating, where we were going, what they were doing at school. And, of course, about the weather, the mainstay of so much of everyone's personal correspondence, especially if there is little else to write about and one is determined to fill a certain amount of space. The weather, like weather everywhere, was unusual that year. That winter, we were told, was the longest and coldest in many years, and sunless days more frequent. Unfortunately Dorothy Lee's letters to me have not survived, so her life was only reflected in my response to hers.

I wrote about the boys. "This morning we bought Claude a suit with long pants and we bought shoes for both of the boys. . . ." ". . . today David and I took a little walk to see what it looked like around here. There are pigs, chickens, a cow, and a garden on the north side of this house, but the boys are forbidden to go there. There is a flower garden on the other side, a swing, a little pond or pool, and chairs and tables scattered about. The boys eat enormously, as you know, and these people have all they can do to keep from staring at such appetites. I told the Benndorfs that I wanted the boys to have plenty of milk, and eggs four times a week. They said that was OK. We had bread, butter, and cheese for breakfast with our milk. . . . David will go to school Tuesday, but Claude will wait a week or two until he has learned a little German from Frau Benndorf." In the afternoon we all went to our favorite coffee house for a snack or to Amerika Haus where Claude studied and I worked. "By Christmas when you come here, both of you will be talking German to one another. . . ." An extravagant expectation, this turned out to be.

I wrote of the school affairs I was attending. In March, for example, "I went to a sort of PTA meeting at Claude's school. It was primarily for the parents of children in the fourth grade because next year these children have to decide whether to go to the Mittleschule or to the Hauptschule and this meeting was to discuss the problems involved in making such a choice."

I wrote about David. Early in the fall she had made a
scarf for Claude and I had suggested she might make a suit
for David. She did, and brought it with her when she came
for the Christmas holiday. By March, I wrote, he was still
insisting on wearing it. He wore the short pants inside his
overalls because the weather was too cool to wear them
outside. "He goes around telling people that Dorsy Lee
made them for him. He is very sweet about it." We humored him, I explained, letting him wear both the pants
and bolero because "it might be too small if we wait too
long." On Mother's Day, "Both the boys and Mr. Lewis
brought me bouquets of flowers, but David insisted it was
his mother's day, so he kept his bouquet."

I wrote about the fun I was having or planning to have.
Tobogganing and mountain-climbing with the boys at the
Semmering, rides in the cable car, the nonstop cinema, a
fashion hat show with models from Vienna, a party for
some newspaper people at Amerika Haus, tea with friends
from the university, dinner with an English family, milk
and pastries with the boys at our favorite coffeehouse.
And about the music. Lots of it: opera—*The Three Musketeers*, Paganini, *The Barber of Seville*—and concerts. "Last
night I went to a concert. It was one of a series in honor of
Franz Schubert. They played one of the symphonies that
we have at home on a record, remember?" Even nightclubs:

I didn't get around to writing to you yesterday, this time
for a quite frivolous reason. Friday night I went to a nightclub and did not get home until four in the morning, so I
was quite tired yesterday. . . . As you said to Ezra, my
age is beginning to show. The reason we went to the nightclub was that a Swedish Negro woman was supposed to
sing and I wanted to see and hear her. As you know, a
Swedish Negro is quite unusual. But unfortunately she was
not there; she was in Vienna making a movie, so I didn't
see her after all. . . .

I wrote about my travels, trying to smuggle in a geography lesson or two from time to time. "Both Geneva and Graz are in very high latitudes, about as high as Maine in the United States, but neither one has as cold a climate as Maine. Do you know why?" Or, "I left Spain last Saturday night at nine o'clock. I rode steadily until Tuesday evening, with four-hour waits in Barcelona and Venice. It took me all that time to get back here. Try to imagine a trip from our home in State College as far as Denver; that was how far Spain is from Graz, perhaps 2,000 miles." Again: "I am thinking about our Christmas trip to Italy. Yesterday I got a lot of information about ships and trips but I haven't yet figured things out. It would be possible for you and me to go to Venice, Florence, Rome, and Naples by train and then we could go by boat either to Venice or up to Genoa. You might look all these places up on the map." In January I wrote about a trip to Yugoslavia. I would go by bus to Klagenfurt to get my visa and then on by train to Ljubljana. I had letters to two professors there and I thought it would be interesting. "Ljubljana used to be part of Austria but it is now in Yugoslavia, which is a communist country, in case you did not know." I wrote briefly about one of the professors, son of a famous Partisan and friend of President Tito, in whose lovely apartment I was a guest, about the dance at the university which my hosts had told me was evidence that things were returning to normal. I did not write about the startling contrast between the holiday Christmas gaiety in even the smaller Austrian cities and the grayness of the Yugoslavian scene. In April I reminded her that if I had not heard from her about her own plans I would not be able to leave, as planned, for my trip to London to attend the meetings of the British Sociological Society. When that little item had been settled I sent her my itinerary: London, Oslo, Stockholm, Germany, reminding her not to expect to hear from me regularly for the next three weeks.

Some of the local trips and expeditions were arranged by Dr. Johann Mokre, a professor at the university, to show me the Marshall Plan in action. Demonstration projects, restored vineyards, newly equipped factories and mills. Although everyone was eager to show how successful his particular project was and to make a good impression on an American professor, I did not say much about them in my letters to Dorothy Lee. In fact, I often felt hypocritical. The project managers were putting on such a good show all for nothing. The only person I reported to was in Geneva, didn't give a fig about the Marshall Plan, and hadn't the foggiest idea of what Nazism had been all about.

I did write about Dorothy Lee herself. About her character, for example. In November I praised her for not being jealous of Claude's trip with me:

I forgot to tell you that I am glad you made a good goalie in hockey. That is fine. I also forgot to tell you that I was proud of you when you said you were not jealous of Claude for his trip to the eastern Mediterranean. Of course you and I are going to have a trip alone to Great Britain in April, so I think that makes it about even for you and Claude. So you have no occasion to be jealous of him.[2]

In the fall I wrote also that I was delighted to learn from the school that she had a good attitude and was pleasant to work with. But in the spring, the news was not so reassuring. "I received your report card and was very much disturbed by Madame Reifenberg's statement that you have a hard time obeying the rules of the school community. Please be a responsible, mature member of the community and respect the rules. I am more bothered by that than by the low grade in French." French was something that could be learned. "Please practice French on Olga."[3] I wanted her to take advantage of the last two months of school. By May I was glad she was doing so well in her lessons: eighteen out of twenty was good in French.

Spelling was not so responsive. I began what was to become a merciless, persistent, insistent, never-ending attack on her spelling that was to go on letter after letter, year after year, almost without respite or pity. Here are snippets from some of the letters:

Do you ever have spelling? It seems to me that you ought to do a lot of work on that subject. Here is another list for you to study. . . . Keep this list and study it so that in your future letters you will know how to write them. . . .

* * *

When I got home from Spain there were lots of letters, including your report card. I was pleased to hear that you have a very good attitude and that you are pleasant to work with. That is important. Spelling and punctuation are important too. And a tidy notebook. Just keep on trying. I am sure you can learn to spell if you will concentrate hard. . . . Do you know that every sentence should begin with a capital letter? I am sure you are learning a lot that does not show in your report card. It would be very nice if you showed a lot of learning in your card also. . . .

* * *

Please concentrate on your spelling. Study words as you look at them and remember to capitalize the first word in every sentence. . . .

* * *

How are the lessons going? I wish you would remember that the first word after a period is always capitalized. Your sentences are very nice and interesting. The spelling is improving. There is quite a way to go however. . . .

* * *

I hope all is going well and that you are learning to spell as well as how to skate. . . .

* * *

I am glad you have a new crop of hamsters, but be sure you train them better than the others. It would be a shame to have them eat all your clothes again. It is fine that you are doing so well on the skiing. I hope you are also doing well on spelling. It is good that your composition pleased Mr. James. I am very glad about that. . . .

* * *

I'm glad that you make a good goalie at hockey but . . .

Anyone can supply the rest of that sentence.

I did not write about my work. There were few references to any of my professional activities, little more than snippets, casual references to chores to be taken care of: completion of a paper for UNESCO, papers to prepare for various and sundry professional meetings,[4] talks to be given at the Styrian Sociological Society, little jobs for Ralph Lewis at the Amerika Haus.

And never—well, almost never—anything about the work not even mentioned in my request to the university for a sabbatical, the psychological work I was engaged in. That was not the kind of thing a mother could share with a child. True, in January I commented—apropos of nothing at all—that we seemed to be such a small family. And, true, I did admit in February that I was "beginning to be somewhat depressed by so many days without sunshine," that I was jittery about starting off on the Middle East trip with Claude. But for the most part, although there was little humor in the letters, they were relentlessly and determinedly cheerful and upbeat. I was "delighted with" this, "glad of" that, "pleased about" the other.

It was not until the end of the year that I was ready—even glad—to leave.[5] I knew when I stopped looking at weather reports (in the *New York Times* at Amerika Haus) for the city Ezra had moved to that I had completed my psychological work. At the end of May I was writing that it would "be fun to get home again." Even without Ezra. I had a lot of professional work lined up for the summer; it wouldn't "be too hard to get it done." I was ready to go. Ready to face solo motherhood on my own. We sailed from Genoa on the Andrea Doria just three and a half years after I had become a solo mother. I was no longer a novice.

chapter two

hard issues, soft answers

I had been uncertain about sending Dorothy Lee to boarding school. I wasn't altogether sure in my own mind whether I would be sending her away for her own benefit or for mine, to give her practice in coping on her own in protected circumstances or to save me from having myself to cope with the issues of adolescent rebellion. The roughest period of competition between her and Claude was over. The year at the International School in Geneva in 1953–1954 had gone well; wasn't that enough? I was uncomfortable with the arguments pro and con. The decision came slowly, therefore, even reluctantly. But I did finally decide to send her to George School, a Friends boarding school near Philadelphia. For during her last year in grade school, especially during the summer, I had become less and less certain of my ability to deal with the problems now beginning to surface. A copout? You might well call it that.

But if I had imagined that sending her away to school would make the problems disappear or become any easier to deal with, I was quite mistaken. They remained: friends, clothes, money, school work, rules, character-training, religion, sex, careers. Documented in detail in the letters.

Making decisions was one thing. Implementing them quite another. All through the fall of Dorothy Lee's first year at boarding school issues arose that called for decisions, all of them equally hard for me to deal with. They were hammered out in my mind, always with a Hamlet-like ambivalence and with a powerful superego overlooking the whole process. I was never completely sure in my own mind of the wisdom of my decisions. I agonized over all of them. No wonder that at the end of her first fall at boarding school I was writing, more for my own benefit than for Dorothy Lee's, of my own uncertainties:

It is very difficult to know what is the best thing to do for a child. I am not at all sure that the policy I have followed is the right one. I have been extremely permissive. I have allowed you to do very much as you have pleased. I sometimes wonder if I have been right. I let you drop dancing. Was that right? I let you drop music. Was that right? When you are older will you regret not having any musical training? Etc. I have never forced you to do anything. Sewing, typing, you have played with and then dropped. Should I have put more pressure on you? Will you thank me for not having demanded more of you? Have I allowed you to be less than you are able to be? If I had forced you to continue with music you might have been able to play piano. Ditto dancing, ditto sewing, ditto typing, etc. Have I really done you harm by not forcing you to develop these skills? I often ask myself such questions as these. And even spelling. I have been very unconcerned about this [sic!]. But is this right? Should I take a more authoritarian position in this matter and, whatever the price, force you to take spelling and punctuation seriously? I really don't know.

The uncertainty was compounded when I had to fight to implement decisions I was so unsure of to begin with. And there were quite a lot of them that fall.

If I had had a partner, equally responsible, to share all

the decisions, how different would they have been? Quite different, I suppose—at least some of them. It seemed to me that I lost on every issue with Dorothy Lee. With support I might have won at least some of them. Would she have been happier? better off? or less so? I have sometimes wondered.

My uncertainty about the decision to send Dorothy Lee away to school meant that the moment she expressed a desire to return to State College for high school I reneged. She did express such a desire and I did renege.

In her first letters she reported that although she liked the school she would like to go to State High next year. Could she? And again, five days later, would I let her go to State High next year? She would explain when she came up for the weekend. Immediately overcome with uncertainty and guilt I replied with overkill. Yes, by all means she could go to State High next year. I had told her this, I reminded her, in almost every letter I had written for about a week. In fact, she didn't have to stay there even this year. She could come home at any time and stay. There was no reason for her to stay there against her will. I would not think of putting an ounce of pressure on her. "Please get that into your head. YOU DO NOT HAVE TO STAY THERE EVEN THIS YEAR, CERTAINLY NOT NEXT SEMESTER."

My vehemence was probably intimidating. So, a week later: "I like it here. I have lots of friends. I am tired because we talk late at night. The work is hard and I have to work hard. I am in other words normal so don't worry. I just want to go to State High next year." In my reply I reminded her that high school *was* hard but she had good natural ability and should have no difficulty keeping up; it just took time to get used to it. But the tenor of her letters continued to disturb me. So, on November 6, after a weekend visit home:

My darling,

I have been doing a lot of hard thinking since I saw you off on the bus at noon today. I have concluded that a Friends school was a mistake for a girl like you. Mary Marjorie's mother [her father's first wife] put her in a Friends school in Washington when she was a little girl— much littler than you— because it was supposed to be such a good school. Your daddy objected to this. He said that she was a child who needed bringing out rather than disciplining or repressing. And perhaps the same is true of you. It may be that the atmosphere of the school is not good for you, not nourishing enough emotionally. I feel very bad about this. I mean about my judgment in this respect. Please let me know if you think you should return here next semester. I would be inclined to say you should. It bothers me that you have doubts occasionally about my love for you. It disturbs you terribly if I disapprove of you, which suggests that you are not sure about my love. And I have become convinced that your acne is a psychosomatic reaction to all of this. I feel certain that if I had you here with me for a month your face would clear up completely. . . . You make a perfect adjustment wherever you are; you are at ease with everyone. But your unconscious rebels and takes it out in symptoms—skin in your case. It distresses me no end to think that I made this mistake. . . . There is no reason why you should go away to school. Now that you know how to study you can do just as well here. . . . I can't promise to write every day, but I will be sending you waves of love all the time so that you should feel them all the time. OK? Don't try to be such a perfect girl, darling. Do the best you can without too much anxiety or strain. . . . We think you are pretty terrific just as you are. I think we can see that you get a good education right here at home. We all love you terribly.

Mother

There was another letter the next day in the same vein:
perhaps I had been setting too high standards for her; I had
taken her too much for granted; I had not expressed my
appreciation enough; I had not told her what a wonderful
girl I thought she was. She replied that she wanted to finish
the year there; she wouldn't want to feel that she couldn't
stick it out for the year. I was not to feel bad about her
being there because she was the one who had wanted to
come in the first place. She knew I loved her but when she
had been away for a long time she liked to hear me say it.
And, again, the next day: "I don't want you to feel I am
unbalanced or anything like that. I am perfectly happy
except I don't feel quite right at G.S. You are the greatest
mother anyone ever had. I just can't help being good cause
I am your daughter." I thanked her for her "lovely tribute."
It was "reassuring for a mother to hear that her children
think she is doing a least a moderately good job"; for it
wasn't easy to know what to do for children or how to do
it. By the end of the year Dorothy Lee loved the school
and was already looking forward to the time when her
brothers would be going there too. But other issues were
not to be so easily resolved. Friends, for example.

Dorothy Lee became fourteen in the summer of 1955.
She was going around with Nancy—the daughter of a
neighbor and dear friend—who had just graduated from
high school and was looking forward to college in the fall.
It bothered me that Dorothy Lee was spending her time
with young people so much ahead of her in their development. She, of course, loved it. I had nothing against Nancy
and her friends except that they were four years older than
she was, that they had served their adolescent apprenticeship, that they were ready for adult experiences—including
drinking at parties.

I had hoped that separation would not make the heart
grow fonder. But some of these friends were in school in
Philadelphia and Dorothy Lee was spending a considerable
amount of time with them on weekends. In one of my

earliest letters I expressed some concern: "I was a little bit worried about your insistence on frequent trips to Philadelphia. I want you to make friends at school and spend time with them. The Philadelphia girls have their own friends and although they will always be nice to you it is better for you to stick with your own age group, or at least with school friends." The objections escalated during the fall and at Thanksgiving they became even more vehement, reinforced by my first letter afterwards. Her angry reply came almost by return mail:

I just got your letter of the 20th. I makes me rather mad that you say I can't spend as much time with Hutch and those kids as I have been and want to do. I will spend time with both because I like both and I think I should be the one to decide who I want to be with and when. I can't see any reason why I can't spend as much time with Hutch and Jenny and the others as I want to. . . . Please write and tell me why you decided I can't spend all the time I want to with Hutch. I like her and I have fun when I am with her and I don't think you have the right to tell me who I can see and who I can't. I hope you will reconsider on this subject. Your present decision makes me very unhappy. . . . I hope you change your mind . . . for this is something I feel very strongly about and if necessary I will fight you. I am sorry. I love you very much and I hate to fight with you but here I think you are wrong. It's my life and I want to have some say on how I live it. I always want your help but you don't have the right to say who I run around with. Love you very much.

So, as much to explain the situation to myself as to her, I did write to tell her why I had decided as I had:

You ask me to tell you why I have decided you should not spend so much time with the older crowd, and of course I am glad to do so. . . . You are entitled to know the basis of my decision about your companions. One of the most im-

portant is also one of the subtlest, and I am not sure you
will understand. It is this: when you associate with these
older girls and boys you are in a special, unusual, position
with respect to them. You learn a kind of behavior which
is not that of an equal among equals but that of a pet,
a "mascot," a sort of privileged, protected, position. You
should be having experiences in meeting people of your
own age as equals, not as a pet, not as someone who is
indulged. I don't expect you to understand; I expect you
to deny it. Furthermore, ask yourself what you would
think of a girl's mother if she were some other girl, who
permitted her to go to parties at the age of 14 where drinking took place. Frankly, what would you think? You would
think such a mother didn't care very much about her
daughter. A girl of 14 has absolutely no business at a party
where drinking is going on. It is not that I don't trust you.
It is simply that this is not the kind of party for a girl of
14 to attend. You will find your own age group dull and
boring if you become used to college parties. I feel as
strongly about this as you do. True, as you say, it is your
life. But I do have the right to say whom you run around
with.

I reminded her of the legal rights of parents which, of
course, I would never invoke. But also of the weaknesses
of parents: "A mother cannot fight a child. She is licked
before she begins. I have moral responsibilities as well as
legal ones and there is absolutely nothing I can do to make
you do anything. I have to take care of you. No matter
what you do I must take it. A mother has no alternative.
. . . I certainly cannot lock you in your room or chain you
in the house. But you cannot expect me to approve of
everything you do."
    In one of the best written letters of the year, with the
least number of misspelled words, she replied:

Dear Mother,

I got your letter explaining your reasons for not wanting me to spend so much time with Hutch. I have to agree with you on some points because I can see you are right. But I think you have to take into consideration how I feel about Hutch and the others. I love her and like her friends very much. You can't make a person break away from a group of people because you know it's best. It has to come from me and I don't feel I can or want to. Perhaps we can compromise. I hope so."

Time was on my side. Little by little Dorothy Lee became increasingly absorbed by her own age-group activities and as the years passed the four-year difference in age between Hutch and Dorothy Lee became less and less relevant. Even long stretches of separation did not destroy the bond between them. They remained loving friends.

Money—the hardy perennial issue between parents and children—was a harder issue even than friends to deal with, not because there was not enough[1] but mainly because of my own distaste for the subject. Thus, when Dorothy Lee went off to school, I put my checking account at the local bank in her name and mine jointly. There was no principle involved. I was not doing this for her benefit but for my own. I wanted to be relieved of the—to me always disagreeable—task of handling money. I thought that if she could draw on the account she would be able to take care of her own allowance and I would not have to bother with it. Absurd as it now seems, I expected her to write checks for no more than her agreed-upon allowance. Before the term was over she was asking me please to close the joint account and just send her a check each month. No wonder. This is how it went:

September 20, 1955

Dear Dorothy Lee,

... And do remember that you must count your pennies. Think of all the big expenditures that you have to plan for—Christmas presents, postage, trips, annual, books, supplies, room equipment, etc. That is part of the training we had in mind in giving you a checking account. I will not consider it at all cute or funny if you run out of money before the end of the school year. I will consider it poor judgment and lack of foresight. As I have told you before, this is almost as important a part of your education as the book-learning. . . . Be sure you have all these things in mind and do not spend money recklessly.

September 24, 1955

Dear Mother,

...I am paying for all my school equipment and it's very expensive so don't yell at me. . . .

September 27, 1955

Dear Mother,

... Do you want an account of my money? I'm keeping one. I will send you a copy. . . .

October 1, 1955

Dear Dorothy Lee,

... I have misplaced the letter with your accounts; please keep a little book and do not send me odd slips. You know how likely I am to misplace or lose things (I think calling Philadelphia is an extravagance). Remember you do not have $30 a month but $25. And that has to cover everything. . . .

October 5, 1955

Dear Mother,

... I don't think I should be paying for my gym equipment because when we were planning my checking account

we didn't count on my having to pay. I am not spending
any more than I have to so stop writing me about it. It
bothers me. . . .

November 8, 1955

Dear Mother,
   . . . The trip back here cost more than I thought it would
because I had to take a cab . . . since the bus was so late.
. . . I hope you will have to pay for my Thanksgiving vacation because I have only $4.00 for the rest of November
and I have to go to Philly to see the doctor yet. I think
I will get on to this darn money business better after Christmas. Until then I will have to do without any clothes or
luxuries. It's harder than I thought to handle money. . . .

After that we alternated between monthly allowances sent
to her at school and a joint checking account, but following a bad scene over bouncing checks:

You make it quite difficult for me ever to rebuke you
about anything because you immediately ask if I love you.
The fact that I am angry doesn't at all affect the fact that
I love you. But you do do the craziest things. As you know
. . . I had just assumed that you were sensible about money.
I never went over your checks to see how much you were
spending. . . . But when my checks began to bounce and
I found myself almost $100 short it was extremely em-
barrassing and annoying. It is extremely bad to get the
reputation for making out checks that bounce. It you do
it often enough you lose your credit and you can't have
checking accounts anywhere. When I found myself so
short I checked your checks and found you had spend
$120 in January. Just imagine that! I just don't understand
how you could do such a thing. . . . I hope you will keep
a careful account of your checks and never, never do such
a thing again.

It made no difference. Whichever system we used the difficulties remained—often focussed on another hardy perennial issue between parents and children, clothes. When
Dorothy Lee reported that she was writing a check for $35
for a formal, I replied:

                                November 30, 1955
Dear Dorothy Lee,
   Yes, indeed, the money situation is getting rather serious,
isn't it? I am sure it did not take $10 to go to the doctor
in Philadelphia, so you must have some of that money
left. And are you sure that you must have a $35 dress? I
can hardly believe that a Friends school would require that.
A 14-year-old girl doesn't need a $35 dress. I have had
only one dress in my life that cost that much. Let me look
around State College to see what they cost here. I would
say that you should not pay more than $15 at most. And
it should be a dress you can wear often. Please do not think
that you are 18 years old, even if you do associate with
girls that age. A formal can be the least expensive kind of
dress since it is not worn often. It is the everyday clothes
that have to be good. I suppose ballerina-length is OK
isn't it? I certainly don't think you should have a long
dress at your age. You are nicest and most attractive when
you are acting your age—which is 14. As soon as you try to
act like the older girls you aren't nearly so attractive. So
please get a dress that is suitable to your age. As I say, let
me look here also. When must you have it? . . . I am sure
Laurie won't have a $35 dress. Nor lots of other girls.
I will let you know what I find out about dresses here
tomorrow. In the meanwhile, all our love, Mother.

True to my promise I did make inquiries and reported
them the next day:

December 1, 1955

Dear Dorothy Lee,

I asked Jean Taylor what girls wore here and she said they didn't wear formals yet. So you will have hardly any occasion at all to wear one. The most you will wear it will be two or three times. Don't you think it foolish to put much money into a dress you will wear so seldom? If it is a dress you can wear another year it might be worth while. But it still seems to me an awful lot of money. Please give me details about the instructions you got. Did the school say it had to be formal? There are ballerina-length dresses that could be worn to parties that would be much more practical. I also saw separate skirts and blouses—tightly pleated skirts and velvet jacket-blouses here that cost much less. If you positively must have a formal—which I disapprove of in a 14-year-old girl—get one; but get the least expensive one you can find. Explain to your friends that your mother is an old fogey who doesn't like to spend much money on garments that will be worn only a couple of times. . . . I send you lots of love and hope everything is going nicely, Mother.

This letter enraged Dorothy Lee. She returned it angrily with her reply written all over it in large letters:

Dear Mother,

I am sending you back your letter. I don't want to ever have to look at it again. It makes me very angry. You can't get a formal for $15. You only use them to formal parties. Everyone gets them. I am getting one my way. I need it for the 15th and I won't have you getting one for me. If you get me one I will not wear it. I can get my own clothes.

In the margin where my letter had said, "I am sure Laurie won't have a $15 dress, nor lots of other girls," Dorothy Lee wrote: "I don't give a damn. Lots of others do." And where I had written, "I certainly don't think you should have a long dress at your age" she wrote, "lots of kids my age do"; to my suggestion that she get a ballerina-length dress she wrote "I don't want one."

But even before I had received this angry letter I had continued my almost daily sermon on clothes and money:

December 3, 1955

Dear Dorothy Lee,

. . . What new clothes will you need at Christmas? You had a considerable number of new clothes in September. Why do you need more clothes within 3 months? Do you know that more money is being spent on you this year than many families have for all members? I am sorry to have to remind you of this. Set your standard at the level of, let us say, Laurie, instead of at the level of Cindy and Ginny. We just are not that rich. If you have already spent $35 for a formal, I think that at least $15 of it should be repaid out of your monthly allowance, perhaps $5 a month for 3 months. And I hope you have bought a formal that you can wear next year also. I disapprove of a formal for a 14-year-old, but if you have one there is nothing I can do. You ask what to get me for Christmas. You can get me an ordinary scarf to wear on my head. Please do not get an expensive one. . . .

All's well, fortunately, that ends well. The fracas over the formal ended well. At least a draw. It turned out that though she had planned to write a check for $35 for the dress, she had not yet actually done so. One point for my side. But the dress she did buy was a long one. One point for her side.

December 5, 1955

Dear Mother,

. . . I got my formal and it's the most beautiful one I
have ever seen. It cost $17.95 and the shoes cost $4.95. I
am very proud of myself. I will use the rest of the money
for Christmas presents so I will deduct it from my allowance. I am very happy and I want you to see it at Christmas. . . .

December 7, 1955

Dear Dorothy Lee,

Yes, darling, I am very proud of you and your ability to
buy a pretty formal for $18.00. That was very good. Was it
a hard job? Did it take a lot of shopping around? Who
went with you? Do the others like it? What color, etc.?
. . . I love you oodles and think you are a wonderful little
girl, beg pardon, young woman. . . .

December 8, 1955

Dear Mother,

Thank you for your lovely letter. It makes me very
happy you are not mad at me. . . . My formal is really
lovely. It's white with silver through it. [Drawing] It wasn't
very hard to get it. Judy and Jill know their way around
Philly very well and they have gotten all their formals
there. Sue, a girl from school, went with us. First we went
to one store where the dresses cost $27.95 and were not
too pretty, so then we went to Gimbels and they had so
many pretty ones for $17.95 that I finally chose the one I
got. All the kids at school really love it. . . .

Dear Dorothy Lee,

The dress sounds lovely. I would love to see you in it. . . .

Finish formal episode. But not the perpetual hassles about money. They were to go on indefinitely.

Of course, there were ups as well as downs. By the end of 1955 I was thinking that "motherhood gets nicer and nicer the older children get." And two months later, still high on motherhood, I was thinking that now was "the time that having a family begins to pay off. . . . I think as a family we are definitely over the hump." I'm not sure which hump I had in mind. But, as it turned out, if we were over that one, there were a great many more left to surmount.

But you can't be serious, people would say when I expressed concern about Dorothy Lee's spelling disability. Spelling wasn't *that* important. I was torn between my own sense of the absurdity of making an issue over such a nonrational set of rules as those governing spelling and of making a big deal over it. When I mentioned it to people they reminded me that Dolley Madison couldn't spell either or Nelson Rockefeller or Virginia Woolf, or lots of others. I knew. It wasn't all that serious if you "recommended" or "elimanated" or "seperated." That could even be funny. Or, in a Dolley Madison, even quaint. And correctable. As a more-or-less natural speller myself, I did not at first take spelling too seriously. But I believed that enough people did for poor spelling to cripple a young woman. I could not rule out the importance attached to spelling in a highly literate society like ours and the penalties incurred by nonconformity to the admittedly absurd rules. Nor, I knew, would there be sympathy for her as there would have been if she had had a visible defect. So I did take spelling seriously. It was a festering issue between us for many years and the one topic that brought tears to her eyes.

My conscience has not been kind with me. I cringe at my own tactlessness as, in letter after letter, I dwelt on the misspelled words. No wonder, in one of her first letters from boarding school, she wrote with fine fourteen-year-old sarcasm: "Nothing makes me happier than to receive your letters, especially when you fill them with my spelling mistakes." I deserved this juvenile barb. My frustration with Dorothy Lee's spelling was three-fourths bafflement. How did it happen, I kept asking, that a child with such a high IQ could not spell. There was no question that she was trying. The tears showed her frustration. She wanted so much to win this battle.

So she went willingly, even eagerly, with me to the university clinic to see what help they could offer. How did it happen, I asked the psychologist, that a child so willing, so bright, could not spell? Why couldn't she? At that time and in that place there seemed to be no way to find out. There were no clinical tests that gave any inkling. They could find no sensory or intellectual reason for this disability. Instead they invoked the still fashionable psychoanalytic one. It laid a heavy load of guilt on me. Dorothy Lee refused to spell as a symbolic repudiation of my career. My academic preoccupations constituted a form of rejection of her. In retaliation she would not join my word-based, literate world. She did not want to compete with me. Refusing to learn to spell was her form of rebellion.

Such a diagnosis, putting the blame on my shoulders, was hard to take. Was there anything I could have done to avoid this seeming rejection? If I had given up my work as, from a financial—if not from a psychological—point of view I could have done, would that have made any difference? If her disability had begun after she had come to recognize the academic world and my place in it, I might have been able to accept the clinic's diagnosis despite its too-rational, too-logical, too-neat explanation. But the spelling disability had begun to show long before the idea of competing with me in academia could have occurred to her. It was not until many years later, after dyslexia had been named and researched, that a more acceptable diagnosis was arrived at. As I look back on it now, the nonrational rules of spelling in the English language became for her a paradigm for a lot of the rules of our society. The rage she felt at her problems with spelling adumbrated the rage she, like so many of her generation, was later to feel against the Establishment.

With the issues between Dorothy Lee and me becoming more and more abstract I found they posed real dilemmas for me. As a professional sociologist, for example, I could be dispassionate about nonconformity. As a mother it was much harder, if even desirable, to be. In a book published only a few months after Dorothy Lee's birth, I had written in considerable detail on the subject of nonconformity, a major area of concern in my discipline. I had even laid out "rules" for nonconformity. When she was eight, in another book, I had discussed it even more fully and again in still another, published when she was sixteen. There was never a blanket defense of conformity; there was always recognition of the inevitability, importance, even at times necessity, for nonconformity. Par for the course professionally.

But for a schoolgirl at an age when rebellion was de rigeur it had seemed to me that conformity to school rules was important. There was quite a bit on that subject throughout all the years of the correspondence between Dorothy Lee and me. When she was twelve, at the International School in Geneva, I had written how sorry I was that she had such a hard time with the rules. Early in October of her first year at boarding school I was again expressing my disappointment that she felt "rebellious about the school rules" and hopes that she was "being a good citizen and respecting the community rules."

Later that year I wrote I was sorry to hear that she had taken to smoking. "You know how I feel about it. Perhaps my objection makes it more exciting, something to laugh about with the others. My wish is that you do not. Can you stand up to not going along with the crowd on this matter? Please do." By return mail, a postscript: "I don't smoke. I just tried it." But during the next year I was called one evening and told by the school that Dorothy Lee and a friend had been caught smoking in their room in the dormitory. The punishment was a heavy load of demerits that would deprive her of privileges for a long time. She was floored that I sided with the school. She had expected me to defend her. It was one of the few times, I believe, when I was not on her side. When the headmaster wrote to me he said that her case would be reviewed after four weeks and I was able to tell her that "if everything is OK it won't even go on your record." The next month, reporting on four senior girls who had been suspended for a week and gotten four demerits for drinking at school, Dorothy Lee wrote: "I feel sorry for them but am thankful I have learned my lesson now. I get off demerit day after tomorrow and am going into Philadelphia." Two months later the subject was still on my mind. "All I ask is that you comply with the rules of the school. If there is pressure on you to smoke just tell them that you have a funny mother who is so silly as to want you to follow the doctor's orders." The smoking issue remained unresolved. I kept sending newspaper stories about smoking and cancer: "Expect clippings of the kind herewith enclosed as long as I live. I can't keep you from subjecting yourself to the danger of cancer but I can make you feel guilty about it, which I propose to do, so that you won't be as likely to smoke yourself into cancer anyway. (Some people are funny that way, n'est-çe pas?)"

If consistency is the mark of a good parent, as we are told, then I was surely not a good one. In one letter I scolded Dorothy Lee for her hostility toward the adult world but in another, addressed to her school, I wrote that she did "not feel the hostility toward the adult world that so many adolescents feel and which impels them toward defiance." In one letter I was rebuking her for her cockiness. In another I was bemoaning her lack of self-confidence. In one letter I was criticizing her for her inability to study. In another I felt "heart-broken when I think of you crying about your grades in French and algebra." I was disturbed by her "increasing disregard for other people." Then I feared she was "too good."

The inconsistency was a reflection of my own self-

doubts. In a letter to the school headmaster when Dorothy
Lee was sixteen, I supported the demerit she had been
given "for being in a group of boys and girls at a place
where they are not permitted to be together," and then
proceeded to explicate for myself as much as for him,
my own child-rearing principles and the difficulties in
applying them:

It is always a problem for a parent to know how much
freedom and how much discipline to impose on a child. I
have tended to lean in the direction of freedom on the
theory that children must learn to stand on their own two
feet and make their moral decisions themselves. But perhaps I have not given her enough support. The problem
in Dorothy Lee's case has been complicated by the fact
that she has had no father since she was nine years old.
When I show disapproval of her behavior it seems to her
that I do not love her and this depresses her and demor-
alizes her.

I assured him that she now sounded contrite, that her behavior was thoughtless, though I recognized that "thought-
lessness can have just as serious consequences as deliberate
flouting of rules." On the copy of this letter which I sent
to Dorothy Lee I added: "Well, so much for that. Let's
not discuss it any more." She was as glad as I was to drop
the subject. It was as painful to her as to me.

   Still, despite letdowns and disappointments from time to
time, I persisted in my belief in permitting as much autonomy as possible.

                                          December 14, 1958
Dear Dorothy Lee,
   The lesson for today is "obedience" and "disobedience."
As you probably know, I am not a great believer in the
virtues of obedience per se. And just as soon as I possibly
can I want to turn over the management of my children's
lives to them. For several reasons: one, I don't like to have

to assume the responsibility any longer than is necessary; two, I have to prepare them for the time when I pass from the scene. You have told me that you are willing to assume the responsibility for your decisions. To the extent that this is so, I want you to make your decisions. I won't always agree with them. But that is beside the point. If I am not going to have to pay for them, if you are going to pay for them, it is not my business. I don't want you to interpret this as rejection of you. I will continue to assume responsibility where you want me to, or at least to share responsibility. But I am anxious for you to take more charge of your life. I would even turn over your money to you except that this is one area where you don't yet assume responsibility. What all this amounts to is that you don't have to ask permission to do things. I would like to be kept informed, of course. But I would like you to be as adult-like as possible. . . . I am not sure that I have made myself clear, but if you study what I have said I think you will get it.

She did, indeed, get it. And I was—five years later—to rue the day she did.

Other aspects of "character-training" drew fire also, like the "increasing disregard for others." In the spring of her sophomore year we were planning a trip through the Panama Canal to Ecuador on a banana boat with provision for eight passengers in four cabins. Two of Dorothy Lee's friends were coming along with us. And so was Stella, our live-in housekeeper.[2] The boys were to share one cabin; Dorothy Lee's friends another; she and I, the third; and Stella, the fourth. When Dorothy Lee wrote asking if she could have Stella's cabin instead of sharing mine, I was incensed and I wrote one of the kind of letters that now make me wince. Under the theme of selfishness, I pointed out that this was probably the only trip Stella would ever take in her life; we ought to make it as pleasant as possible for her. Dorothy Lee herself would take lots of trips in her life so a minor inconvenience like sharing a cabin with me wasn't all that big a deal. I sailed into her for her self-centeredness and lack of concern for Stella's comfort. It was not one of my most loving letters.

Ethics and religion were easier to deal with than these subtler and more personal qualities. From time to time, Dorothy Lee asked me for help with her courses. Reading lists, for example. Philosophy, psychology, the nature of groups, all, of course, suitable channels for didactic responses from me. Especially current events: was it good that the labor unions in the South wanted to break away and form a Southern Federation of Labor? Barbara said labor had too much power. Was that right? She didn't think so, did I? The weight of the world began to bear on her. She began to feel "guilty to hear about the way some people live because I have so much and take it for granted." Her question about religion elicited a lengthy reply.

Dorothy Lee's father had become an agnostic as a boy when his high school teachers introduced him to Herbert Spencer; religion was a sociological rather than an emotional concern to him. I was eclectic.[3] So when we had first come to State College I was quite willing for Dorothy Lee to shop around at the several churches for the Sunday School she liked best. It turned out to be the Presbyterian one. Mrs. Inga Johnson knew her way around a Sunday School class and Dorothy Lee came home with enthusiastic reports and lots of art work. But after a year or so she became more peripatetic and visited around with her friends. At Geneva she had gone to Mass with her roommate, Olga. And now at George School she was attending Friends' Meeting; from time to time she went to Mass with friends. Not until she was a senior did she become interested in Judaism as part of her course on religion. She wrote that her teacher had promised to tutor her because she wanted to know more about Judaism. She asked me to tell her about it. I was, of course, happy to comply. And I did—in smothering detail:

February 26, 1959

Dear Dorothy Lee,

It is awfully nice of your religion teacher to give you tutorial attention. If you can express my appreciation to him without seeming to be apple-polishing I would appreciate it. Now as to Judaism. This, as you know, is a complicated topic and I don't know just how to begin. Because Judaism, like, let us say, Hinduism, has become so intertwined with customs that it is hard to tell where religion leaves off and culture begins.

There was a Semitic-language tribe in the pastoral stage of development; that is, they were nomadic cattle and sheep growers who moved with their flocks wherever the grazing was good. Once when it was very dry they went down to Egypt. They remained there a long time, much exploited. They finally left Egypt and wandered in the desert for a long time (more than 40 years). These people worshipped animals (Golden Calf story) and had graven images and lots of gods. Little by little, though, they came, or their leaders came, to conceive of a single God. Also they developed a pastoral code of ethics. After a long sojourn in the desert they came to Canaan. The people in Canaan were an agricultural people, with agricultural ethics, and many local gods, called Baalim. The pastoral Hebrews were shocked at the agricultural Canaanites. There was much conflict and controversy between the Hebrew concept of Yawah and the local concept of Baal. They even had a contest to see whose god was better, remember? I think it was Elijah. Both the Yawah and the Baal followers prayed for a sign and Elijah's altar burst into flame, which was a proof that his God was better. Well, after a long time the Hebrews took over Canaan and little by little their ideas came to prevail. (By the way, the story of Cain and Abel is an allegory illustrating the conflict between the herdsmen, represented by Abel, and the farmer, represented by Cain.) It was a long, hard, struggle, though,

because the people were always backsliding and the prophets had a hard time keeping the ethical standards up and
local gods out. At the time of Joshua (I think) all the
written documents and traditions were collected and the
religion began to be codified. The story of Moses was one
of the important books and all the important laws that
had developed were attributed to him and taken to be revealed by God to his people. The Pentateuch (first five
books of the Bible) came to be viewed as sacred. They
constitute the Law or the Torah. Carrying out the Law
came to be the most important duty of the Hebrews. They
considered it the most precious thing in the world, a shield
against barbarism, etc. Well, as you know, there came the
Roman Empire and much distress. There arose another
prophet. Jesus. The Hebrews had been looking for a Messiah (Christ) and now many of them accepted Jesus as the
Messiah. But many of them did not. So the earliest Christians were a branch of Jews. But many Jews rejected the
idea of Jesus as the Christ. And that was the beginning of a
great cleavage. Christians came to blame the Jews for the
death of Jesus and the Jews kept themselves as far apart as
they could. After the Diaspora, or Dispersion of the Jews,
the Torah became increasingly dear to them. Rabbis or
teachers spent a lot of time analyzing, interpreting, and
applying it. This rabbinic literature came to be known as the
Talmud. And with just these two bodies of literature, the
Jews all over the world for 2000 years maintained their
identity. It is quite a sociological phenomenon that they did
so without any homeland of their own. No wonder they
practically worship the Torah and the Talmud. The essence
of the Jewish religion was once stated by a great rabbi, Aki-
bah who was asked to tell what it was while standing on one
foot. He said: Love God with all your heart and your
brother as yourself. The Jewish form of the Golden Rule is
in the negative, i.e.: "Do not do anything to someone else
that you would not want done to you." Jews have been
accused of being legalistic. And many of the laws have had
the effect if not the intention, of keeping them segregated

and apart. Their dietary laws, for example. "Thou shalt not seethe a kid in it's mother's milk" from Deuteronomy, for example, has developed into a vast ritual of not mixing any dairy foods (milk, cream, butter) with meat. Also, many kinds of meat may not be eaten (if they do not have cloven hooves, I think). Or sea foods. Even separate dishes and cooking utensils have to be used for dairy and for meat foods. Keeping these elaborate dietary laws came to constitute the major contents of religion for many Jews. Since they could not eat with gentiles, they kept to themselves, were "clannish." Also their meat had to be slaughtered in a special way. In general, the kind of life demanded by their religion made it necessary for them to have close community ties. This and laws against their ownership of land meant that they were not farmers but always town dwellers. This also had its effect on their mentality. A whole host of other regulations kept the Jewish culture intact for many years. Then in the latter part of the 18th century, under the influence of the French Enlightenment, some Jews wanted to emancipate themselves from the centuries of almost superstitious worship of the ritualistic laws. A movement developed in Germany known as the Reform movement. These people wanted to strip away the non-essentials from the essentials of Judaism. They wanted to retain belief in a single God and the great ethical teachings of the prophets. But they wanted to cut away the ritualistic adhesions that had gone along with the Jewish religion. They were willing to accept Jesus, not as the Messiah, but as in the tradition of the great prophets. They reintroduced music and choirs. They did away with the skull cap, which had been considered a mark of respect to God since man was not worthy to go uncovered before God. They did not separate men and women in worship. Instead of a synagogue they called their place of worship a Temple. In the United States at the present time you can hardly tell a Jewish Temple from, let us say, a Unitarian Church and often rabbi and minister can exchange pulpits and no one tell the difference. The East European Jews,

however, retained their orthodox practices. As they rose in
the social scale, however, their children rejected their form
of worship and there arose a sort of middle ground known
as "Conservative" Judaism. It is a compromise you might
say between the extremes. They retain more of the old
forms. Because of their attachment to the Law (Torah)
and their refusal to accept Jesus as the Messiah, the Jews
have been called stiff-necked and stubborn. They, on their
side, have blamed Jesus for the discrimination they have
been subject to. Many of the older orthodox Jews hated
him and wouldn't even mention his name. The long history
of study of the Torah and the Talmud has given a certain
cast of mind to Jews. The scholars who studied the Talmud
got practice in making fine points, in subtle interpreta-
tions, in casuistry. This was excellent intellectual training,
even though sterile so long as it was limited to the ghetto.
When they burst out of the ghetto, though, this long intellectual tradition became useful. Especially in science.
Especially in the social sciences. Consider this: three of the
four great revolutionaries of modern times were Jews.
Marx, Freud, Einstein (the other was Darwin). Some of
this was due to their ability to see cultural phenomena
objectively since as Jews they were really outside the system as well as inside of it. Like all religions, Judaism
changes with the time. No one knows what it will ultimately become in this country. It will always be mono-
theistic; it will always emphasize justice; it will always
insist on the social obligations to the community. It will
always reject Jesus as divine or as the Messiah. But it will
be a great step forward if and when it can cease to reject
him and accept his message. The contrast is sometimes put
in the form that Jehovah was a just (in the beginning a
vengeful) God but Jesus' God was one of love. There are
ever so many sociological complications involved. The
Jewish religion has no place for the theory of original sin
which plays such a large part in Christianity, especially
Catholic Christianity. Jews do have a Day of Atonement
in the fall when they fast in order to atone for their sins.

But otherwise there is no emphasis on this. The Jewish
religion is tailor-made for children. It is filled with holidays
for the delight of children. I can't remember the names
but there is one in February when fruits and nuts are
eaten. There is the Passover feast which is one of the
pleasantest ones imaginable during which the exodus is
recited with a charming ritual (perhaps you can visit one
someday). There is an autumn festival during which bowers
are built outside of vines, etc. for celebration. Then, of
course, Hanukkah, or the festival of Lights. Every Friday
night there is the ceremony of the lighting of the candles
to introduce the Sabbath (Saturday among Jews). It was by
means of these charming celebrations in the bosom of the
family that the emotional conditioning was done which
tied the child to his religion, just as it is the same sort of
thing that does the same sort of thing for Catholics. The
Jewish religion is not demanding emotionally. You do not
have to search your soul. You do not have to feel unworthy. You do not have to feel yourself an unworthy sinner
begging for God's forgiveness. The Jew takes it for granted
that he is saved. He is one of the Chosen People. God made
a covenant with Abraham and he holds God to it no matter what. Nor is there any virtue in self sacrifice, as among
Christians. Nor any virtue in asceticism. Jews believe that
the good things of life are made to be enjoyed. This often
looks like crass materialism and ostentation to non-Jews.
All too often it is. They believe the good things of life
were made to be enjoyed and that God wants it this way.
In Israel there is a conflict between the orthodox Jews who
want the state to be run according to the old religious rules
and the modern Jews who want to be modern. I don't
know the details but it will be interesting to watch. The
separateness of the Jews has been both externally and
internally enforced. They wanted to live by themselves; in
time they were forced to. They were always sort of foreign
enclaves no matter how long they had lived in the country.
After the Diaspora they were dispersed all over the world.
Most of them followed the rivers into Europe and settled

in Spain, Germany, and especially East Europe. They
were expelled from Spain in 1492 (some people attribute
the decline of Spain to the loss of the Jews). There are
Jews in the Orient, in Africa, in South America. They tend
to come to look like the peoples among whom they live.
In Israel all races are represented. In this country interesting developments are taking place. Jews want to retain
their separateness but they also want to be integrated. They
advocate cultural pluralism for our country, that is, the
living together in amity of many different kinds of culture, opposing enforced similarity. But the difference in
world outlook and values makes this difficult in many
cases. What looks to the non-Jew like clannishness looks
to the Jew like reaction to discrimination. Many Jews have
found a religious home in Ethical Culture Societies, in the
Unitarian Church, and also among the Society of Friends.
In general, Jews react against emotionalism in religion;
they tend to be rationalistic. One of the greatest theologians today is a Jew, Martin Buber. I have not read his
book but the great point he makes is called the "I-Thou"
relationship. Ask your teacher if he can explain this to you
since I cannot. Non-Jewish theologians find this point of
view very interesting too. Well, I suppose this is enough?
All my love, darling. Mother.

When you come home, if you are interested, I will show
you two chapters in a book I wrote dealing with the culture of Jews. OK?

After all this, written in large script came the question:
"Have you looked in any encyclopedias under Judaism?"

Sex had never been a hang-up in our family. I had dutifully answered the children's questions when they first
asked and they had promptly forgotten, relearning the
facts of life from their own sources when they were ready
to. LLB and I had not made a point of appearing nude in
the presence of the children but, if or when we did happen
to, there was no issue. At the age of four, Dorothy Lee had
asked if she and Darryl could get married now while they

were still young. When she was five I had returned home
one afternoon to find her and Michael seriously examining
one another's bodies carefully, Dorothy Lee remarking
bemusedly that his—circumcised—organ was different from
her—uncircumcised—brother's. She had played with boys
her own age along with girls in the long summer evenings
and she had been to parties with older boys the summer
before she went away to school. At fourteen she was going
to a dance with a boy in her French class named David.
But I was indignant at an invitation from Bill to attend a
high school fraternity party during the holidays in Philadelphia:

December 5, 1955

Dear Dorothy Lee,
 . . . About the Christmas plans. I am still opposed and I
hope you will not be disagreeable about it, but since I
don't want to seem arbitrary and unreasonable, here is my
position. First, I think it most thoughtless of anyone to
suggest stealing four days from me during Christmas vacation. Strange as it may seem, I like to have you around just
as much as anyone else does. I might consider allowing you
to go down for one party, although I am not certain even
of that; but four days! In the second place, the whole idea
of high school fraternities is ridiculous and having conventions at this particular time is most unusual. I very
much doubt the judgment of any adults involved in this
ridiculous business. And, in the third place, as I have told
you, I will not stand in the way of any relationship between you and Bill, but neither will I do anything to advance it. [Since you have known him longer than the
other boys.] He already has the advantage of history on
his side, as I explained to you once before; and it is not a
good policy on my part to expand or elaborate that advantage. I know you count on using your charm—a not inconsiderable weapon!—to invite him up here for a visit.
Hanukkah is all over by Christmas usually, so he could
come up between Hanukkah and his convention in Phila-

delphia. Again, let me say how well I think you are developing and how much fun it is to be the mother of such
a lovely girl.

At fifteen, she had liked a junior "a little taller than I.
Dark hair and eyes," but she did not think it would last
long. It didn't. A month later she didn't like him any more
but there were other boys around she did like. At sixteen:

All the boys in my class especially seem a lot more fun. We
get along well just joking and hacking around. Frank (in
my grade) has been telling me his problems lately. As you
say, most people lean on me. What is it about me which
attracts this kind of attention? Also Fran's boy friend, Bill,
who is another buddy of mine, has been having his troubles
lately. I seem, as always, to be in the middle of things. . . .

I forebore telling her that she was already performing for
the boys in her life the traditionally supportive feminine
role. Without any particular romantic interest in them.
Attractive as she was to the young men, she herself was
not at all boy-crazy.
    As early as the age of fourteen there had seemed to be
some uncertainty about dating. At that time I had written:
"Sometime I will write you a very long letter explaining
some of your problems to you. I think, for example, that
you are not ready yet to face the problems that go with
dating and that this is part of your malaise. I hope you do
not feel that you must date if you do not really want to."
To which she replied: "I don't have to worry about dating
(I don't)," leaving unexplained whether it was worrying or
dating that she didn't do. Now at sixteen, the same malaise
vis-à-vis boys surfaced again. It evoked this from me: "Perhaps also in your unconscious there is a little concern
about the transition from a friendly to an adult relationship with boys which may bother you, but I am not sure."
And, a month later:

... I'm not sure I know you very well. But this is the way
it seems to me. . . . In Nancy's [college age] group you
could go along as a little sister and have the company of
boys without having boy-friends. So for several years you
went around with a crowd much too old for you, not because you were on an advanced level of development but
because you were not. Like me, you are slow in developing
an interest in boys as males. (I was 17 before I even dated.)
You like boys as human beings, as interesting companions,
as representing a different point of view, as friends. You
are still growing, wanting new experiences, wanting to explore new personalities. I am glad. I wouldn't want you to
be any different. But when boys are too insistent in their
maleness it interferes with the kind of stimulating relationship you crave at this point. . . .

At seventeen, she asked permission to drive down to
Florida with another girl and two boys; in my reply I
noted that the school would certainly object and gave my
own reasons for raising questions about it:

February 28, 1959
Dear Dorothy Lee,
 . . . You know what the mores are and how hard they
are to buck. So far as I am concerned, as I have made
abundantly clear over the years, I have perfect confidence
in your judgment, common sense, and ability to deal with
crises. I think the trip would be interesting and valuable.
But I foresee any number of difficulties. A suspicious gas
station attendant or garage mechanic, a minor brush with
the law, which might happen to any driver, a cautious
motel or hotel keeper might precipitate a lot of trouble.
The Mann Act, and all that. (The Mann Act forbids trans-
porting a female across state borders.) I agree with you
completely that it would be ridiculous and uncalled for;
that the boys are gentlemen; that the relationship would be
friendly and circumspect. But adults often can't under-

stand this kind of idyllic relationship and with all the
publicity now being given to juvenile delinquency people
tend to be overly suspicious of anything. So what I suggest is that you get Terry's relative to give you a regular
invitation, according to the school's rules, and that you go
down on the train. . . . If you are sure that Terry's relatives would have you, that would be all right. I would
like to have you lie in the sun and sleep. But I'm afraid the
driving down with the boys would not be allowed by the
school and I can understand their position. I hope you can
make all this clear to the boys. I wouldn't want them to
think that I had any doubts about their behavior. But
neither would I want to put the school in the embarrassing
position it was put in with respect to the New York trip.
I can understand the school's position very well. They
have under their care a great many young people who require a good deal more supervision than you and their
policies have to be based on maximum security, so to
speak. That is, it is better from their point of view to for-
bid acts even if they would be all right rather than permit
acts that some children might take advantage of. Please
let me know your reaction to all this.

There was no protest. There may even have been some
relief.

At seventeen Dorothy Lee began to wonder if she was
normal; my reply:

Now about the "I wonder if I am normal" deal. As you
know, I believe everyone is entitled to privacy with respect
to his or her sex life so I will just write in generalities and
you can judge whether any of it applies or not. Different
people mature sexually at different times, some very early
and some late and some not at all. The last-named or so-
called frigid women we can disregard; there is usually
some psychological block there. But normal women vary
greatly. Men are more standardized. They reach their peak
of sex expression at around 19–21 or thereabouts. Most

women, though, are later. Some, though . . . reach sexual
maturity very young. This is too bad because it is distracting and inhibits learning in other areas. Sex can become extremely absorbing, as you have no doubt noticed,
and, unfortunately, at just the time when there are so
many other things that have to be learned. In your case I
would be willing for it to be delayed for several years yet,
although I wouldn't be too disturbed if it came earlier.
If you still found the sexual advances of men trying four
or five years from now we might make enquiries about
your "normalness" but definitely not at 17! As I have told
you, I believe, it is important not to make men feel that
you disapprove of them or condemn them or feel superior
to them because of their strong sex drives which, after
all, were built into them and were not of their doing. And
women wouldn't want it any other way. Some girls feel so
insecure or so bored or so rebellious that they need boys
not necessarily as sex objects but as something to organize
their lives around. Fortunately you have never suffered
from these needs—I think, although one never knows one's
own child that well—and so you have never had to have
"boyfriends" to buoy you up or supply supports. I wonder
what you mean by being "able to out-run, out-climb, and
out-yell the boys?" Do you feel competitive with boys?
Do you envy them their freedom? Do you feel you must
out-do them? This would bother me a little if true. Because
I would like you to enjoy being a woman and not envious
of men or competitive about them. It has been my observation that despite the fact that you would like someone to lean on when you get married you are always going
to be a strong person that others are going to lean on. (In a
good marriage each leans on the other, of course; no one
can be a strong oak all the time. Says so in a book you
can read when you are ready!) Does any of this help? All
my love, Mother.

If she answered the question I raised, the letter recording it
has not survived. But my description of her—whether it

helped or not—did prove to be correct. She was a strong person and others did continue to lean on her.

When we discussed college, the question of women's versus coeducational schools came up for extensive talk. I blew hot and cold. In April of her senior year I was arguing in favor of Penn State:

April 24, 1958

Dear Dorothy Lee;

. . . This is how I have figured you out. You will reject this analysis because you don't like it, but here it is anyway. I believe that it is beginning to dawn on you that growing up into adult responsibilities isn't much fun. Just being pretty and charming—which you are in large degree—isn't enough. You also have to meet stiff tests. And I think in your unconscious this is beginning to worry you. You have been able to meet most life tests so far just on the basis of being a lovely, attractive girl. But that isn't going to be enough. And I think the prospect of having to put more in rather frightens you. Perhaps also in your unconscious there is little concern about the transition from a friendly to an adult relationship with boys which may bother you also, but I am not sure. I think the main anxiety you feel is about the difficulty of adult responsibilities. I am more and more convinced that it would be a good idea for you to go to Penn State and live at home, at least one year. . . . So why don't we think not "Penn State if everything else falls through," but rather "Penn State because it's a good school."

Still, a month later I was writing that I was glad she liked "the idea of Sarah Lawrence. . . . I am beginning to think that perhaps a woman's college might be all right for you. . . . You are still eager intellectually and I think you might be happer in an environment where contacts with men were not so persistent and distracting."

The choice of Sarah Lawrence was hers. I strongly approved but, characteristically, almost at once, in response to a depressed letter from her, began to have second thoughts. Thus, early in November of her freshman year: "I am not sure a woman's college is a good place for you. Your happiest relationships with boys were the casual, day-by-day kind that didn't have the artificiality of dating about them. At SL this is lacking and for a girl like you is this good? You aren't interested enough in men to make the necessary aggressions. But there are no other ways to have such contacts. I wish you would consider with me the possibility of transferring at the end of the semester to some other school. . . . I wish I knew the best thing to do." She remained at Sarah Lawrence.

There were few references to young men during the first year, and those there were, were incidental and casual. "Went to a mixer last night and had a good time; talked to a boy who was with me at George School, now at Yale . . . was pleasant." "Went out with . . . a boy from Yale. We went into the city, listened to music, and ate. Had a pleasant time." Nor were there men that year who appealed to her especially. There were always men on the campus, especially weekends—some slept under the beds—and there were frequent weekend trips to Harvard, Yale, and Princeton. No big deal. Not particularly attractive.

Dorothy Lee had entered Sarah Lawrence in 1959. The late '50s and '60s marked the high point in the era of the feminine mystique. At that time the birth rate, which had been rising for some time began, finally, to recede. Women were now beginning to be rebuked for their "return to the cave." Within a few years Betty Friedan was to deliver the coup de grace to the age of togetherness. But not before it had left its imprint on Dorothy Lee's college generation. The feminine mystique still pervaded the world of college women. Thus, after a visit with young married friends, Dorothy Lee was saying, "I think it would be kind of nice being married." But she added immediately, "Don't worry or get excited. No one in mind."

More serious though, was her reaction to her first disappointment in the adult world. When, as a sophomore, her

grade on the legal aptitude test proved to be only average,
she reconciled herself with the still highly approved retreat
into femininity. The high school girl who had been "able to
out-run, out-climb, and out-yell the boys" now wrote:

November 14, 1960

Dear Mama,

I am feeling somewhat better about the tests. Vicki says
the boys who took it at Yale thought them difficult too.
And who am I to claim equality in a man's world? Which
brings to mind a decision I arrived at recently. I have no
desire to compete as an equal in a man's world. I'd just as
soon be a woman and be treated as one. I am beginning to
fathom the psychology of getting one's way without fighting or perhaps I am trying to beat intra-departmental
rivalry. Not that I don't want to work, but I am beginning
to realize that there is something to be said for the old
adage a woman's place is in the home. I am basically a
sweet child but still I think only as a child because the
future seems far off and not worth too much worry.

In a sophomore one could take all this with a more-or-less
tolerant sense of humor. A year later it was going to have
to be taken more seriously.

In the letters from Sarah Lawrence in the first two years
one could see, limned clearly against the background of
those years, the "identity diffusion" Dorothy Lee was
struggling with, her effort to put herself together.

Although I had always placed a great deal of emphasis on
autonomy and independence, I had not made much of the
means of achieving them by way of work. I said little
about work, for example, or jobs or careers. I think now
it was a mistake not to have been more insistent that she
take earning money more seriously. At the same time I
think also I was probably putting more pressure on her
than I was aware of. She wanted to do great things; she did
not care to be bothered with the banalities of daily living.
In August of the year before she entered college, taking

charge of moving books, clothes, and the like from State College to Princeton, for example, she had felt overwhelmed by them: "When I grow up I'm never going to be happy running a house. Too much of a strain. The problems of the world I feel I could handle but not the problems of running a house." Now, two years later, discouraged by her inadequacies, she asked for emotional help: "If it's not too much trouble I would appreciate a letter giving me a little moral support."

Beginning in high school there had been snippets of concern in Dorothy Lee's letters about the best use to make of her life, but little attention to actual jobs. From time to time I tried to get her summer work—interviewing for a university research project, working for an acquaintance in the Washington office of the AFL-CIO, volunteer work for the Friends' Committee on Legislation. She had decided early, at fifteen, that, though she had liked her course on mechanical drawing, she did not want to be an engineer; she thought she might like to be a psychologist.

In college she did a little baby-sitting; she did some tutoring; she ran a movie projector. She expressed some interest in political science and in law, but she was becoming restless with the narrowness of her life experiences so far: "Every now and then I get upset because when I think about it, all my life has been spent in the same way." Her tutoring experience convinced her that she could not be a teacher. She had insight into her uncertainties; she recognized that the depressions she was increasingly subject to resulted from her inability to work up enthusiasm for anything. Still she remained uncertain about what she could do with her life: "At the moment I am very unsure about what I can spend my life doing. There are so many thngs which interest me."

On July 23, 1961, Dorothy Lee ceased to be a "teenager." She was on her way to London for her junior year at the London School of Economics. It was the beginning of the '60s, a fateful decade not only for her but for all of us everywhere.

chapter three

odyssey

What happened to the '60s, was "one of those deep-seated shifts of sensibility that alter the whole terrain. . . . Less than epoch but more than an episode, the '60s are likely to remain a permanent point of reference for the way we think and behave."[1]

Odyssey may not be the best word to use to describe Dorothy Lee's junior year abroad. She was, to be sure, returning home from a struggle, but not like Ulysses from a war. Nor was she, like him, wily and deceitful but open and seeking. She was wandering more in the German sense of the student's *Wanderjahre*. She was, like the German students, seeking experiences to grow on, to find herself. The year—1961-1962—was a fateful one not only for her but also for young women generally. A pivotal year of stresses and strains in the transition between the ebbing feminine mystique of the 1950s and the waxing youthful protest movements of the 1960s.

No one individual, however "typical," can truly represent a whole class or group or generation. But Dorothy Lee's experiences during her year abroad in 1961-1962 were, I think, illustrative of the experiences of at least one part of her generation. Her letters trace the uncertainties young women were experiencing—as many still are—as they were torn between two forces operating on their generation—the feminine role as defined in the feminine mystique and the intellectual and social interests they had been socialized to value, between the search for the love of the man whose children they would bear[2] and the search for a cause.

The early 1960s were a time when parents were first becoming dimly aware of the changing life-styles then emerging for both young men and women. Just as my sister had brought the new world of the 1920s home to my parents so my children were bringing the new world of the 1960s home to me, especially, because she was the oldest, Dorothy Lee. Through her letters I became aware of their fantastic mobility, for example, and more frighteningly, of the part drugs were beginning to play in their lives. Of the freedom in the relations between the sexes. Her letters gave me a personal view of much that the media were only beginning to report about that turbulent generation.

Kerouac's *On the Road* had appeared in the late 1950s. Presently great swarms of young people were, like him, also on the road. Route 66 was to become, symbolically speaking, the great main street of a whole generation. Driving across country became as matter-of-fact as driving across town had been in earlier generations. Riding the rails had been an old custom among migratory workers when I was a child. But now the great interstate highways were making the automobile the major vehicle for the astonishing mobility of these young people.

Networks of friends and acquaintances developed so that you could hitch-hike anywhere in the country and be sure to find someone you knew all along the way. All over Europe also they were finding one another—even in parts of Asia, especially India. Young women as well as young men.

In the offices of the American Express Company in Paris

and London, for example, they congregated to learn where
the cars were going. If there was a car going to the Greek
Islands, you could go there. North Africa? There, too. The
USSR? Of course. And all the trips were coeducational.
For, along with all this mobility, went extraordinary free-
dom in the relations between the sexes.

Soon after Dorothy Lee had arrived in Paris she was off
to the USSR. Just like that. A casual invitation accepted.
"Do you remember Peter Henley, the boy from Harvard?
Well, he is here with a friend. They are getting a car and
they invited Joan and me to drive to Moscow with them
and we accepted. We will leave Paris and drive to Berlin."
Then the itinerary: Warsaw, Minsk, Kharkov, Kiev, Lvov,
Dehelm, Budapest, Vienna. Actually, the trip proved
inauspicious and was finally aborted. The car broke down
in Moscow; parts to repair it were not available nor, for
that matter, were the skills. So the car was sent to Helsinki
by train. "The boys are hitch-hiking and we are going back
to the free world by train." A horrendous week-long trip
lay ahead of them before they set foot in England:

Your only and thus favorite daughter (you remember the
girl who used to drop by occasionally, the one who can't
spell?) well anyway she has made her way to that well
known world capital, London. How she survived the jour-
ney is still open to wonderment. It was a mere 29-hour
train and boat trip from Copenhagen. There is nothing like
sleeping 8 people in a compartment. The crowd is so bad,
it's lack of air. Well, that was child's play when compared
with the crossing. Our valiant ship left the Hook of Hol-
land to traverse the North Sea. Fortunately Joan and D. L.
had taken pills before boarding as a precautionary measure
which, as it proved, was extremely wise. Very exciting
voyage. I have never experienced in my long and varied life
time such a rough sea. Everyone was terribly ill but what
was better was everything kept sliding back and forth. The
ship had to change course. I climbed up on a luggage rack,

anchored myself between two firmly planted suitcases and went to sleep. We arrived finally on the lovely green shores of England.

That was her first summer. The second summer's trip began just as casually. She and a friend, Leslie, were thinking of going to the Greek Islands. A chance encounter changed their plans. Now it was to be Spain, just as casually, and North Africa, instead.

Well, after a rather hectic channel crossing . . . I arrived in Paris [from London]. I went to the American Express, as it is the center of information. This was at 10:30 a.m. Tuesday. . . . It was about 11:00 when John (Jenny's boy friend whom I'd seen in London) came saying he and a friend were leaving for Madrid that afternoon in a car they'd rented for the summer and we were welcome to come. Leslie and I thought it over quickly and decided, why not. After no sleep [the night before], an all-night trip, I set out for sunny Spain.

Why not, indeed. Between the two summer trips there had been others: "a weekend in the country with Mike . . . driving down to visit a friend on the East Coast"; a holiday in Fomentara where she and three friends had stayed "with a Canadian boy, a friend of a friend . . . [who] was trying to write, has a house." In June, Dorothy Lee and a young man "hitch-hiked all the way back [from Sweden] to London. It took three days almost non-stop," This peripatetic generation were like nomads. Trains, planes, cars, ships. . . . They seemed to be at home with all of them.

It was in Dorothy Lee's letters that I had my first brush also with another aspect of the culture of that generation, the drugs that were becoming so salient in their life-style. From Paris, Dorothy Lee had written: "Hanna and her brother managed, or rather I managed to do it for them, to acquire some marijuana from the boy who lives next door. I don't like the idea myself but find it is a constant topic of conversation. Quite dull but some people are quite strange." The casual, almost incidental, tone of this item—three lines out of thirty-three in the letter—struck me as much as its contents. She took it for granted that I knew all about the customs of her generation. We had hassled cigarettes and I had lost; we had never had occasion to deal with alcohol for she had had no taste for it. The subject of marijuana had never even come up. All I knew about it was what I had read in the professional research literature. My reply, almost by return mail:

I must say I am not at all impressed by your procurement activities for Hanna. I can't say I like the idea of your getting marijuana for her or anyone else. As you know I am not at all restrictive in my ideas; I want you to have all kinds of interesting and worthwhile experiences. But experimenting with drugs is not one of them. There are plenty of worthwhile stimulations from the outside world and one doesn't have to resort to drugs to have interesting experiences. I must say also that Hanna's preoccupation with marijuana doesn't speak very well for her and it disturbs me that she rather than Joan is your roommate.

Expectably, information about the use of drugs was no longer forthcoming in her letters. My next encounter with marijuana was to come much later, with David.

The early 1960s constituted a special moment in the lives of young people. The middle and late '60s were to be so much more shocking than the gestating early '60s that we tend to forget how shocking the early '60s were at the time. Protest was just beginning to trouble our consciences. A generation characterized by antiestablishmentarianism was just surfacing. The beatniks protested by withholding conformity to, and hence legitimization of, the norms of the conventional world and, if necessary, withdrawing from it. Students were beginning to drop out of college not so much as in the past to earn money to continue in school as to make a political statement, to show their rejection of the establishment, to refuse to validate it by even formal deference. Others were more aggressive in their assault on the establishment. They did not want to just sit there; they wanted to *do* something.

Among the issues agitating the campuses at that time were: premarital sexual relations, the censoring of college student publications, capital punishment, opposition to nuclear testing, peace, and, in the United States, the Reserved Officers Training Corps. Suddenly, at least so far as the rest of the country was concerned, the issues exploded in the San Francisco "riot" on the steps of City Hall as young people protested the House Unamerican Activities Committee hearings in May 1960. It was a galvanizing experience for many of the students. "The minute you join a picket line or circulate a petition you're not 'beat' any more, because you're actually working for something you believe in."[3] The protesting generation was off to a flying start. "The search for a crusade was an important sustaining force."[4]

The HUAC hearings and the free speech issue were close to Dorothy Lee. A sophomore project at Sarah Lawrence in one of her courses had been on the Smith Act and free speech. She was already a veteran picketer, having served an active apprenticeship and become something of a connoisseur of picket lines. Protest was as much a part of her world as mobility. But so, paradoxically, was the feminine mystique.

It is true that every generation is a transitional generation. But the generation of college women in the late '50s and early '60s seem to have been in an especially vulnerable position. For although the era of the feminine mystique had reached its zenith and was now on its way out, the decline was not yet easily visible, let alone clear-cut. Or, for that matter, even generally recognized. Betty Friedan was still researching her landmark book.[5]

Still, in a book dealing with an avant garde—academic

women—written during the early 1960s, I had vaguely
sensed an emerging change, the beginning perhaps of a
reversal of trends. After noting the dismal decline of
women in academia, which I called the "great withdrawal,"
I had expressed the idea, on the basis of admittedly slender
evidence, that there were "some indications that changes
are in the making." I saw "augurs" of such changes about
which, however, I was so uncertain that I offered them
only tentatively. It might be, I suggested, "that younger
sisters, seeing large families at close range and in close
quarters, may find them less enchanting than their older
sisters did at their age."[6] Similar changes were also taking
place at that time in Great Britain, where Dorothy Lee was
spending the year. Interviews with both working-class and
middle-class women in London in 1960–1961, were showing that even then "these women no longer saw their
lives dominated in the long term by the role of wife and
mother."[7] The expected decision was the decision to
"work." "The *special* decision was the one to remain at
home."[8]

This, in barest outline, was the world of young women in
1961–1962. They were being buffeted by the conflicting
forces then playing on them—the revolutionary idealism of
the student movement all over the world and the receding
but still powerful feminine mystique. Protest and adum-
brations of the new feminism. Causes and crusades versus
togetherness and motherhood. Dorothy Lee along with the
rest of her generation.

Dorothy Lee came to London after two years at Sarah
Lawrence. Sarah Lawrence took education seriously. It
was socially conscious. It was "not an island—a special land,
a country all to itself. Like every good institution," its
president had said, "we must know how to make our particular contribution to solving the problems, and must be
part of the common effort."[9] Sarah Lawrence took young
women seriously too. And taught them to take themselves
seriously. They were encouraged to think. No intellectual

terrain was viewed as beyond their grasp. Marxism, Kafka, existentialism, whatever, were all grist for the intellectual mill.

But the young men they associated with—or other men, for that matter—were often not ready for them. So long as the young women were seen as just that—attractive young women—there was no problem. The men could be attentive, chivalrous, generous, especially so if a young woman were a damsel in distress. Dorothy Lee's letters were filled with incidents illustrating this point—in Paris, London, Gibraltar, North Africa. "It is really amazing how easy it is to meet people, mostly men. Hanna and I just walk down the street and we are invited for a drink. . . . It gives me an excellent chance to speak French." The first day in London a young man offered to drive Dorothy Lee and Joan about in his car to help them in their search for an apartment. Later two young Pakistani offered instant hospitality. A taxi driver on Gibraltar gave Dorothy Lee a free tour of the Rock. When she left Tangiers with no money, having forgotten to change any, an Air Force officer bought her breakfast. "After a day which proved the goodness of mankind," she wrote, she met a writer of about fifty, a naturalized American of French-Egyptian extraction, who drove her around Morocco. "I don't care for him too much but he's pleasant and tolerant. I manage to meet people and to communicate in my limited French. Perhaps that's the luckiest thing about being a girl. No one worries. They all are friendly." These men extracted no price.[10] The mere company of an attractive young woman was enough.

It was only when they had to associate serious intellectual pursuits with young women in the prime of youth and beauty that the men found it hard to deal with them. Young men, as always, were responding to the beauty of the young women but the women were having to struggle with their own identity as they experienced it, as intellectual as well as feminine beings. The "moratorium" in the dedication of women to the interests of men that Erik

Erikson had told them we permitted college women was
more apparent than real. True, in theory they did have a
few years to explore the world of ideas between the protection of the parental family and the establishment of
their own. But actually they were permitted no real moratorium. Even the years of the moratorium reflected the
feminine mystique. If young women were going to be intellectual, they were made to understand, they better be
intellectual in a charming, unchallenging, disarming,
appealing—strictly feminine—way. A classmate of Dorothy
Lee, Sally Kempton, has shown us how it worked:

Sarah Lawrence appeared to me and to most of my friends
there as a sort of symbol of ourselves; like the college, we
were pretty and slightly prestigious and terribly self-serious
in private, but just as we laughed at the school and felt
embarrassed to be identified with it publicly . . . so we
laughed publicly at our own aspirations. "I like Nancy," a
Princeton boy said to me, "except she always starts talking
about Kafka promptly at midnight." And I laughed, god
how I laughed at Nancy—how *Sarah Lawrencey* to carry
on about Kafka—and, by implication, at myself. For I too
expressed my intellectualism in effusions. Men expected
the effusions, even found them charming, while treating
them with friendly contempt. It was important to be
charming. A passion for Marxism, stumblingly expressed,
an interpretation of *Moby Dick,* these tokens we offered
our lovers to prove we were not simply women, but people.
Yet, though we displayed strong feelings about art and
politics, we behaved as if we had not really done the reading. To argue a point logically was to reveal yourself
as unfeminine; a man might respect your mind, but he
would not love you. Wit, we believed, is frightening in a
woman.[11]

The "gentleman-and-scholar" model had just about run its
course by the 1960s. (Sputnik had had something to do
with it.) There were, to be sure, some who regretted the

loss of that male style. But the "lady-and-scholar" model lived on. It was all right for women to be scholars provided they did so in a ladylike way. "Sarah Lawrencey" meant a blend of the traditional feminine with masculine-type intellectual interests.

An image that keeps recurring in my own mind is of a young man holding up to the face of the young woman a mask that represented what he wanted to see in her—and responding to that. Behind the mask the young woman in my image finds it impossible to overcome the barrier of the mask. By the end of the decade young women were going to be furiously tearing the male-imposed masks from their faces and trying to look as unlovely, as nonfeminine, as possible. They wanted to appear before the world under their own colors, not under colors forced on them. The year 1960–1961, however, was not the end of the decade but only its beginning.

Dorothy Lee's experiences with the Soviet bureaucracy in Moscow had been disillusioning. It was her second trip to a Communist country, the first a student visit to Cuba the winter of her sophomore year in college, which had been made exceptionally pleasant by the Castro regime. The unsponsored, un-cosmeticised trip to the USSR was less ingratiating. From Leningrad she had written:

At the moment Joan and I are at the Leningrad Station waiting for a train from Moscow to Leningrad through Helsinki. Our car broke down the first day we reached Moscow. They couldn't fix it so we had to send it by train to Helsinki. The boys are hitch-hiking and we are going back to the free world by train. All I can say is I am sorry I won't get to see the rest of Russia but then I have many years and at the moment capitalism and the decadent west seem pretty wonderful. I have spent a little over a week here and most of it running from one Intourist office to another and then to the American Embassy, etc., and it is increasingly a wonder to see how they ever get anything done here. I'll say one thing. They are way ahead of us in

the technique of passing decisions off on the next person.
Moscow I guess is a nice city but . . . much too heavy for
me. . . . Camping had been good though and I am glad I
came. . . . Joan and I are rushing across Europe—Helsinki
was beautiful. The free world. We are waiting for the boat
to Stockholm. Then the train to Copenhagen. I love you.
Will write. Freedom is lovely.

Dorothy Lee returned from Russia "more than ever firmly
convinced that the only fair way to govern is to encourage
diverse points of view." But her own experiences were no
match for the theoretical presuppositions of the young
men she met at school, practically all of them Marxists
who automatically discounted her accounts of her own
personal jousts with bureaucracies in the USSR. They
made the "Sarah Lawrencey" blend difficult. Of one such
young man she wrote: "He was a Marxist and was quite
disappointed in our report on the USSR." Her conclusion:
"I'll have to learn to discuss it gracefully because I have a
feeling that I'll run into it a lot at LSE." She was right, she
did. Thus, half a year later, the same story: "Jim and I
constantly argue about everything. I always lose because
he won't admit I am right." How could any attractive
young woman be right, whatever her background? Or
whatever her experience? She had the reputation of being
a conservative, even—spare the word—a Rightist.
    Dorothy Lee, like Sally Kempton, was in the Sarah
Lawrence mold. She was intellectual but always in the
correct "feminine" way. She had been reared to be both
"feminine" and interested in intellectual concerns. She had
masculine-type intellectual and political interests which, in
"Sarah Lawrencey" fashion, she could not show too seriously in public. But they were real to her and constituted
a considerable portion of her letters to me, however
"stumblingly expressed." But during the fall she was to
learn that the rewards for being just an attractive young
woman were great, the punishments for having intellectual
interests equally great. Without the support Sarah Lawrence

had provided for her intellectual pursuits, she found herself struggling to maintain them in the face of young men
who would never concede when she was right.

LSE still has me somewhat in a muddle. I've been going to
lots of lectures and am trying to work out a program
which will contain the best of them. . . . The thing I have
been noticing here is that all the lecturers are very concerned in establishing their subject as a valid part of the
social sciences and proving that the social sciences are valid
in themselves. I've never run into such fine distinctions
before. Sociology seems to enjoy a high regard here so the
social anthropologist has to show where his subject differs.
Sometimes I fail to follow the argument but I enjoy it
all. The best lecture so far was the one in social anthropology. . . . I am taking a lecture in sociology called social
stratification. It hasn't met yet but the reading list looks
good. I sometimes feel out of things because the big issues
here are things like the Common Market and the reaction
of British public opinion, all of which I know very little
about. . . . I hope the lectures prove to be interesting.

Brave new world. Her favorite lecture proved to be a
sociology course on medieval society, but she liked international relations also. She began to do some of the reading and felt a little more like she was fulfilling her purpose.
At first she wanted to sample widely, to get a taste of a lot
of lectures, but then she decided to stick to subjects she
had some background in. She had just started American
Society Since 1939, in which they read Riesman and
Whyte; she felt it might be a pleasant experience. Her main
problem was that she loved American history and missed
not having courses in it. Laughter! The course in American
society proved a great success; five students, all from the
western hemisphere (strange); they were going to cover
subjects that interested her, including the Rightist movement and her old friend Robert Walsh, but also population,
urbanization, education. It did seem a bit silly to come to

England to study America but she was learning more. And
she was really happy. Less than two weeks later she was
"suffering from great depression resulting from reading
The Organization Man. I hope it has a happy ending. I see
certain traits of mine in the book but somehow the whole
concept of [organization] society revolts me. . . . The
reason all this . . . annoys me is it doesn't give you a life
of your own. . . . I am my father's daughter as well as my
mother's and for me to live I must do so by earning what I
achieve, not materially so much as emotionally. I can't
compete with others but I have to prove myself to me. I
want the task to be difficult and I want to work alone. . . . I
was thinking about communism and war the other day and
it occurred to me that if right is relative and change is
inevitable, communism in some form may well become the
future. It might be right for my children or theirs but just
because I live when I do and come from the society I do,
I know I couldn't live under it. There have to be some
things more important than life or life couldn't be so
important." A good deal of intellectual searching went on
in those early weeks. Had a good discussion of C. W. Mills's
Power Elite. Also had been reading MacIver's *Web of
Government*—sounded like Mills. Nothing was that new.
Mills seemed to her like a mixture of Jeffersonian democracy and midwestern populism. Still, who did make decisions and who did assume responsibility for them?

The "great depression" Dorothy Lee was suffering from
may have been due to *The Organization Man.* But there
was more to it than that. A gradual change in mood began
to creep into the letters at the end of October, reflecting
the difficulty involved in protecting her intellectual interests from the demands made on her by the young men
who surrounded her and the two friends who shared the
apartment. Life was quite confused. The problem of living
outside a dormitory was that so many things kept happening to distract attention. She found it almost impossible
to do any serious work and "as a result constantly feel
frustrated." Her whole life had come to depend on intel-

lectual pursuits for its meaning and enjoyment. That was
the one place she felt at home, where she could do something well and know that she had succeeded, a place where
method and result were certainties. Not that she couldn't
get along away from this, but much as she enjoyed people
she found very few who offered a challenge or who could
hold her interest. She was sometimes afraid she had cut
herself off because it was easier to deal with ideas than
with people. It didn't involve the same kind of involvement or giving. This hidden curriculum was far more
difficult than the official one.

The lecturers at the LSE may have been teaching
Dorothy Lee a great deal about medieval society, about
organization man, about the power elite. But there was
another faculty following another curriculum and teaching other courses. Late in September she had written:
"Another thing which I find interesting is that all summer various foreign men have told me that they find
American women frightening. After about 21 or so at
least. I guess the very freedom which attracts them to
American women also causes them problems in knowing
how to treat them. . . . What is there about American
women to frighten people?"

Whatever the answer might be, the question itself soon
became evident: how to deal with the "frightened" men?
Dorothy Lee's answer was in the traditional feminine
style: pacify them, reassure them, "stroke" them.

I do have another problem. One of the Americans kept
coming over here with one or two friends (one an English
boy). Well, we were quite good to him even though he was
a little difficult. He persisted in an attempt to get at the
real meaning of everything we said. He was sure there was
more in every remark than met the eye. He also was extremely touchy so you couldn't joke with him. . . . Through
it all I maintained a politeness and charm for which I am
becoming notorious. . . . Yesterday things came to a head.
Billy dragged me aside and we had a long talk. He isn't

coming over any more. . . . I don't want to feel obligated
to pacify him, yet I do.

To protect herself against the demands the young men
were making, Dorothy Lee was turning more and more to
her intellectual interests. There were few men who "offer
a challenge or who can hold my interest." She could "give
to others what they need, or do the most pleasant and
right thing" or be "polite, because it is easy." But she
"could not become emotionally involved." She went to a
concert with an American from school but "he never
seemed to be talking about the same subject I was." Billy
gave up "speaking to me and won't come to the party
because I'll be there. I feel sorry for him but he is doing
the whole thing himself." Somehow or other connections
were not being made. Why was she not becoming involved?
Why did she have intellectual interests but not romantic
ones? What was *wrong* with her?

I am trying to understand . . . this problem which has
recently developed for me. I have had several boys (Americans) tell me I was the hardest person they met to get to
know. I am very charming when they meet me; I am excellent with people, better than they are: extremely perceptive—what is more I am bright and funny—and most
of all, good. Oh, yes. I also understand life. Now, after all
these compliments they proceed to try to find out what in
my past caused me such difficulties. Why aren't I normal?

Whatever it was Dorothy Lee was being criticized for by
the young men, the general impact of their demand for her
"feminine" stroking and of their "friendly contempt" for
her intellectual pursuits combined to lower her own self-
esteem. The hidden curriculum worked its way. She was
being taught her "place." The letters came to be filled with
expressions of self-dissatisfaction, alternating with occasional letters reaffirming her strengths, her self-confidence.
But with accompanying appeals for reassurance. "Will you

write a reassuring-type letter?" she asked in November, as
Sylvia Plath had asked her mother: "I guess I just need
somebody to cheer me up by saying I've done all right so
far."[12] And, perhaps also like Sylvia Plath,[13] Dorothy Lee
wondered if I would think well of her even if she didn't
manage to do brilliantly that year.

By the end of November the Sarah Lawrencey solution
to the conflict between the demands of the "feminine"
style being so relentlessly drummed into her in the hidden
curriculum and the intellectual interests catered to in the
official curriculum broke down. By then the young woman
who in high school had written that she could "out-run,
out-climb, and out-yell the boys" was writing: "It's funny
but just from the few months I've been here I am convinced that at a certain age boys take over from the girls
intellectually because the really creative thinking seems to
come from them."

She continued to write of doing worthwhile things at the
same time she lashed herself for her inability to discipline
herself to do them. She could not get herself together
enough to think seriously in career terms. She could not
concentrate on her intellectual work because the psychological work she was engaged in was too demanding. There
were alternating expressions of self-confidence and self-
dissatisfaction, great swings between happiness and depression. The letters highlighted the struggle between her
intellectual interests and the demands of the feminine role
into which she was cast. She listened, she supported, she
reassured, she built up. At the same time, she rebelled
against the emotional costs they involved. She found it
impossible to hurt even unwelcome guests. She hated to
hurt men even when she could no longer bear them. She
was meticulous in carrying out the assignments of the
hidden curriculum.

The "friendly contempt" Sally Kempton had noted in
the young men Sarah Lawrence women went with had left
its imprint. She was beaten down. She just didn't know
what to do with herself or with what she was learning. She

felt such a waste; she had not done anything properly all year. She just didn't think she had it in her to do as much as she felt she should. Mountains of research have been produced to explain the "achievement motivation"— or rather, its lack—in women. It is not at all hard to understand.

The term *career,* defined as a profession with possibilities of advancement, my Oxford dictionary tells me, came into the language only at the beginning of the nineteenth century. It was borrowed from the racing world; it implied a long-time commitment; it required you to run the course. A course, as it came later to be recognized, that was laid out for men and not always suitable for women unless they were willing to exclude marriage. Since there was little probability that women would find themselves in professions with possibilities for advancement, the issue of careers was not salient in the lives of women until almost a century later. Only then did careers become an issue. And even then for only some women. But it was always contingent, contingent on whether or not they married and, if they married, who.

Researchers continue to remind us of the contingent nature of women's lives even today—and how such contingencies make career planning for college women problematic at best. They have accumulated an impressive corpus of work on: career aspirations, achievement orientation, marriage plans, and fertility. Yet, after all this scrutiny, it is still not clear "what the precise effects [of college] are. In the broadest sense of life style . . . college-educated women . . . differ predictably from the non-college educated. But life style in terms of the relative priorities given to advanced education, marriage, family, leisure and work is far less predictable."[14] Only by eliminating marriage could the contingent nature of their lives be obviated and planning become straightforward. This anomaly was basic to the old "marriage versus career" issue that young women used to argue. If you were planning to marry there was little use in planning for a career. It all depended on the man you married.

Although careers were not an issue for many women in the nineteenth century a considerable number of them did espouse causes. Some even made a "career" of espousing causes. (It occurs to me now as I write that the very term *espouse* means, literally, "to marry.") Abolition, temperance, and women's suffrage were among the most outstanding of such causes. But there were also others ranging all the way from bloomers to gluten flour.

In their ideal-typical form, causes and careers differ considerably, the first propelled by a strong emotional dynamic, the second, by a more intellectual drive. Actually, since women have so frequently chosen service-type careers—teaching, social work, nursing, for example—they could use their careers in behalf of causes as, in fact, Catherine Beecher, Clara Barton, and Jane Addams had done. Jane Addams, in fact, created her own career and used it to support causes. Sophonisba Breckenridge and Edith Abbott used their academic careers in the same way. As did some of the early faculty women of the women's colleges who made these colleges "hotbeds of radicalism."

The young women of Dorothy Lee's generation were still seeking causes. "Career" for them still meant a helping career. They wanted causes more than they wanted achievement in business or industry. They wanted to serve rather than compete, to dedicate themselves to some great movement. "I long for a cause to devote my energies to," seventeen-year-old Sylvia Plath had written to her mother.[15] Some of these idealistic young women found their causes by attaching themselves to the cause-intoxicated young men they fell in love with. In this way they found a kind of integration of their idealism with their female identity. The New Left became the matrix in which they fought the battle between their idealism and the remnants of the feminine mystique. There are few stories more poignant than those of Jane Alpert[16] and Diana Oughton[17] who did, indeed, marry cause with love, with—in their case—tragic consequences.[18]

Like other young women of her own and earlier generations, Dorothy Lee had come to college seeking a cause. In the spring of her senior year at boarding school she had written: "Do you think I could get a job with the Friends' Committee on National Legislation? This approach appeals to me. . . . I am intensely interested in the fate of the nation." Little by little she had become unnerved. She longed for help. During the fall in London, she expressed her need: "I would love to have someone around me to guide me, to give me direction or a cause. . . . I feel guilty a little that with all the training I am receiving I have no ambition to save the world or change people." The acid of the social criticism college was exposing her to and the more personal criticism of her conservatism from her peers were disillusioning her.

Men can't do anything without some kind of belief which gives purpose or direction, because just to be alive isn't enough. When you're young, i.e., at George School, you learn to look at the world in a certain way which reflects an ideal. You can and are encouraged to think that if only all people were let alone to do as they really wanted, their basic goodness would guide them to act in the general interest. World government, ban-the-bomb, integration, are all good without question. Then you proceed to college and you discover that these things, though still good, don't necessarily fit the reality of the world. . . . What I am trying to say is that when you are forced to see facts, to interpret them within their context you discover the gap between the ideals and the realities. If ideals have never been realized, if people have believed on one level and acted on another, if Jefferson could write such beautiful things yet faced with facts act pragmatically, then ideals are only an indulgence and luxury. . . . School teaches you to question, and being fair and reasonable, you try to give

fair consideration to all sides. Then no longer is it possible
to know anything for certain. Then it's no longer possible
to believe, or rather, it doesn't matter which things you
believe in. I don't mean that. I just mean nothing seems to
be very important. Now when you reach this point you
begin to wonder what am I doing? Why? What will I do?
Well, there isn't anything I especially want. There is nothing to get passionately excited about.

I hear resonating through these words a dozen discussions
with young men in which her own arguments and ideals
were shot down, one by one. Who could take them seriously from an attractive young woman—like a family pet
who seems to think it is a human being?

   Still she longed for "some great important flash of truth
or wisdom" and commented on how dreadful it was to be
so undone. "What I want is something to live in terms of,
to give up some of my damn strength and independence,
for something to take me outside myself, to make me
really feel." She had thought seriously of the Church but
could not get herself to accept its teachings. Like Sylvia
Plath, who at seventeen, had written to her mother that
she longed for a cause to devote her energies to, Dorothy
Lee wrote that she was still an idealist in her desire for a
"noble cause." To which I replied, almost by return mail,
how about a hitch in the Peace Corps, surely that was big
enough. And added: "I feel there is something troubling
you but I'm not sure what it is so I don't feel I know
enough to discuss it with you." Like other young women
before and after, she was to find her noble cause—in the
Coalition for Nuclear Disarmament—by way of a young
man.

   "We've seen large groups of 'ban-the-bombers' all over.
It seems to be the chief function in town," Dorothy Lee
had written almost her first day in London. The Coalition
for Nuclear Disarmament had been one of the first causes
that had attracted her when she arrived. "This afternoon,"
she wrote a few days later, "we're going over to Trafalgar

Square to watch the 'ban-the-bombers.' We figure this is
the chief social gathering place in the city. They have been
forbidden to enter a certain area of the city so we shall
see."

Her own apprenticeship in activism had been in the form
of picketing. As a freshman at Sarah Lawrence she had, in
fact, become a connoisseur of picket lines. Of one such
experience—picketing the New York Women's Detention
Center—she had said, "It was the best picket line ever." So
in London she was already an old hand.[19] This was her
report on the Trafalgar Square meeting:

The rally at Trafalgar Square was huge. There were 14,000
people there and about 4,000 police. It had been raining
so everything was muddy but here it is the accepted custom to sit, so we sat. It was a strange mixture of people, as
are most affairs of that sort. Lots of young people; some
who came to be arrested, others to heckle, others who
were convinced. The hard core, though, were older people
and they stuck it out. I was interested most in the attitude
of the authorities. They banned the meeting and proceeded to promise arrest to anyone who attended. This I
think they should have realized attracts even more people
and . . . defeats that wonderful western concept, Free
Speech. So my protest was along this vein.

Dorothy Lee's participation in the CND was not so much
as a radical or rebel or passionate pacifist as it was as a
seeker, a cause-seeker—at least this early in the year. For
despite her Friends' Sunday School and boarding school
background, she was fast losing her pacifist leanings. She
had "done a lot of reading on NATO, balance of power,
disarmament, and arms control." But still just didn't know
where she stood. "On principle I disagree with war, and all
that goes with it. But the question seems more complex. It
may well be the best way to protect peace is by a certain
amount of armament." In spite of her misgivings, though,
about the antibombing activity as a cause, she continued

her interest and more-or-less desultory activities in the
CND movement, spending the last two days of the year
1961 at a CND outing:

The last two days I've been with some CND (ban-the-bomb)
people. We drove to the Midlands Stock-on-Trend for a
rally, then through snow and ice to Northern Wales for a
day of mountain climbing. Then back to Birmingham,
more CND, and today, home. I was the only non-CND
person and as the result received extra special care and
attention. I must say it was lovely just to get away to talk
to people who aren't trying to understand you, and the
rest.

Still, as yet, the CND was only one of the causes she was
exploring:

Went to a labor-socialist party weekend school last Friday
and Saturday. It was in the country. Quite charming, like
the advertisements for visiting quaint historical England.
Aside from that it was the most intellectually stimulating
thing all year. Not so much the discussion of socialism but
things like how to resolve theory and practice, what should
be sacrificed in order to get into power, and is intraparty
democracy compatible with a parliamentary system of
government. I am still sorting out my thoughts. There is
just so much I don't know. The sociology of politics seems
to be a fascinating field. Missed a marvellous debate in the
House of Commons Monday, a censure on the government
on Lord Homes' speech. Everyone was there including
Churchill. Hope to go to the Old Bailey Monday to hear
the trial of a member of the Committee of 100. And so it
goes.

And, a week later, her report on the Old Bailey trial:

I have been to the Old Bailey to sit in on the trial of six
members of the Committee of 100. They're being charged

on conspiracy to break and incite others to break the Official Secrets Act. This is in connection with a civil disobedience sit-down at an air base. It's kind of involved but in my line of interest. Although not involving civil liberties it's all tied up with war, peace, etc. I am sure they will be found guilty. They are so, legally. We have to get up at 7, go down there, and stand outside until 10 in order to get a seat but it's fascinating. I am also taking a great interest in the labor party and British politics, as far as I can follow them. I have been taken in hand by a few members of the socialist labor society at school. They are very tolerant of my to-be-expected American rightist attitudes. Really all I do is keep reminding them of the more expedient side of politics. Makes me feel very old. . . . Joan's picture and mine were in the Daily Worker, taken while we were standing in queue at Court. I always seem to be picked upon. Will you have me back?

Still, despite these new interests, she remained drawn to the CND and its activities. "The CND had a weekend of marches and demonstrations to greet the announcement of the Christmas Island testing. . . . They feel the choice of Christmas Island is an attempt to share blame which I imagine it is. I just don't know where I stand."

Between the Socialist-Labor party and the CND as causes her balance was turning toward the latter, in part because of her inability to share so much of the anti-Americanism of her socialist friends:

Perhaps I told you before of my interest in the Socialist-Labor Party. . . . I think about American society and listen to it being attacked by people here. I can't really defend it because I don't understand it but I am sure it isn't static, that it changes, slowly perhaps, to meet the problems it presents. It's just that America is pragmatic; it acts more often than not without an explicit ideology. We might eventually arrive at socialism if it filled the need, but we probably wouldn't call our actions socialistic. Even so, somehow terms like socialism, class struggle, exploitation, ruling class don't really seem applicable in the 1960s. New definitions should develop to explain the 20th century because what we're doing is trying to explain it in terms of the 19th century. All very interesting.

But the CND seemed to be winning out—partly because it was not so Marxist but mainly because her "favorite boy," Cecil, was so active in it.[20] He was organizer for the London region of CND. And though she found "it very hard to find understanding there," she thought she was right. Life wasn't "as simple as personal conceptions of morality."

After the winter of her discontent, she was "working a little more . . . mostly on international institutions, U.N., etc.," and finding things she "sort of knew before falling into place. When I've sat down in moments of calm and worked out my thinking I think I'll find I've learned more this year than it now seems." She was writing a paper on "League Was Instrument for Maintaining Status Quo: U.N. An Instrument for Changing It." She was "impressed with the extent to which we live in a world of revolutionary ideology."

Now that she had definitely opted for CND work, she embarked on a full calendar of activities. Upon her return from her Fomentara holiday (March 29 to April 13) she was "off to demonstrate against bomb testing," still wishing she understood what was right and wrong but concluding that there never was really a clear-cut line between them. She was working in the main office of the CND when she was not off demonstrating somewhere. It was:

. . . unskilled labor. Very unskilled. Quite embarrassing to be so highly educated and able to do so little. I am quite competent at addressing envelopes, making phone calls, counting, sorting, even a little typing. But good grief, who taught the child to spell? If I weren't such a charming person I'd never get away with it. The reason I took on this task was one of curiosity and a desire to be useful and it is all quite entertaining.

In the same letter she noted that she and her friends were all arrested for peace demonstrating. I was, however, not to worry. Being arrested was "perfectly acceptable. All the best people take part." One of her friends had spent the weekend in jail because she refused bail. Dorothy Lee herself and the other friend got out on bail. "The fine was only one pound and the whole thing interesting." Later in the spring she took part in the Aldermaston march:

Well, I went on the Aldermaston march. In fact, I was a site marshall. Which means I had to get people lined up and off in the morning, get 10,000 to 15,000 people through lunch and tea, then to bed at night. I didn't march because we drove from site to site. But I sure did a lot of running around, shouting, answering questions. The last day at the rally in Hyde Park there were around 70,000 people. I was terribly impressed and what a job it was to get them all in. I was down on the assignment list to read out greetings from the American group but they cut that part out of the rally. Not enough time. The chief marshall thanked me for coming on the march, said it was lovely just to have me around because, as you know, I am a happy, good-natured person, a pleasure to have around.

She had picketed the American Embassy last night; it was covered by CBS for television. She was still helping in the CND office. All this was hard to reconcile with her philosophical position, but she enjoyed being busy every minute. It was "also a fascinating sociological study of the organization and composition of minority groups, also in mass psychology." May 6 she was still hard at work with the CND and "more and more beginning to understand people and problems involved with protest groups, anyway those to the left." She had been on the CBS television program on the demonstrations at the embassy. The people at the

top of CND were not "nearly as anti as one would expect
from talking to younger people who dread to think they
might have something in common with 'The Government.'"
She and her friends were the "golden darlings" of the
organization, which was gratifying. They were also "considered real swinging," which was like being considered
"clean beatniks." Perhaps envied for living as they liked in
a "rather naive, unconscious way." Toward the end of
May she had managed to become quite necessary at the
CND office:

I am in charge of the office when the rest have to be away
on speaking jobs. I type stencils (if copy has been written
out and spelled correctly), I type letters, fill envelopes
with circulars, run errands, and in general keep people
happy. The most important fact to keep in mind when
hiring office help, I have gathered from observation, is to
find someone who can find things to do without being told.
I am getting to that stage. When the Russians announced
they were going to test I took it upon myself to see that
instructions were sent out announcing a demonstration at
the Russian Embassy as soon as the tests actually began.
You see we must give equal [demonstration] time to the
Russians.

From June 5 to 16 she went to Sweden for a peace march:

Just had most lovely time in Sweden. We drove up through
East Germany, took about four days. The march was only
two days so not too tiring. Met quite a few Swedish kids
who gave us place to stay in Stockholm. We all slept on
the floor, had parties, walked around the city, sat in tea
houses discussing world affairs, modern poetry. Life's the
same all over.

As late as the end of May she had planned to go to a CND
national research conference from the middle of June to
the first of July, but apparently by that time her enthusi-

asm had begun to wane. The last mention of her activities
came at the end of June when she had gone "to Greenham
Common, an Air Force base, to help on a [sit-in] demonstration which began Saturday. Not many people came. It
was rather sad. I didn't sit and felt rather indifferent. I
reckon it's one of the hardest things in the world not to
sit when all your friends are and calling for you to." The
explanation for her waning enthusiasm for CND activities
came in a letter when she was about to leave London in
which she wrote: "I am very taken by Cecil, which is a
good reason to leave the country."

Dorothy Lee had first mentioned Cecil in a letter in the
middle of February. Her apparently hero-worshipping
attitude toward him became more "ordinary friend-type"
with time, when she wrote in April:

As for Cecil, well there is nothing like seeing someone in
their own surroundings to turn them into ordinary friend-
type people. The thing is I can't help liking people I know
but I understand them and that puts them on my own
struggling level. Not super-human, to take from my shoulders the trials of this life. Oh, well, never mind.

He was not the "someone" she had longed for in the fall
who would guide her, give her direction or a cause. He was
either more or less. In any event the relationship was
equivocal. Writing from Fomentara during spring holidays
she said that she would be glad to see Cecil but she didn't
know how things were on that score. Still, he had taken
them to the train when they left, "at some sacrifice to
himself, which must count for something." Upon her
return, Cecil was still problematic, ". . . as I like him. He
works all the time so I see him little. What he feels for me
I don't know, at least something to occupy my mind,
sadness. . . . All is well except for Cecil. I feel a bit of a
failure there, mostly because there are things I'd like to say
and can't find the words and no matter what, I still feel
alone. Oh, so sad." My puzzled reply.

I wish I knew more about Cecil and your feelings for him and his for you. If you are attracted to him only because all the other girls have a man in their life and he is as near as you can find to an acceptable one, that is one thing. If you like him very much and wish he paid more attention to you, that is another thing. If you find yourself in a position where you could easily fall in love with him, that is still another. I can't figure out from your letter what to make of his attitude. You said he took you to the station at some sacrifice to himself; that looks favorable. But in the next letter you say "all is well except for Cecil. I feel a bit of a failure there mostly cause there are things I'd like to say and can't find the words and no matter what I still feel alone and oh so sad." If the reason you can't find the words to say to Cecil what you'd like to say is that you love him, why don't you just say that? Since, as I take it, you aren't demanding anything in return, that is, no commitment, no anything, you needn't feel ashamed or embarrassed to say it. It is my theory that only when you have an exploitative motive in the back of your head is it embarrassing to say you love a person. That is, when you want more than you are willing to give. Or when you want someone for what he can do for you. But if it is a genuine, out-going, generous feeling it seems to me quite all right. I know this is contrary to the mores (mainly, I think, because the mores were designed to help protect men from designing women). It may make women seem aggressive, something which everyone dislikes. But you surely are not aggressive. I wonder about Cecil himself. I wonder if he is one of the men with a "working class" background that you once referred to.[21] And, if so, perhaps he feels inhibited on that account. Class, as you have observed, means so much more to the British than to us. He probably looks at you as from a higher class background than his. As you can see, I am just making stabs and may be wholly wrong. I am only eager to help you. Especially if you really think you could fall in love with Cecil. If I am quite far out and wrong you can let me know. In any

event, please tell me more about Cecil if for no other
reason than it helps me to understand you better. You can
tell a lot about a person by the kind of person he (she)
falls in love with. Is he a student at LSE? Is he from a
"working class" background? Does he share your interests?
What does he look like? Etc., etc. There's a song in one of
the musical comedies, perhaps *South Pacific,* which has
words to the effect that once you have found him (her?)
never let him (her?) go. If you want Cecil you should try
to get him. I am sure that whatever way is congenial to
you will be charming, attractive, and very winning to him.
If you succeed, fine; if you don't, well just chalk it up to
experience. Some of the most beautiful, talented, and
wonderful women in the world have failed to win the men
they wanted so you would be in good company. As I said
above, I feel as though I am just making stabs in the dark
since I know so little about what the situation is but the
comments are for your consideration. Use them or not
according to how they fit the situation and your feelings.
In any event, it is not a world-shaking problem and however it turns out everyone still loves you and thinks you
quite a wonderful girl, though causeless. Just be yourself,
develop autonomy, don't feel you have to be like the
others; take your time about developing and all will turn
out well, with only the usual quota of heartbreaks which
are the condition of mankind.

Not until two months later did I get any feel for the situation. She had visited Cecil's family:

Saturday night I went to Cecil's home, which is in Chelten-
ham, West England. Lovely country, a little like Pennsylvania. Met Cecil's mother and father, both very sweet. . . .
Cecil's terribly spoiled and gets away with it by being
loving and charming, a little like me only I'm not spoiled.
His mother plays the piano beautifully. I enjoyed it. It was
lovely to see how proud both the father and Cecil are of
her. The father is a printer and has an immense garden in

which he takes great pride. They live in a recently built
house with a dog and a cat. Sunday Cecil and I went
driving and walking in the hills around his house. He told
me stories about the area, why and when the Romans
came, the history and geography. The places where he went
when he was little. Then we went to look at Gloucester
Cathedral which is one of the best I've seen, part Norman,
the rest perpendicular Gothic I guess. Anyway Cecil knows
all about that as well. A little disturbing because my great
passion for cathedrals springs from a love of the thought
that people believed something enough to spend lifetimes
building a beautiful monument more than any intellectual
appreciation. I feel very close to the good and beautiful in
the world when I am in a cathedral—funny. We came back
to London yesterday morning. I told Cecil some about
Daddy and you, mostly about my trip to Cuba but it was
really the first time I've felt free to just talk on and on,
which is funny because with most people I talk very freely.
Somehow now it's important I be able to say what I mean,
what I want to say, not just something to keep people
happy so they won't ask too much about me or things I'm
not sure of. I once told Cecil I would like to say more to
him but somehow most of the time there didn't seem to be
any need. It's nice to feel good being quiet. I also feel very
inadequate and inferior, like some sort of idiot child which
makes me annoyed with myself. Cecil says I'm amazingly
vague. Perhaps I am but when he asks me what I am thinking, chances are I am just being happy, not really thinking
except what a pretty sky or what green grass or only being
appreciative of being with him. I don't understand why I
should feel so secure with him. I know he is very unde-
pendable but I've never been so calm and sure of things
and if not sure at least not worried by my uncertainty.
He's very strange, he's weak in a way. He'll please people
at the moment even if it will hurt them in the future. He's
afraid of letting them down. I guess I'm like that anyway
and he seems to follow the pattern. I recognize the symptoms. He's in a muddle most of the time, forgets things,

loses things, gets sick when things get unpleasant, worries, hates asking people directions, changing money, making arrangements, not very well organized. I notice, too, when he talks to people outside of CND or academic subjects he can't really communicate. He either can't understand people or he's not very sensitive to what they are saying. I don't know. Mutual friends have said he's a disturbed person, very strange. I know when he's with most people he is a little tense. I only feel it because I feel him relax when we're alone. It must be because I'm such a gentle person at heart no one can be afraid of me. He says he never feels as relaxed as when we're together.

It looked like true love to me. She seemed to have no illusions about his character and personality, she was drawn to him anyway. Not until just before her departure were all the complexities of the situation presented to me. And even then I could not understand them. I was still not knowledgeable enough about the new life-styles of this generation. Toward the end of June, this from Dorothy Lee:

Well, as you may have guessed, being as you're naturally sensitive to me, I am very taken by Cecil which is a good reason to leave the country. As lovely as things are when we go away together, in London it's very painful. He's living with a very nice girl. I know her a little. Very good person. He also has rather absent-minded and passing interests with other girls. I don't mind this when I'm happy because I am quite fond of several other boys and most of the time I think of and treat Cecil as Veronica's boy friend and CND organizer, but this can only go on if he lets me. Once he wants me to be more, life becomes very complex with growing intrigues. He never lets me expect more than what is there. He said you've always known what I am which may be true but I tell him how lovely he is and how happy he makes me because it does me good to be able to say it. I am always a little afraid of being hurt but I know he wouldn't do anything purposely. I don't quite trust him but then it's all been quite lovely. He wants to come to the States to do graduate work. Wants to work at Swarthmore because they have lots on peace movements, public opinion towards mass bombings, and other things about which I don't quite know. Anyway social psychology or political sociology. Says he might come in the spring, get a job, then go about getting into school in the fall. I think it's all more difficult than he thinks and when he runs into difficulties he'll give up. I hope not, I want very much to have him come over. My personal feelings aside, I think it would be a good thing. If he's definitely serious I'll do all I can to help settle things. Well, this letter turned out to be a little like true confessions but it's about what is most on my mind.

"Naturally sensitive" to Dorothy Lee I might be, as she had said I was. But I was nevertheless somewhat non-plussed. So my only comment on the Cecil episode was disapproval of "taking him away" from another woman. "I don't know what to say about Cecil so will reserve any discussion until we can talk face-to-face. My only major reaction is that it is wrong to take a man away from another woman. Does Veronica know about your interest in Cecil or his in you?" Still, whatever her feelings might be with respect to Cecil, by the time she returned, if she would like me to I could try to get him a fellowship at the University of California. The last mention of Cecil was in a somewhat cryptic letter sent just before she left London: "I made a very matter-of-fact good-bye to Cecil as I am a child of great resilience and above all hate unpleasantness. I am a fatalist in that I know things will pass and can never be caught again. At the moment I feel much loved by many lovely people." I never asked on whose initiative the relationship was broken off. She saw him once again when he visited her in Chicago the following year, at which time she wondered why she had ever been so attracted to him. By then she had found Brick.

Dorothy Lee's junior year abroad ended in a trip to
North Africa. Her letters, neither travelogs nor reports on
the emotional and intellectual travail of her generation,
were illustrations of the free-wheeling life-style these
young American *Wanderjahr-lings* were beginning to
introduce to an astonished world. In the almost hit-or-miss
manner characteristic of planning at the American Express
in Paris, Dorothy Lee and Leslie on an hour's notice left
for Madrid in a car rented by a friend's boyfriend. Paris,
Tours, Poitiers, Bayonne, Biarritz. They wanted to see a
bull fight and then on to Toledo, Madrid, Granada, Málaga,
Gibraltar. Across to Tangier. Might even visit Fez. She'd
let me know when they had decided. Madrid to Málaga on
a third-class train coach with ten people in the compartment was pleasant. The other passengers were quite taken
with them because they were foreigners and couldn't do
enough for them, so they ate and ate. It didn't matter that
they could not speak Spanish; the Spaniards just talked
louder and faster. The Alhambra was lovely and romantic
and made *Arabian Nights* stories quite real. So far they had
had little trouble with the males who followed them. It
could be annoying, but never mind. Lots of guilt feelings
about having so much when others had so little. She really
had to take herself in hand and decide on something constructive to do. Looking forward to Tangier; hoping something exciting, like exposure of a CIA plot, would happen.
At Casablanca and at Rabat they saw the Arab part of the
city. In Casablanca smelly little boys had thrown stones at
them but at Rabat the natives were more hospitable. (In
Casablanca they had met a Moroccan government official
who had invited them to visit him in Rabat, so they did.)
Rabat a perfect town, clean, well-planned. Now after an
all-night trip they were back in Tangier. All very tiring and
she sometimes wondered why she kept going. Now they
were off to the beach. Late in July, Leslie went to Greece
and Dorothy Lee remained in North Africa where Raoul,
the French-Egyptian naturalized American she had met in
Málaga took her on a tour of Morocco: Centa, Tetouin,

Chovian, Ouzzane to Fez. Raoul was a little strange, rather suspicious of people's motives, and worried about things it never occurred to her to think about. He was critical of America. But he was a writer and they had to rebel. She didn't care for him very much but he was pleasant and tolerant. After the desert which, though beautiful, was too strong for her taste, civilization and Marrakesh were welcome sights. She was getting a bit tired of Islamic art: too much color, cramped design. Perhaps it was her Puritan austerity that made her appreciate a little silence for the eyes. Funny to see a Muslim girl in veil and long dress riding on the back of a motorcycle. She was beginning to get a feeling for the transition from a backward to an industrial society.

The summer of 1962 had been good, but she was getting excited about going back to school. There was much she wanted to work out and experiences she wanted to use. This last year had been one of the most disturbing times in her life. She wouldn't have missed it but she needed some quiet now to fit things together. She wanted very much to talk to me. Perhaps I would be able to tell if she had changed. "Thank you for making all my wandering possible and for being there when I return."

The most important news of all did not appear in any of the letters from North Africa, the news that all the thinking and doing and feeling of the year had been relentlessly leading up to. In Tangier she met Brick Johnson and fell profoundly and overwhelmingly in love with him. The options snapped closed. This was the event that everything had depended on. That contingency was now resolved.

In July of 1962, before her senior year, Dorothy Lee was still writing that she really must take herself in hand and find something constructive to do. But during her senior year at Sarah Lawrence there was to be no more such talk of career or even of noble causes. Brick was to supply the raison d'être for her being, the center for absorption, the cause she had been looking for all year.

chapter four

a losing battle

I had been able to understand Cecil—understand his background and the class matrix that so puzzled Dorothy Lee. I admired the movement he was so active in. I understood the working relationship between him and Dorothy Lee, so seemingly similar to the working relationship I had had with her father. I was, to be sure, distressed by some of the qualities Dorothy Lee had so clearly limned—and impressed by the insight she showed into the weaknesses of the man she loved and her ability to love him anyway—but if they had married I would have welcomed him warmly into the family, even if it had meant her living in England.

Brick was different. I did not understand him, nor the counterculture generation he was a prototype of. (He was, for example, one of the earliest of the generation that began to take time off from their college work to seek their identity.) Brilliant, beautiful, talented, he came out of the Southwest, more as troubadour than as Lochinvar. He sang, he played the guitar. When he came to Harvard as a scholarship student the culture shock was well nigh lethal. He drank; he used drugs. After three miserable years he left college for Europe, where he played first for the armed forces, then on the streets of Paris, and finally in North

Africa. That was where Dorothy Lee had found him, living in a communal household, sick and demoralized.

I first learned about Brick in a telephone conversation with Dorothy Lee in September, when she was back at Sarah Lawrence. In a letter dated September 23, 1962, I apologized for the tension that had shown up in my voice: "You were right about the state of affairs which my voice registered and I am sorry I was so edgy. I can explain if not excuse it." I then proceeded to recount all the crises and emergencies that were bearing down on me. Then: "But Brick was also a casualty of one of your bad habits. You never introduce a topic. You just begin to talk as though your listener had all the background. . . . You never once introduced Brick. I just picked up from the odd bits of conversation that there he was." But the more she told me about Brick the more panicky I became, though I was determined to at least put up a calm front:

I confess I still feel I must plan for you, which is absurd, and I hereby promise solemnly with my eye on a bible, that I will desist. Not even suggestions. Not even for your children! I will treat you as a grown woman with the right to make your own decisions, to plan or not plan, and live your own life. And that, my dear is a promise.

I am sure I really meant the promise and that I did intend to abide by it. But the promise became harder and harder to keep.

Brick wove in and out of the letters. Dorothy Lee's highs and lows were, I came to learn, responses to her relationship with him. When he wrote, she was elated; when he did not write, she was depressed. In reply to a telephone conversation I wrote:

I was sorry to hear you were bored and depressed. I know you hate to have me sociologize, but since I am almost as much a sociologist as a mother I can't resist—knowing as a mother that you don't like to have me do it—pointing out

that what you are experiencing is the classic woman college senior funk or doldrums. Lots of people have researched it, most recently Nevitt Sanford, at Vassar.
Remember? While you are "suffering" through it, remember his conclusion: "The uncertain senior . . . is on the
road to becoming a richer and more complex person. . . .
She is striving for integration on a higher level."

In your case this senior depression is confounded by
your year in London. A whole year with no responsibilities,
no obligations, nothing to do but grow, have experiences,
adventure, excitement; carefree, unshackled. It is almost
a prescription for Utopia. But it is the sort of thing that
can happen only once; it cannot be extended. It can happen only to one at a certain stage of development. If you
look at it that way, as a terrific experience, but a non-
reproducible one, I think you can take your time to digest
it, incorporate it into your self, quarry it for all it is worth.
But not think nostalgically about it. We did discuss the
come-down that S.L. would be after a year at a cosmopolitan university. But it seems to me that S.L. is an ideal
place to retreat to after that wonderful year to interpret it,
see it in perspective, and assimilate it. Of course S.L. now
is a totally different experience than S.L. your first two
years. But every year has its own quality and can make
its own contribution. If you let it, that is.

Your senior depression is complicated also by the fact
that it coincides with a certain phase of your sexual development. . . . As you well know, I have never been one to
believe that a few years of virginity before marriage were
worth fifty years of inhibition after marriage. So I am
not being critical, just explanatory. I know all these words
don't make being a senior any easier but they might make
the diagnosis more understandable. . . . I sent you a book
on Nigeria this morning. Hope it proves interesting and
useful. So much for now, my dear daughter. Lots of love,
Mother.

How little I understood Dorothy Lee's depressions I was
only to learn later. The same day, buoyed apparently by
contacts with Brick's friends, she was feeling better, "comfortable and cared for . . . quite befriended":

Things have pretty much settled down. I've begun to do
some reading but don't really feel involved. Guess I will
when classes begin. Everyone is as I left them but with
a year's backlog of experiences to discuss and analyze. So
far I've spent much time sitting around talking some,
listening more. Jenny is wonderful and makes living quite
enjoyable. She's planning to get married next year or the
year after. Many others are engaged or getting married.
Anyway it's a prevalent topic of conversation. I find it a
little terrifying so I've become silent on the subject and
only occasionally mull it over in my mind. Saw Jimmy,
friend of Brick's from Paris, in the city. He was very sweet
and I felt quite comfortable and cared for; he has a flat
with Ronald, another friend of Brick's, in Cambridge
which I'm invited to visit. Also Hans, Joan's boyfriend
from LSE, is in New York. He's at Columbia doing an M.A.
in International History. His courses sound lovely and
he's invited me to come to any I want. All in all I feel
quite befriended and when my trunk arrives and classes
begin I should start to feel a sense of belonging.
    I run into Mrs. Bozeman around campus. She's so
friendly it sometimes frightens me—not sure of the proper
relationship to be established. Hope I can do well, as I
would like to please my teachers. It seems like they all expect so much and I'm not sure I'm as bright as they think.
Oh, well. . . .

Still not fully informed on the situation vis-à-vis Brick, I
had no way to understand what was troubling her. With
only vicarious contact with Brick—by way of his friends—

she was trying to come to terms with the fact that Brick's commitment did not match hers.

I feel as if I've passed through a crisis. Got a lot of self-pity out of my system and have proceeded to a more contented, cheerful attitude. After a perfectly terrible weekend spent sitting here complaining, not being able to get down to work, and feeling a total failure as a result, I spent several hours sobbing my heart out. I felt so awfully trapped. Even if I did not want to be here, I knew I could never quit; even if I didn't want to work my head off, I knew I would. As you said, this is all a part of being at the crossroads as it were. I wouldn't mind so much if I could be sure of anything but I don't guess life ever falls neatly into place. Well, anyway, after my outburst I felt much better.

It also helps that my conferences are getting under way and catching me up. I talked to my Shakespeare teacher; he's wonderful; quotes chapter and verse; explains Shakespeare's relationship to everything. We are playing with the idea of my writing a contract on the satirical elements in Shakespeare which intrigues me. I shall mull it over. I have done much reading for Mrs. Bozeman, not so much following the assignment but taking off as my interests wander. The former French colonies are my present love, especially the French Sudan. My tribe is the Fulina, very conservative but wonderfully proud, having a tradition of political organization going far back. It's still in bits and pieces but it's coming.

For Mrs. Lynd I am in the process of writing a paper on my creative thought processes. Most difficult. Perhaps I haven't any. It's funny but so far, at any rate, I'm finding the actual technical part of writing comes much easier than before. Who knows, there may still be hope.

I talk with Hans on the phone almost every day. He tells me how Columbia graduate school is improving and I inform him of the superiority of S.L. We find mutual consolation and it's good.

Jimmy called today asking me up to Cambridge. It seems
he and Ronald are feeling low and want my pleasant presence to cheer them up. I think the change of air would
do me good so I'm off this weekend. Jimmy said to bring
my books and make myself at home. He assures me there is
a rather good library in the vicinity. . . . Thank you for
the book; it's got something on the Fulina which I de-
voured eagerly.

Not until the end of the letter did she give a clue to the
depression she had been suffering from: "I still haven't
heard from Brick and am worried that he is cold, hungry,
and unhappy in some foreign land but there is nothing I
can do and he can take care. Anyway, I hope so."
    To which I replied—exhaustively—two days later:

Dear D. L.,
    I knew something was going on emotionally but couldn't
know the details. I wrote you yesterday and today your
letter of the 10th arrived and helps me understand, at
least a little. . . . I wish you had told me what the self-pity
was all about. Self-pity is one thing I never noticed in
you before and I would like to know more about it. I'm
sure Brick is not cold in Tangier, nor hungry; he may be
unhappy, but for reasons that, I believe, you can do nothing about. And they probably have to do with the same
reasons that make you unhappy. But I won't say more
about this until I know more. As I said in one of my earlier
letters, the senior year is very hard for college women (it's
the end of the sophomore year for men). So many decisions have to be made. And in cases of sheltered girls
like you, graduation from college presents the first really
major test and they are very unsure of their ability to pass.
About your creative thought processes, it seems to me
that the general area in which they would take place was
largely influenced by the kind of family background you
came from. Although you fought sociology—a major
competitor in your life for my attention—you found your-

self powerfully attracted to it and have therefore skirted
it all your (intellectual) life.

But you have rejected a psychological approach; you always resented the idea that an outsider could know you
better than you knew yourself. You felt it violated your
autonomy to have your motives analyzed. What seemed
to me to be an attempt to give you insight into your
motivations, seemed to you a humiliation. In almost
all your letters from London you complained of the endless analysis of motivation that went on in your circle
of friends, a probing of psyches, etc., which you found
distasteful.

Another factor in your thought processes is the fact that,
living in a one-adult family, you never heard adult-adult
discussions or, for that matter, personal gossip. I hardly
ever discussed personalities with you, which also meant one
less dimension in your thought repertory. Also, I think,
your sheltered and protected position in the world had the
result of shutting out a great deal of experience that sharp-
ens the wits of those who have to make their own way, or
at least some part of it. You have to believe the best of
people. You are incapable of seeing evil in anyone. It has
been pointed out that all one's social theory rests ultimately
on one's theory of human nature. Since you believe that
it is fundamentally good, all your creative thinking takes
place within this framework. Just as those who believe it is
fundamentally evil, think within that framework.

I think also that your creative thought processes are influenced by the strong necessity you feel for being loved.
You cannot bear not to be liked. You can stand up to
people—as, according to your reports, you have often done
—but you must feel that they like you. . . . I am sure that
there are a great many other factors at work influencing
your creative thought processes, but these are the ones
that occur to me at this moment. Perhaps at this point in
your career sexual factors may also be involved, although
you might not want to put this into your paper.

Then I launched into a new interpretation of her depression. Some of her emotional malaise may have resulted from an unconscious recognition that it was the exotic circumstances of her meeting Brick, the moment in her own development when it occurred, recognition that under ordinary circumstances she would not have fallen in love with him:

If you have occasion for self-pity it seems to me this is it. I mean, falling in love with a person who, in your natural habitat, may not be appropriate. This is just a guess, a stab in the dark. I think the same malaise may be back of Brick's not writing you. He has probably gone over the situation in his own mind. Can he assume responsibility for you and still live the kind of life he feels he must? Can he, alternatively, allow you to take care of him and still retain his own self-respect and autonomy? These are serious questions. I imagine they haunt his unconscious, as they do yours. If I am way off the mark, you can let me know. In the meanwhile, I think it an excellent idea to have interesting contacts with other young men, including Jimmy, Ronald, and Hans. So much for now, my darling, and let me know about your visit in Cambridge. Oceans of love.

By the middle of October, Dorothy Lee had heard from Brick and her morale was restored, she was working hard, and she was rebuking me for my attitude toward Brick:

At the moment I am thoroughly exhausted. Thursday is my hardest day. After a class and conference with Mrs. Lynd and a conference with Mrs. Bozeman my poor mind has overdone itself with concentration. I have an elated, frenzied feeling, like I can't wait until I know all the things we talk about but Oh, God, the work.
Mrs. Lynd is letting me do the early sociologists, i.e., Weber, Durkheim, etc. if I still want to after a little investigation. I think she decided to let me follow my inclina-

tions when I explained my long love-hate relationship with
the subject. She had a smile on her face so perhaps she
thinks I'm trapped. No, seriously, I would welcome any
suggestions. What I thought I might do was take several
men and show . . . that sociology and related studies are
valid and necessary in understanding modern thinking. . . .

Mrs. Bozeman and I chatted about my future. She told
me I had been nominated for a Woodrow Wilson so I explained that I didn't want to go to graduate school just
yet and would rather work for a few years. We then proceeded to try to find out what I should do. Nothing much
was decided except that she thinks I'm quite capable of
anything that interests me and I should look around. She
says my strong point is "this new sociology." It's uncertain as to what she means. Also I am a talented historian,
a good scholar as well. All of this went straight to my head
and I beamed. Praise is such a lovely thing. . . .

I might go up to Cambridge again tomorrow as I have a
ride. . . . I feel much more relaxed when I can get away for
a little time. You ask about Jimmy [a senior studying
German literature] and Ronald [a graduate student in
psychology]. All I can say is they're like older brothers.
They enjoy having me because it's good to have a girl
around and more relaxing if that girl is a friend. We study
a lot, talk about nothing serious, laugh a lot, eat a lot. They
show off Cambridge and in general spoil me. It's very good
for me because one of the things I've regretted, thought
lacking at S.L., was male companionship.

Then the real source of her euphoria:

Brick wrote Wednesday. He's all right. Very tired. Didn't
say why he'd not written but I don't worry and wish you
weren't so quick to criticize. When you know him better
perhaps you'll be more indulgent. You are [indulgent] with
me when I don't always show the greatest amount of consideration. Must return to duty.

Then, after loving regards to both David and me, a casual postscript: "Did I tell you I've been asked to be one of two delegates from here to a conference on American foreign policy at West Point in December?"

Early in December there was a "moral crisis" on campus over defense scholarship money, "whether to accept it. Some of the students are strongly against it on principle, considering it a breach of civil liberties. The faculty voted to take it. Now are going to hold referendum. I've been pulled into the discussion because I know the people in the student body most strongly opposed and Mrs. Bozeman who has been delegated to represent the 'for' side. Now this means I've got to find out what the whole controversy is about. Ugh. Also madly trying to prepare for West Point."

Much of the communication between Dorothy Lee and me during that fall was by telephone. And there was much to be communicated. I seemed at times to be winning points. Brick's silence, to be losing points for him. Then, in the middle of November, I learned that Brick was returning to the United States. In reply to a letter from me, she wrote: "Your letter was very comforting" and then: "I'm quite nervous about Brick's coming but it's something that's got to be worked out by me. I do appreciate having you behind me. In many ways I feel very young and uncertain. We'll see. I'll call as soon as Brick gets here." I may have won against a silent, missing man. Against even the hope of Brick's return my resources were to prove puny.

As usual when confronted with a critical decision vis-à-vis the children, I canvassed my options, uncertain of any and all of them:

I can't help but keep thinking about your sadness and wishing I could do something about it. I know how hard it is to find one's self and achieve identity (which, I know, is a joke among college girls but which, by now you must know is a very real problem). It seems to me that there are three things I can do. One is to be a spontaneous mother and try to solve all your problems for you. Definitely not. Another is to give you something to rebel against by, in effect, fighting you. This would definitely hurry the process of finding yourself, but neither you nor I have the temperament for this sort of thing and it would leave scars that might prevent us from being friends and I don't think there is any need to hurry the process. The other alternative is just to let you work out these problems by yourself, however long it takes, and keeping my hands off. I just want you to know that if I do succeed in doing this—which I may not do!—it does not mean that I am rejecting you or abandoning you or deserting you or that I am indifferent or not involved. It's just that I think that will be the best for you. You are having an especially hard time because you have to become independent of a very strong mother but console yourself with the thought that succeeding will mean that you are also very strong. At any rate, darling, know that I am here, loving you very much, yearning like any other mother but abstemiously holding back my impulses to jump in with both feet. Another thing. Would it be proper or not to get a Christmas present for Brick, knowing that he probably can't afford to get us one? If it would be, what do you suggest? Oceans of love, dearest.

To which Dorothy Lee replied with appreciation. The letter was "most comforting" and reconfirmed her belief that I always managed to do and say the right thing at the right time. But she really didn't want me to worry so much about her and what I should do. She was quite resigned to growing-up problems and didn't expect miracles or a bed of roses. "You must not try to formulate policy because I have a feeling it makes you feel uncomfortable. Anyway, if there's one thing that does disturb me it's a formal relationship based on certain conscious rules of procedure. I love you and do try, in spite of appearances, to be a good daughter."

Because Brick was a country singer I made it a point to learn what I could about it. Thus:

This morning I picked up the Nov. 23 *Time* and read the story about country singing (organized around Joan Baez) and I feel I understand you and your world much better. And also Brick. There are still some things I don't understand about your attraction toward it; I have ideas but won't bother you with them since you resent my analyses so much. All I ask is that you try to be as tolerant of the values I stand for, my world—rebellious as you may sometimes feel toward it—as you would like me to be of yours. That way we can remain friends—something I very much want and hope you do, too—while recognizing that we are different. I have been misled by the fact that you are always in the "in" group; you always "belong," no matter where you are. I misinterpreted this to mean that you yourself . . . well, here I go again, violating my own restriction. I *won't* do it. I mean inflict analyses on you. I just had to let you know, though, how much better I understand your world and despite *Time*'s characteristically snide approach to it how sympathetic, if not sharing, I am of its problems.[1] OK? Oceans of love, my darling. I hope you are on top of things.

Dorothy Lee replied that she did not consider herself "in" Joan Baez's world. She was not "cool" enough and refused to take life seriously enough. Maybe she didn't even take herself seriously enough. In general she tended to be conservative. Whether or not she was "cool," conservative, or serious enough about herself, she was definitely serious about Brick's return.

But Brick's return proved to be more of a hassle than either Dorothy Lee or Brick's friends had bargained for. Where was he to get the money for his passage?

Mama love,

In spite of what I may say I am quite a happy person and really rather content with my lot in life. It was very good to see you and I do hope you realize I love you very much even when I'm being defensive or complaining. It's just a little difficult to know what to think, to believe, to do at this point in my life and I guess I tend to get very touchy when I have to consider questions to which I don't have answers.

I've thought over the question of Brick and money and would like to send him enough to come home. I'll send it so that he can make the arrangements in time to get the ship leaving on Dec. 12th. His money may come in time, then again it may not, and I don't want to expect him and not have him come. If his money does come in time he won't need mine. And any problems arising from the issue can certainly be best worked out with him here. Now of course the problem is can and will you lend me the money? We could work out some arrangement either for Brick to pay you back or for me to and then Brick, me, or something. I think the boat is $120 and would like to send it off as soon as possible. Please do help. I think it's a good thing and it means a great deal to me to be with Brick.

Thank you for a lovely vacation and I think I have a very impressive family.

(Then, never one to neglect my education even in a crisis, she added a postscript: "Enclosed *Glamor* test on masculinity-femininity.")

The third of three letters in three days from a mother who seemed to be groping in a dark room for a black cat that, as she saw it, wasn't there, had to do with Dorothy Lee's request for money for Brick:

About your request for money to send to Brick. . . . Even if I had the money I don't think I would do such a thing to Brick. I know that my world differs from yours and his but surely even in your world it would be humiliating and embarrassing to meet a (probable) mother-in-law for the first time indebted to her? And wouldn't it highlight his ineffectualness? Shouldn't he be shielded from even knowing that I knew his predicament? . . . I suggest that you write to Ronald and Jimmy who, you once said, were willing to send Brick transportation money. Ask to borrow the money from them to send to Brick or, better still, to lend the money to Brick themselves. It would be much better for your relationship with Brick to have the money come from them than from you. I confess again that I do not understand your world. But do you really want to start a (probable) life-time relationship in the position of a creditor to him? Just to save a few weeks of time before you see him? Do you really want to establish a precedent for protecting him from his own ineffectualness, for bailing him out of contingencies? . . . How long can this continue if you have to be a mother to him? Please really think over these things. I will do what I can to help you, but this, in my opinion, is not the way to do it. I know this is a very serious problem for you and my first impulse is, as always, to rush to give you what you want. But this is one problem I cannot solve for you or even help you solve. You will have to deal with it yourself. This is one of the responsibilities of independence and adulthood. I know you will feel resentful because you are unaccustomed to having me turn you down on anything. You may hate me for a while. I can take it, darling. Be as angry as you like. But ask yourself, too, if it's me or circumstances that make you mad. Believe me, dearest, I do love you.

Of course, she replied, she didn't hate me for not giving the money. She was not so much of a child that she got annoyed when her wishes weren't granted. Perhaps it was just her rather fatalistic nature but she believed if things were meant to happen, they would. She could make attempts to speed things up, change them, but in the end it was of little importance. "So we shall have to wait and see."

Beginning to recognize my impending defeat, I replied:

Thank you for calling Sunday night; it is very therapeutic
for me to hear you and to mitigate the picture I have of
you. I know you are a very stable and equable girl but I
also know that you are under lots of pressures and, whether
I want to or not, I do feel concern. In fact, on the bus and
train going and coming to and from State College when
my eyes give out and I can't read any more I have lots of
time to mull. But you are quite right; it's silly. And, further, it occurs to me that what I am doing is carrying on
the discussion you and I have had off-and-on during the
fall without letting you know what I am really talking
about. The secrets, so to speak, that seem to pervade my
letters. What I am trying to do—and I can see I haven't
made it clear—is to learn how to be the mother to young
people who are "beat." Brick is, it seems to me from what
you have told me about him, the archetype beat and if he
is to become a member of the family I ought to know how
to live with him. This is what has set off the train of thinking in the letters. I can't pretend to like or approve of the
beat living pattern but I can try to understand it and be
tolerant. (In turn, of course, I would expect beats to toler-
ate me and my standards.) Does that make it any clearer?
It's my problems, I suppose, not yours, fundamentally,
that are concerning me. I have to examine my own biases
and work out accommodations to relationships which I
have always viewed coldly, from the outside, as a sociological analyst rather than as an involved participant. Do
you read me? . . . I hope everything is A-OK with you,
darling and I send oceans of love.

In December there was no reference to Brick in the letters. She wrote about the West Point conference she had
attended which proved interesting; it had "now become
historic on account of Dean Acheson's talk." I wrote
about "the only time I ever visited West Point . . . a thousand years ago, like about 1922 when I went with the

Ezekiels to Rafael Ezekiel's graduation." I wrote about understanding evil. I wrote about her contract papers. I wrote about David and his Christmas shopping. I wrote, in brief, about the trivia that could hide my growing malaise. It was as though we were both holding our breaths.

Brick did not make the December 12 sailing departure date. He was delayed almost a month, not arriving until early in January. Dorothy Lee was jubilant:

Mama dear,
So sorry for not writing but kept waiting because so much has been happening. Nothing terrible. If so, you would have heard.
Well, Brick got back OK. Was lovely to see him. He had a terrible time in Tangier and it took all the food he could eat on the boat to revive him. He looked good, though. We stayed in New York for several days then went up to Cambridge. I met old roommates and friends. Was fun but a little hectic. Back at school and Brick trying to get a job in the city. He has friends to help so things looking well. Also he may even go back to school next year. We will come down mid-term. The first of February, I think. We want to get married. When, I'm not sure, but soon. Will see you first and discuss. I hope I can keep everything going. School and Brick I mean. Got my Shakespeare paper back. Good contents, bad spelling. Brick is going to help me correct it all. Then I have one long paper due before vacation and one right after. Much work. I will most likely call you tonight because I'm excited and want to talk to you. Sorry again for not writing. Love you very much.

Thud.
I had made such an issue of independence for Dorothy Lee that I should have been pleased when she showed it. Yet, now when she was finally exercising independence in the most crucial situation of her life—marriage to Brick—I was not only not pleased with my success but, rather, reduced to near-panic, especially after meeting him when

Dorothy Lee brought him home for a visit. I wrote a flurry
of anguished letters to friends calling for help.

Dear Janice,
    This is an SOS. I need help. Is there anyone—psycholo-
gist, psychiatrist, marriage counselor—that you could
recommend to me for my daughter? Someone warm and
understanding? Preferably, for this case, a man? . . . She is
planning to marry a young man. . . .
    As I see it, this is something she has to do in order to
liberate herself from me. This is healthy. I want her to. She
minds her dependence on me but doesn't know how to
free herself. With the help of this man it must seem to her
it will be easier. . . . Apparently she is really not sure of
herself, feels overwhelmed. . . . There is no hostility toward
me in any overt or conscious sense. She is quiet and well-
mannered. We discuss these matters openly. . . . Of course
I want her to be independent of me. I have never tried to
keep her dependent. I have always given her the greatest
freedom. . . . The one thing that is good about her relationship with Brick is that she does feel free with him.
Their relationship seems to be tender and gentle, strangely
innocent, rather than passionate. . . . He wanted her to
marry him between terms, in order for him to feel more
secure. Fortunately that was averted. The plan now is to
wait until she graduates in June. If she could be getting
some kind of help between now and then, at least she
would be better prepared for what she is in for. She knows
she will have to support him. The fact that none of all this
seems abnormal to her is part of her problem. So if there is
someone you could recommend I would greatly appreciate it. . . . What I want for her is someone who can help
her gain independence from me, able to face the world
on her own, get a job to prove herself to herself, help her
gain confidence in herself, etc., so she won't need this
marriage.

There followed the characteristic expressions of guilt which were never far from my consciousness. "I have sometimes thought that perhaps the next few years, if married to Brick, should be interpreted as part of her education and that I should not try to prevent it. But, like any mother in this situation, I feel terribly guilty. I went wrong somewhere along the line. Since the conflict between me and Brick is so hard on her, I feel like the true mother in the case set before Solomon. I try not to push her too hard with my objections. They do not move her in any event and may only harden her determination and they make the marriage that much more necessary for her. . . . Whether the marriage is averted or not, I think help is much needed. . . . I hope I don't sound frantic or panic-stricken." And then the apologia, in a postscript:

P.S. I should say that she interprets Brick in the light of Quaker teachings, which are anti-materialistic. His lack of concern for physical things—from time to time he feels it necessary to be cold and hungry as payment for his sins and wrongdoings, about which, however, he seems to have no anxiety—fits in with Quaker ideals. When I point out the realities of the situation I think I assume the role in her eyes of the conventional mother-in-law who insists on money in a son-in-law. It is hard to reach her when she has the defense of her Quaker upbringing to use against me.

The appeal went unanswered.

At the same time, I wrote also to a psychiatrist who had helped a neighbor's child, hoping that Dorothy Lee would talk to him, and through him be able to help Brick. I gave him my version of Brick and his problems:

He finally arrived, soon after Christmas. No money, no job, no visible means of support. I had never met him when my daughter telephoned one night to say they were

thinking of getting married between terms. Why, I asked.
This is a bad time for Brick, she said, and she thought
marrying him would give him more security. Fortunately
this was averted. She brought him down with her between
terms and I met him last night for the first time. We talked
about an hour. . . . Very vague about money. . . . About
getting a job he was inconsistent. At first he said he
wanted to get a job and save some money. A little later he
said he supposed he really doesn't want to get a job. He
starts out in the morning to look for a job, sees a friend,
and spends the time with him instead of looking for a job.
He talks of going back to California to work in the oil
fields. He talks of assembling a jug band (improvised
instruments) which would make a lot of money. He talks
of a teaching job at the University of Beirut. He talks of
returning to college but knows he couldn't stand it for
more than a couple of months. Why did he leave Harvard
with only one year to go? They were teaching him wrong
things, things he had to unlearn. It wasn't good for him,
etc. He wants to be a writer. But the conditions are hardly
ever right for writing. What has he written? He told me of
one novella called "Four Christmases" which was obviously an effort at self-therapy, the main character trying
to get over his own confusion. Brick is often cold and
hungry. But apparently this is a form of self-punishment.
(His friends tell him he is too Puritanical.) Why self-
punishment? For his sins and wrongdoings. I pushed no
further. . . . He seems to have a "God will provide" sort of
attitude.

I pointed out that he was soft-spoken and nice-looking
though his clothes were not clean. "I would be willing to
pay for psychiatric treatment for him although I doubt if
this is likely." I added that Dorothy Lee—who had had to
live up to very high intellectual standards her father had
set for her and who had probably found it hard to be the
daughter of a mother who was a professor—was a babe-in-
the-woods so far as the world was concerned and did not

accept my judgments about Brick. "She thinks it is my
old-fashioned view of the world." Nor was Brick much
more mature himself. Naturally I hoped she never married
him: "But if she insists, she is of age and can do so. I want
never to punish her. I love her and will always be ready to
help her. Nor do I want to punish him. I feel terribly sorry
for him." Plans were made for Dorothy Lee to see the
psychiatrist but nothing came of them.

February proved a dismal month for all of us. From
Dorothy Lee:

I am managing to get some work done but most of my
attention goes to Brick. It's just very difficult to lead two
lives and I hope I can last. Right now Brick is going through
a bad time. He can't bear to sit around doing nothing but
can't bring himself to get a regular job. His reason for
going to Cambridge was to try to find people interested in
forming a jug band.[2] But mostly it's the planning. I don't
think even if he found people they'd ever actually get
organized. I am not sure if he's coming to some point of
deciding but it's all painful for me cause I wish there were
some way of helping and there isn't anything I can do
but love him. It's also difficult for me to realize how much
his having been poor affects him. I suppose it's a matter
of status, etc. I know he's insecure, and unsure of what he
is or perhaps he doubts his ability to compete. I don't
know. Right now he has to find out something about himself. He's staying in Cambridge this week because he doesn't
want to come back to New York. No one to talk to and he
has to face days of doing nothing. The only thing that worries me is that I can't give more time to him and be with
him but it will work out. All this is new to me and I don't
know what to do really or even if there is anything. I love
you very much and don't want you to worry.

Five days later, in reply to my note telling her about my
correspondence with the psychiatrist:

Thanks for your note. I haven't heard from the psychiatrist. Perhaps tomorrow. I do have lots of questions but I
suspect most of the answers will come in time. Brick has
been in Cambridge all week and I presume he's well although I haven't heard from him. It's been very good for
me to be away from him. It's been so long since I've had
time to think without my mind full of Brick's problems. I
guess it's one of his charms, the ability he has to completely overwhelm me, to absorb me in his life until mine
seems so simple by comparison. At this minute I am just
beginning to have some sense of who I am and what I
am doing. I have been looking into job opportunities for a
liberal arts graduate. Not overwhelmingly bright but then
they do exist. I will take the Civil Service examination.
Then there may be a chance at teaching in private schools.
Anyway, I am doing something. . . . I finally got my literature paper back. He said that with a few small reserva-
tions, "Excellent." Very nice.

Floundering in my own uncertainties I was writing to
Claude, against my better judgment—I had no right to inflict my own concerns on an eighteen-year-old—mainly to
express my anguish:

Dorothy Lee? A complete question-mark. I spend a good
deal of time worrying about her. She never writes or calls
unless she wants money. . . . It's no use trying to communicate with her. She pays absolutely no attention to
anything I write, even when it's important. Sometimes I
weep for her. It is so terribly sad to see her caught in this
situation. I am of the opinion that Brick should be hos-
pitalized as soon as possible . . . to assure protection for
him. Dorothy Lee can't give him adequate care. He sleeps
most of the time. But even so, he needs care. I am trying
very hard to get Dorothy Lee to go to a psychiatrist . . . I
located here in Washington. I asked her to make an appointment for spring vacation. She hasn't so far.

The next day I received a letter from Dorothy Lee. Utter dejection. Brick had left. Not just for a few days in Cambridge. Rather, so far as she knew, forever.

Dear Mama,
    Brick's gone, left to go home, the West Coast, or just anywhere. I was waiting for him to decide what to do so it wasn't too much of an upset but right now I am very sad. It all seems so out of my hands. There is no where to find fault. No one was wrong or unkind. He loves me in his way or as much as he can love anyone but himself. For him I was a symbol of all he didn't think he was. Good, beautiful, honest. He left because he doesn't want to make a life or has to move or wants confusion, destruction. I really don't know. He wrote a letter which I'll bring home. It's all the explanation there is. I feel exhausted and a little relieved. I don't guess I ever believed it would work but so much was lovely I didn't want to have it end either. I held on, letting Brick work it out in his mind. Perhaps I should have done more but what, I don't know. It all has made me have vague realizations about myself and life in general, but I suppose that's to be expected. School goes on. Not much work now, but there will be so I think I'll try to get ahead over spring vacation. Can you help me with a paper or two? . . . I'll live but now I don't feel much like doing anything. Love you very much.

Saddest of all was the postscript. She had written the Florida Avenue Friends Meeting in Washington asking if she could be married under their oversight. Now she had written to the Meeting "telling them not to bother."
    Her friends rallied around her. A flurry of parties and signs of solidarity buoyed her up. Nancy's birthday party was large, noisy, and fun. She looked like a birthday cake in pink dress, orange beads, but pretty. Hope Cook was to leave to marry the prince of Sikkim in a week and Dorothy

Lee had promised to visit her some time. She was going to have dinner with a friend who knew Brick a little and he was trying to show solidarity. Ronald had called because he loved her and had known what was happening all along. Claude had also called; she loved him, he was so good. Her grades had been good—perhaps two As and a C—though Mrs. Lynd said her work was uneven, whatever that meant. Ronald said Brick was in Cambridge and acted "as if a weight had been lifted from his mind. He just couldn't care for me but then Ronald said he'll never be able to care for anyone the way he did for me. Oh, well, it's really beyond me to understand." Ronald had invited her to Cambridge during vacation; Brick would have left. In three months she would be out of school. Lord, she was tired. She did not think it necessary to see the Washington psychiatrist; if I insisted she would go to the school psychiatrist. To which I replied in a telegram: "Insist you see Dr. N. Don't break appointment. Don't go to Cambridge."

Dorothy Lee's letters during the spring were filled with accounts of her work, of plans for graduation, of visits with family. By the middle of April I was writing to Claude that I thought she was "coming along well; she still grieves in her unconscious and it comes out now and then. But, as the saying goes, 'time cures all.'" As, of course, I had had occasion to learn myself. In May I told Claude that Dorothy Lee was "going to take some of her inherited money for a trip to Mexico this summer." It was, I thought, a delaying action to avoid having to decide about a job. But I did not press her, feeling her problems were hard enough without such pressure.

By the end of May all the psychological work she had done was undone. A letter that began with a lot of cheerful news indicating how much she had achieved academically in the last three months ended with the news of Brick's return, plunging her once again into confusion.

Mama dear,

I am exceedingly proud of myself! Just finished typing
Mrs. Lynd's paper and I think it's good. Mrs. Bozeman was
very pleased with the paper for her (46 pages). I also did
my work sheets, so I am through except for a few odds
and ends and of course packing, organization, etc. I am
sending graduation invitations to Anita and family plus
Nancy and Joe. Who else? Should I ask about Uncle David?
As for hotels it would be cheaper and probably easier for
you to stay in New York because there isn't much out
here. I am excited about it. . . .

Now my future and plans have been thrown into a state
of complete confusion because Brick is back. He came
back to see me because he says he realized that I am most
important to him. He is much better. Stopped drugs and is
able to be honest about himself. It's difficult for me because I still feel strongly for him. I don't want to marry him
at least not in the near future, but I can't just leave him
and I don't want to. If I am the reason he has for doing
what he should do, i.e., get job, start to write, I want to
help him. I see things much more clearly and feel stronger
in myself. I am frightened because I just don't know how
strong I'll have to be and whether or not Brick is capable
of sticking with anything even if he wants to. I am seeing the doctor next week. Though I don't suppose he'll be
able to tell me what I should do. I wanted to write you first
before I talked to you so you would have time to get over
any strong reactions. I need your support so much now
and also feel wrong for being so dependent. Please help me
to work it out because I am just not sure. Would you
mind if Brick came to Washington after graduation for a
little so we could have some time to get things a little
straight? I'll call on the weekend. I love you.

My reply, two days later:

I'm delighted that the Lynd paper turned out good and that
Mrs. Bozeman was pleased with hers. It is a very great
victory for you. You picked yourself up and won. For a
while I wasn't sure you could make it. Congratulations.
You are much stronger for it. OK, we will plan to stay in
NYC and commute. It would be friendly to ask about
Uncle David. I will be delighted to meet your teachers.

You ask me "please help me to work it out." I will do
what I can: but you know that no more than the doctor am
I "able to tell you what you should do." All I can do is
help you analyze the situation. Here is what we have to
work with:

1. "I still feel strongly for him."
2. "I don't want to marry him . . ."
3. "I can't just leave him . . ."
4. "I don't want to."
5. "I want to help him."
6. "I am frightened . . ."
7. "I just don't know how strong I'll have to be . . ."
8. "I just don't know . . . whether or not Brick is capable
   of sticking with anything. . . ."
9. "I . . . feel stronger . . . but I need your support."
10. "I . . . feel wrong for being so dependent. . . ."
11. "I am just not sure."

This is the order in which the items occur in your letter.
Items 1, 3, 4, and 5 indicate the positive pull; you want to
do something for him, to help him, to support him. But
you aren't sure you can (items 6, 7, 8, 11). You feel guilty
because you need help yourself (items 9, 10). But even if
you could help him you don't want to marry him (item 2).
Since no matter how much you want to help him, you
aren't sure that you can, why not wait until you feel sure
that you can? It would be no favor to him to break down in
the attempt to pull him up. It would only make it worse
for him. . . . But if you will carry a load of guilt around
with you all your life, [unless you try to help him] you
may as well learn for yourself how hopeless it is. In my

opinion it would be wasting a normal person (you) trying
to help an incurable one (Brick). Since I have so much
love invested in you, naturally I deplore it. And no more
than you do I know what would constitute helping him.
Supporting him? Getting him a job? Giving him money?
Paying his rent? Feeding him? Living with him? Defending
him? Protecting him against the world? Clothing him?
My own feeling is that you should go ahead with your plans
as made, giving him three months to work things out.
When you return in the fall you will have a better perspective on it. As for his coming to Washington, that is out
of the question. There is just too much to be done. David
has to be gotten ready for camp, plans for the house have
to be made, Claude's graduation, deadlines in my work
to meet, etc., etc. You could "get things a little straight"
by letters as well as by face-to-face discussion. In fact,
better. Especially since it isn't at all clear what would
constitute getting things straight or what kind of help he
needs or can use. Like you, I would like to help him; but I
have quite a load of problems of my own right now and
couldn't take on another. This is a battle you have to fight
out yourself; the only help I can give you is this kind. Wish
I could do more. In the meanwhile, oceans of love. We are
looking forward to graduation with much pleasure.

Later, in May, feeling, perhaps, prematurely successful, I
was able to say in a letter devoted mainly to graduation
details, "Best wishes to Brick, really. I do hope he can
learn to come to terms with life."
    Brick came to the graduation. He served as an usher. He
was utterly charming. Afterwards he disappeared once
again. "Wish I could do more," I had written. But what? I
was to perform any number of postmortems on my dealing
with the whole Brick segment of Dorothy Lee's life. Would
it have been better if I had not tried so hard to control my
rage? Did my support give her a wrong assessment of the
situation? If she had felt that I would cast her off if she
persisted in her ties with him would she have been so vul-

nerable to his appeal? If I had been more willing to risk losing her would I have had a better chance of gaining her? Did my dread—for both myself and her—of reliving once again the trauma involved in severing a parent-child relationship unnerve me?[3] Did my determined logic confuse her? Or would nothing I did have made any difference? I still do not know.

Once more let down by Brick's disappearance after her graduation, Dorothy Lee accepted an invitation to visit friends in Chicago. Though all three were in the throes of job-hunting they spent a good deal of time on the beach, with more or less sporadic attempts to find jobs. Dorothy Lee tried a number of them—airline ticketing, National Opinion Research Center interviewer, and waitress at the Second City, an avant garde theater. But through it all, still the longing for Brick. Just before her twenty-second birthday she wrote:

I miss Brick and hope he comes, as well as I know he has faults and isn't a safe bet for a secure future, I want to be with him. As you have said, perhaps there is something about me that needs someone like Brick. The only thing that bothers me is that it worries and makes you unhappy. I know that you understand and most of your worry is because you want the best for me.

Her hope was realized. Brick reentered her life on her twenty-second birthday, by way of a gift.

Mama, thank you so much for the plant. It's mostly green —growing in moss with little yellow flowers. Very pretty. I feel very settled now I have a plant of my own. Claude sent me a birthday telegram. We had a party. I baked a cake. Ronald and Gene gave me two large coloring books, one of *Alice in Wonderland* and the other of *Wind in the Willows*. . . . I like them. Brick sent me a record which is nice too. So all in all I had a lovely birthday. I feel much older. . . . Work is going well, getting to be routine. I don't

think I'll be a waitress all my life. Will have to think about
what to do.

A week later Brick reappeared on the scene in person and
Dorothy Lee was once more cast into a maelstrom of conflict and uncertainty. But now she looked to Brick to help
her understand:

Mama Dear,
    I have been thinking lately that I have learned much from
this summer. Mostly that men are much different from
women and it is small wonder that communication is difficult. Always before I had thought that there wasn't all
that much difference, but now, after having lived in a house
full of boys and being the only girl, I have revised my
thinking. Boys are less straightforward or maybe it's just
that they are dealing with problems which don't concern
me or that I have gotten over. I am not sure what it is they
are trying to do—understand themselves I guess, but they're
in such a rush. Mostly I feel that there is time and I can't
be expected to know everything at once nor answer all
questions this minute. I am much more accepting. Sometimes it's a strain to always have people questioning. Also I
just don't have anyone to talk to in the way I can talk
with Joan or Lesley. Not necessarily about important
issues, just talk. Now that Brick has come I talk to him and
because he tries hard we sometimes manage to understand
each other. It's lovely to have someone to whom you want
to explain yourself.
    I also think there is a lot of hostility toward women on
the part of men. Never specific, certainly not open or
towards me but it's there. I asked Brick and he says it has
to do with boys and their relationship to their mothers. Is
that true? Do girls have hostility toward men? I am sure
they do, but why? Is it all a part of the problem of communication? There are many things I am thinking over but
[I] don't yet have formed ideas about.
    I realize how naive I am. I somehow manage not to see

what I don't want to see. Now I am trying to see what
is there and to work with it. It's just very hard to grow up
because so much is uncertain. Sometimes I wish I could
come home and have you settle everything for me. But
that wouldn't satisfy. Mostly I guess I want you to appreciate how difficult it is for us young ones to find a way.
I love Brick and want to be with him in spite of all warn-
ings, doubts, uncertainties. Perhaps it's not the best I could
do but I feel it is. I am trying to plan and to understand.
I will probably stay in Chicago, get an apartment, and
look for a new job come September. I won't get married
without seeing you and talking it over with you. But I
do want to be with Brick. The hardest thing is that I know
you don't approve so it makes me feel that I am hurting
you which I don't want to do at all. I love you both and
wish you would love each other.

Two weeks later:

Mama dear,
   I am looking forward to talking to you. I feel that so
much has happened to me and that I have come to understand the meaning of such all-encompassing terms as
"growing up," "being on your own," "the real world,"
etc. Sometimes it all seems so hard and not worth the effort and all I want in the world is to come home and be
protected. I know you understand the process of children
leaving home but home seems to represent ultimate security and certainty.
   Sally Kempton was just here for a few days on her way
back to N.Y. (She's been in California.) It was great to talk
to her and made me realize how lucky I am and no matter
how unsure I am about the future at least I love Brick
and that makes a difference. As you know, love isn't the
cure-all but it makes me able to function and gives me
courage. I am finding out that Brick's problems are one
thing and that I have my own as well but I am learning and
want very much for things to work. I think that always

before I haven't been sure enough of my own mind to be
able to seem at all sure to you. And your arguments and
worries were true enough to make me doubt my own
judgment. But I am coming to be very sure because I know
more about myself and about Brick. It's hard for him but
he understands himself quite well and realizes the need
for order and self-discipline and for just doing things even
if they're hard and unpleasant. It's getting better because
as he gets stronger and has more self-confidence he comes
to rely on himself. He helps me and I feel sure that he'll
be there when I need him. All in all I am happy. As you
see we have much to talk about.

Within a month Dorothy Lee and Brick were established
in a small apartment. I visited them and promised to send
odds and ends to make it more attractive. I must have kept
my anguish under good control.

Mama dear,
     Thank you for sending the rugs, etc. We've got nearly
everything up and in order. It is all beginning to look
homey. The living room drapes, are, I think, too heavy but
the brown ones are right. At any rate I'll get it all worked
out.
     I want also to tell you how happy I was with your visit.
It takes so much off my mind when I can feel you and
Brick can manage to like one another. I guess I have been
quite self-centered through this whole business but I just
didn't know what else to do. I will be very glad and relieved
when we are married. I got the letter from the Meeting
and it looks as if we'll have to start from the beginning. I
hope we can manage everything.
     I'm still working although the weather has cut down on
the number of customers. I don't know when or if I'll start
looking for another job. We were both interested in the
idea of writing articles but I'm not really sure I know anything. At least not enough for a whole article. We've discussed it a few times and perhaps we could do a rough draft

of some sort which you could look at. I also am thinking
about taking a history course at Loyola. Its being a Jesuit
school intrigues me. I've been reading quite a bit, cooking,
and not much else. Sunday we went to the dunes with
some friends. Had a lovely day walking around, swimming, and eating. We drove back and looked at the University which is quite huge. Lot of new buildings.

How are the boys? Tell Claude he is welcome to any of
my books. David, too. Just not to lose them. I'm very
interested to hear about Johns Hopkins. Please do write
me as I am anxious to hear from you. I don't want you to
stop loving me because of all this.

And so the girl who had longed for a noble cause, who had
agitated her soul to find worthy use for all she had learned,
became a happy nestling.

Dear Mama,
. . . the rugs look lovely. I've done quite a bit to make
the place look nice. Put up some of Jill's woodcuts. I have
the largest collection of original Jills. Anyway we're more
settled. We've been having people over and everyone likes it
so well they don't leave but sit around saying how comfortable it is and how nice we are. I am flattered, of course,
but then it's true. We also have been invited out several
times.

She was going to look for another job; Brick might get a
job as editor for some publication; she was beginning the
process of getting permission to be married under the oversight of the Meeting.

In October she was stricken with hepatitis and came
home for care and convalescence. When she was well
enough, plans were made for the wedding—announcements,
invitations—and for the oversight of the Meeting. On returning to Chicago she was pleased that Brick had "even
attempted to clean the house." He was pleased with the
plans. She wanted to thank me because it was lovely to see

me and to feel I was behind her, and just to talk to me.
She sometimes forgot how interested and busy I was.
"Anyway one should come home every now and again to
find out some perspectives." The letters were long, filled
with the details of her life: gifts I had sent (tea things,
lamp shade, books); interviews with members of the Meeting; clothes for the wedding. And, of course, Brick:

Last night we went to a folk music club and Brick played
a little. They liked him. The manager wanted to know if
he would take over a blue grass band and told him any
time he needed money, a job, etc., just to ask. I don't think
Brick will get too involved, partly because of the time and
partly because of the whole association with the scene.
It would be fun if he could just play with people for enjoyment without making it his whole life. I was really very
proud because everyone thought he was good—vicarious
experience.
Brick and I have talked about his seeing a psychologist. I
don't think it is absolutely necessary that he does because
as I've told you he can see himself quite clearly but I would
feel better if he did try it out. He would too, I think, just
because he's now beginning to understand that there
are a lot of his motivations or whatever that he recognizes
and can control but doesn't really know where they come
from. I am afraid I'm not making this very clear. Perhaps the best way to explain is that he's come to the point
where he is strong enough that he can be curious about
himself without becoming completely overwhelmed. I
think I am a little jealous of the idea first because I almost
unconsciously want to keep it just the two of us and second because I resent the attention he would be getting.
But we've discussed this and so we know where we are beginning at least. Now what I want to know is what is the
best way to find a psychiatrist? Would a clinic be good
enough? Can we find one who is good without being too
expensive? Where should we begin?
It's funny and perhaps the best thing about loving some-

one that the more you come to understand the other
person the more you understand yourself and because you
understand yourself better you are able to love the other
person more. I hope you don't worry about all this. There
really is no crisis. Just better understanding.

Brick continued to play at coffeehouses from time to time,
Dorothy Lee becoming more nervous than he. She worried
that the audience would not appreciate him enough. She
sat and listened to all the performers, bad as they were,
because she felt they should have an audience. Brick said
she was too tender but since she herself would dread having to perform she felt those who had the nerve to do so
should get all the support possible. Brick was thinking of
returning to school to study criminal psychology or
criminology but it was all very vague so I was not to take
it too seriously, "but suggestions welcome." She was
knitting Brick a scarf. She was going to put up the green
and brown drapes. "I have a lovely house." She was sending the item about the wedding, clipped from the *New
York Times,* to Brick's mother.

Toward the middle of November, Ezra came to visit:

Brick went Friday for his interview with representatives
of the Meeting. . . . He said it went well. We were going to
Meeting this morning but I was too exhausted to get up so
I slept until you called.
Ezra called Friday night about 8:00 and I went down to
his hotel. I was a little nervous. After all I haven't really
talked to him for 11 years. He was smaller than I remembered and has white hair but very attractive. He was nervous too I think. We went up to his room and talked.
We talked about how fast you did everything and how it
was sometimes difficult to keep up. Also he mentioned
daddy several times but I somehow got the impression he
resents or is in some way hostile towards him. I imagine
Daddy gave Ezra a rather hard time so I didn't press the
subject. We talked about how hard it is to find some-

thing one can do or to find one's place. He said he thought I'd had the best kind of education, etc. Then he told me about this project he works on, teaching older people, which I think is his pet. I also told him all about Brick, drugs and all. Then he told me about alcoholism. I think he felt a kind of understanding of Brick and wanted to assure him he wasn't the only one who had ever gone through that kind of thing. So when I invited him for dinner he accepted. As he was walking me to the El he said how much different it was between how he'd remembered me and me now. I was a very understanding and charming young woman. It almost made me cry because I felt so guilty and bad for having not been more understanding when I was younger, but then I really didn't know what was going on. I couldn't see anything but myself. I'm not doing a very good job of this letter but it really was right somehow to be able to talk to Ezra and to try and understand both myself now and when I was little.

Ezra came about 7. I'd cleaned the apartment and it looked nice. We all talked for a while about the weather, etc. Then I went in to make dinner and Brick and Ezra talked. Things were a little strained until after dinner. Then Brick and Ezra really began to talk and enjoy it. I was kind of left out because they were talking about how they felt, about when they were younger, etc. I think Ezra was trying to make Brick's actions and motives the same as his and in many ways they seem alike. At any rate they both talked for hours. Brick told stories about people he knew at Harvard and Ezra talked about people at his university. He also talked about a cottage he'd built. Finally Ezra and I fell to remembering the department at Penn State, Mr. Green, Mr. Clark, Mr. Coutu, etc. Brick laughed. Ezra told stories and I told how it had all seemed to me. Ezra left about 1:30 and I think he'd really been pleased with the evening. I told him as I walked him to the underground that I wished that Brick and you could talk with the same openness and he said he doubted it because you were my mother but he would write you and tell you what he

thought. Anyway I was happy and Brick really likes Ezra.
I would like to talk to you about it when I see you because
it's difficult to write it down.

On December 27 the wedding was rehearsed and the
next day it was solemnized under the care of the Florida
Avenue Meeting. The only remaining letter from me to
Dorothy Lee for the second half of 1963 was dated December 29, the day after her marriage. (During the summer
and fall there had been so much moving about on Dorothy
Lee's part that my letters had apparently been lost in the
logistics. And also, on my part, a good deal of the communication had been by telephone.) The last letter:

Dear Dorothy Lee and Brick,
    It was in every way a lovely wedding. Everyone said how
much they had enjoyed it, how impressive the ceremony
was, and how pleasant the reception. I believe they all
meant it. . . .
    I wish for both of you much happiness. And I want to
explain why I fought this marriage for almost a year, tooth
and nail. On the basis of the only facts I had at my dis-
posal the prognosis for such a marriage was not good.
Everything I knew about Brick was problematical. It looked
to me that he had been in a tailspin or at least a downward
spiral for several years, with a knack of putting himself
into positions which left him no choices, no alternatives.
There were long stretches in the fall when Dorothy Lee
didn't even hear from him, there was all the uncertainty
about his return, there was his condition—physical, emotional, and mental—when he did return. When, therefore,
Dorothy Lee initiated the process of getting married under
the care of the Meeting I could not give my consent. I
was fearful that marriage would mean she would not complete her college work. There seemed to be nothing in
favor of the marriage. When Brick left in the spring, it
seemed to me to validate my judgment. It was heartbreak-
ing, of course, to see how hard this was on her but it

seemed to me the best solution and that she would get over
it. When he returned, my misgivings returned; it seemed
one more evidence of his instability. During the summer I
was further confirmed in my misgivings by hearing from
Mrs. Hutchison that Brick had told Nancy he had traf-
ficked in drugs. When Brick went to Chicago I was fearful.
But little by little, as Dorothy Lee's doubts began to clear
up it occurred to me that if she had no doubts, why should
I. I became reconciled. And little by little it occurred to
me that perhaps we were in the presence of an authentic
miracle. It appeared that Dorothy Lee's love, trust, faith,
and confidence were really helping Brick rehabilitate himself. That is what I now believe and that was what made
it possible for me to accept this marriage and do everything I can to make it not only a happy and successful one
but the happiest and most successful one that is possible
for both of you.

I find that Brick, too, had had a similarly creative influence on Dorothy Lee. He has made it possible for her to
recognize what a truly beautiful woman she is. . . . I must
say that even when I was fighting Dorothy Lee the hardest
I couldn't help but admire the way she fought for what
she wanted. She is the kind of person I wanted her to be.
And I know that she will grow and develop and mature
and gain in pose, self-confidence, and understanding for the
rest of her life. I don't think that life is going to be
especially easy. But Dorothy Lee is an enormously self-
disciplined person; she never really flinches. I am laying my
bets on her ability to lick the odds.

I hope you had a wonderful time in New York. We
will send the packages later in the week so they will get
there about the time you do. Everything seems very quiet
now. There is time to review and remember.

My faith, so extravagantly expressed, proved misplaced.
There was no authentic miracle, as indeed, I must have
known in my heart there could not be. I lost that bet. It
took Dorothy Lee a long time to see that no miracle had

happened or was about to happen. Resilient, gallant, indomitable though she was, she was no match for the enemy she was facing. She fought the battle for Brick against one of the most formidable and powerful of foes—alcohol—and, in the end, she lost.

When the marriage was over, the grief lived through, the psychological work completed, there was no anger on either side, no resentment, no hostility, no recrimination, certainly no hatred. No feelings of bitterness, no sense of "wasted years." The fact that the marriage ended in divorce did not mean to Dorothy Lee that it had been a failure. They had had, as she once tried to tell me, in many ways a good marriage. Worth the cost which was, admittedly, high. She had had the experience of total love in the Pauline sense. Not everyone, even in long-standing intact marriages, could say that.

Now, with all passion spent, I can also, like Dorothy Lee, view Brick through a clearer lens. As the emotional film that once clouded it disperses a more balanced image comes through. I can see him in a more dispassionate light. I deplore the waste of talent his life represented. So beautiful as a young man—tall, slender, blond, blue-eyed—gentle and soft-spoken. So brilliant. I have long since given up trying to explain.

part II

Claude
and I

autobiographical
introduction

When Dorothy Lee—everyone's ideal of what an infant should be—blue-eyed, golden-haired, with rose-petal skin—proved to be such a delight even to her originally reluctant father, there was little argument about a second child. None at all, in fact. I can scarcely even remember that pregnancy. My work went on apace. The students were again concerned that I was running up and down the stairs too fast and asking weren't my heels too high? But they were even more concerned about the young men serving in the military and they sat around the college snack bar arguing endlessly the pros and cons of marrying now so that at least they would have his child in case he himself never came back.

It was an uneventful pregnancy that terminated July 2, 1945. Several weeks later I emerged from the tight little postpartum cocoon that envelops the mother of a new-born—always joyous in my case, never depressed—only to discover Hiroshima and Nagasaki. I was utterly dismayed. How come, I demanded, that no one had told me? The Bomb was to shadow my mind during all the years of the childhood of my children.

It was also in Claude's early childhood that the enormity

of the Holocaust had struck me, not only for what it meant for the human beings involved themselves—horrendous as that was—but also for what it implied for my whole intellectual *Weltanschau*. LLB had written his doctoral dissertation on the "transition to an objective standard of social control," which meant, in effect, that with the advent of the social sciences it was now going to be possible to determine objectively the best way to achieve desired societal ends. It reflected the point of view of Auguste Comte, often called the father of sociology. The work of Comte in the nineteenth century had had an impact on many thinkers similar to that of Newton in the seventeenth. He had envisaged a world of phenomena more abstract than a world of planets and stars but one equally susceptible to scientific, especially mathematical, study. He spoke of the "positive method" and he foresaw the result of applying it to the study of societies as "sociology" or a "science of society." But there was another side to Comte. The science of society, the Positive Philosophy as it was called, was only a prelude. The purpose was to introduce the true masterwork, the Positive Polity. As Comte described it, it looked absurd, fundamentally a blueprint for a totalitarian society modeled after the Catholic Church, in which scientists replaced priests. Comte's intellectual disciples were embarrassed by the Polity and rejected it. It was like a deformed child that the family tries to keep out of public view.

Still, reject Comte's Polity as they might, proponents of the new science did, like him, look forward to the time when science, if not scientists, would chart the human course. Coming upon this vision was the most dazzling of my college experiences. My own faith in science—I use the term *faith* advertently—remained unchallenged, unexamined, for more than a quarter of a century. It took a catastrophe as overwhelming as the Nazi Holocaust to shake that faith. A whole network of intellectual, emotional, and moral roots were dug up and exposed in the process. The faith on which I had built a life was shaken, the nineteenth-century faith in the benign nature of science, a belief that it was intrinsically good. And belief in the intellectual infallibility of the man—teacher as well as husband—who had shaped my mentality.

As in a frozen movie frame I remember the very moment when the nature, dimensions, and implications of the Nazi final solution struck me. It was in the university library one evening when I first ran across an article describing the psychology of the extermination camp.[1] There was no category in my mind under which to classify this article. Was it scientific? Was it for real? Was it accurate? I was literally at sea. I could not handle it. I had no intellectual preparation for it.

I do not remember discussing any of this with LLB. He never knew of the alienation I experienced in those years of emotional and intellectual *Sturm und Drang*. I never spoke of either the alienation I experienced from the sociological positivism he had instilled in me or the emotional alienation from him as a result of it. For here, in effect, was the "objective" standard of social control in practice. Here was science in the service of—evil—men.[2]

During the first few years of his life, therefore, Claude did not have a serene mother. Nor was the situation ameliorated by the death of his father when he was five. The months following this event were excruciatingly difficult. One parent was just not enough. When their father had been alive there had been a rough sort of balance. Each child had had a parent. Their father belonged to Dorothy Lee and I belonged to Claude. That was the way we had lined up on walks, picnics, family expeditions. The loss of one parent upset the equilibrium of the whole structure. Now, bereft of "her" parent, Dorothy Lee began to horn in on Claude's property. The competition between them for my time and attention—only partially relieved by Ezra's taking Claude under his wing—became almost intolerable. As Dorothy Lee saw things, Claude now had both a father and a mother while she did not have even her share of me. (Part of her hostility to Ezra arose from this double father-loss.) I tried sending Claude to camp when he was seven, "which turned out to be an awful mistake," as I later wrote to David and "it took a long time for him to get over my deserting him like that." He was too young. It was to be a long time before we "balanced" again, a long time before Dorothy Lee and Claude ceased to keep accounts. The struggle for the love and attention of the only parent available broke out from time to time for many years, despite my fetish of complete equality among all the children, my determination to show no favoritism.[3]

If there had been uncles and cousins and grandparents to close ranks the void would have been less gaping. More than just increased demands on me was involved. The lack of "family" seems to me now to have been one of the most serious deprivations the children had to suffer. No family on their father's side; their one paternal uncle and aunt had died before Claude was born. In my childhood the sense of family, though fading even then, was still real. My parents had retained contacts with their relatives. I had had aunts and uncles on both sides and there were occasional family gatherings, which were festive and gay, with all ages from infants in arms to seemingly ancient grandparents, even a great-grandmother. True, family in this personal, immediate sense was not to survive long. By the time I grew up there had been losses by death, by mobility, by centrifugal pulls into new professions, new careers, new interests, new kinds of children. But at least I had known what a family could be. My children never did. The nearest Dorothy Lee remembers was a neighborhood Thanksgiving celebration at which, as in a large family, all ages were celebrating together. She loved it, it remained one of her happiest childhood memories.

I had never had any question about my ability to provide economic support for the children. The inadequacies I feared were less remediable. I could never be more than a single, lone, separate, isolated individual. I could never be a father, or even cousin, aunt, uncle, grandmother, in addition to mother to my children. I could never be a family.

I could never provide a network of relationships. With my children I stood alone.

There were feeble attempts to revivify contacts with relatives. Before their father's death we went, all of us, to Kentucky to visit the Bernards. There was a whole clan of them and, for the moment, there was family. Later on there were visits to Minneapolis where my several cousins created instant family ties. And while they lasted they were reassuring. But fragile as gossamer, a momentary, insubstantial web with little residue, impossible to sustain into the future. The demise of the extended family was not a sociological abstraction to me. I had lived through it.

chapter five

handyman,
assistant, surrogate

Although Claude played an important part in my life—as handyman, assistant, surrogate, and confidant-mentor—he appears to be offstage a good deal of the time in this story. He was not separated from me as often or as long as the others. He did not travel as much as they did. He was away for only short periods of time and for the most part remained within telephone range so that there were few occasions for letters. "I'm not in the habit of writing," he wrote to Dorothy Lee when he was fifteen. "In fact, I never write home. OUCH." But, he added, he often called home. When he did write, beyond the earliest years, his letters tended to be impersonal, factual, with a minimum of feeling, but often quite funny. Humor was as good a distancing device as any. Rarely, if ever, reports of either depression or elation.

There were several strikes against Claude from the beginning. Not the least important, health problems. He suffered from crippling allergies that sometimes made mere breathing a life-or-death struggle. From Graz I had written to Dorothy Lee in December that Claude was not feeling well. "He had a hard time breathing all night and he has been coughing hard. . . . If he continues sick I will try to get him into a hospital where he can get good care." In addition, he had had polio one summer which, though it had left no permanent damage that we could detect, did restrict his activities that year.

An even more serious strike against him was the loss of his father at an age—five—which psychoanalysts told me was the worst possible time for a boy because at that age he had not yet had time to work out his relationship with his father. And in Claude's case it meant that I came to lean on him in many ways. I depended on him for help ranging from the trivial to the profound. This dependence on my part placed him in the equivocal position of both needing support from me and supplying it to me.

Equally serious was his position vis-à-vis the other children in the family. He was, first of all, from the age of five on, a middle child and had to come to terms not only with a sister four years older than he but also thereafter with a brother five years younger. As a child he found both Dorothy Lee and me almost equally intimidating, her power less chastened than mine and hence more fearsome. When I once rebuked her for pummeling him, pointing out to her that it was doing him no good, her reply was: "I know, but it makes me feel better." I was not unaware of the hazards of his position, writing to him at fifteen "that it has not been good for you to have two dominating older females in your environment." Perhaps we had undermined his self-confidence. Having an older sister may have made him too passive. I asked him to think about all these things.

Although at the age of nine Claude became freed from the daily presence of one of the dominating females when Dorothy Lee went away to school, he was still exposed to a little brother whose smaller size worked in his favor with adults if not with Claude himself. Sometimes the relations between them became murderous. In a letter to Dorothy Lee when Claude was twelve and David seven, I reported: "This morning I was playing definition with David. You know. What is a house? a rug? a boy? etc. I asked, 'What is

a brother? 'Someone who tries to kill you' . . . was his
reply."

Although in time Claude's letters were to become quite
inexpressive, still, early on, undated, there was an attempt
at loving poetry which made its point quite affectingly:

> MOTHER I LOVE YOU
> YOUR SO DEAR
> MOTHER I *LOVER—you*
> Your [son Claude]

The first of the bona fide letters from me to Claude were
to camp. They were attempts on my part to overcome the
reluctance he had felt, though bravely suppressed, at being
sent away from home, the first letter timed to arrive on his
birthday:

Dear Claudie,

> Happy birthday to you!
> Happy birthday to you!
> Happy birthday, dear Claudie,
> Happy birthday to you!

How does it feel to be so old? I bet you are having a lot of
fun being seven years old. We surely thought Camp Lanape
was a wonderful place. It was hot all the way home. David
insisted on having all the car windows open, so my hair
practically blew away. We came home a different road;
it was pretty, too, like the road we went on going there.
We stopped at a place called Rickett's Glenn to eat our
oranges and then came home. We found that there had
been a bad storm in State College; it blew down a tree in
Euwema's yard. We were glad we had missed that. This
morning David took all our empty milk bottles over to the
Hutchinson's step, so the milkman was all mixed up about
how much milk we all wanted. It is pleasant and cool here

today. I bet it is wonderful at camp. I hope you are having
a wonderful time. I will send your belt today. Lots of love
from Mother.

And, ten days later, a post card:

Dear Claude,
   I am glad you are having fun. I hope you are learning to
swim. How are the horses? I bet the boat trips are wonderful. It is fine to have movies. David still is very mischievous.
He spilled paint on Dorothy Lee's rug. Dorothy Lee played
in her basement house today. It has rained here which was
good for the plants. I love you, Mother.

My enthusiastic sales pitch was not altogether successful.
Though he tried bravely not to let me down, not to show
how miserable he felt at being cut off from the old familiar
patterns of his life which I so tactlessly reminded him of—
including David's mischief and Dorothy Lee's playhouse—
the camp counselors had, finally, to concede that it would
be better if he did not remain for both sessions. Although
he had been sent to camp in the first place to ameliorate
his position as middle child, the effect was rather to
aggravate it.
   As a result of his position, the injustices of life were
brought home to him early. It wasn't fair. At fourteen he
wrote to me at Kabul in protest:

Because David and I really miss you we scrap even more
than usual and then too because of this long trip taken by
Dorothy Lee. And Hutchie is on edge and comes over at
any moment when David cries and separates us like tonight
David fell and hurt his side partly because of me and some
his own fault but Hutchie came over and made David go to
sleep in his bed and not to sleep in my room where he has
been for several days. . . . Even though she is to guard us I
wish she wouldn't always interfere. You know David's

crying and how nerve-wracking it is but when she threatens to keep him at her house it is (I think) too much. (Do you agree?)

I understood if I did not necessarily agree. I knew he would be blamed, as the older one, no matter what. So all I could do was appease him:

Now, Claude dear, I know what a difficult spot you are in and, believe me, I do agree with you. . . . Try hard to be as patient as you can with David and Hutchie and try to show it with her if possible. . . . Also, if it is possible, be tolerant of David. I guess he suffers most of all from my absence because he is the youngest. So try to help him as much as you can. It was good of you to take him to the pool. Go as often as you can.

About a month later Claude wrote, from Princeton, to me at Lisbon:

This happened to me. Every morning as I awaken I find a great big object upon me. I struggle to think what it is and what I see makes me try to turn around, but alas I cannot for it is already upon me. All manner of noise utter from its noise-maker. Then, all at once it is at a dozen places at once. Then when I awake, I realize that it is not a baby whale but my little brother who caused my suffering. The end.

Now that they were in Princeton I wrote, "please, boys, try not to yell and fight so that you make a bad impression." Two years later almost to the day I was writing to Dorothy Lee how delighted I was that the boys' friends were back. We had surely missed them, for:

Not having outsiders to associate with, Claude and David have scrapped day and night until I had to shriek at them. David feels so inferior and discriminated against that he is paranoid, and Claude, being unable to handle the situation, strikes out in frustration. Leaving me in the middle. But now that their friends are back I hope all will be well.

Poor Claude. Poor David. Poor mother.

Still, despite his frustration, there was an underlying affection and concern for David and even companionship. "Since David has control over his sleeping hours," he wrote to me at Hong Kong, "he is often grouchy and very temperamental. He misses you to the extent of violent coughing in his sleep. . . . Last night David and I went to see the *Diary of Anne Frank*. . . . I suspect David and I will be going to *Sleeping Beauty* before long."

Sensitive as I was to the hazards of the middle child and fetishistic as I was about equality, it is surprising to me as I reread the letters to find how different my relations were with Claude than with either Dorothy Lee or David. Harsher, it seems to me, and "meaner."

Problems with money took on a different cast with Claude. Early on he and I had worked out a credit system in dealing with them. It arose originally in connection with his passion for toy automobiles. Almost from the moment he could clutch anything in his hands, toy automobiles had enthralled him. The first document in his file was an attempt to start a magazine devoted to automobiles. It included four drawings—a taxi, a cab, an unlabeled car, and a car embellishing the C in "Claude." It was this thralldom that precipitated the first monetary crisis in our relationship, when he was nine. He needed money to support his habit of buying Dinky toys. So on August 5, 1954, he signed the following document written in my hand: "Having received advanced allowance to buy a jeep I promise never again to ask for an advance. If I want to buy anything I will save in advance. [Signed] Claude." Next spring there was another transaction, this time formalized in a typed document:

On this day Charles Henry Claude Bernard borrowed
$2.50 from his mother, Jessie Bernard. Beginning Friday,
March 4, he promises to repay this amount at the rate of
$.25 a week in ten installments, the last to be May 6, 1955.
Repayments will be acknowledged below.

(Signed) Claude

My own signed acknowledgements of payments follow
from March 4 to April 29. The last payment, due May 6,
was never recorded if, indeed, it was ever made.

Claude's credit was, nevertheless, apparently unimpaired,
for on June 21 of the same year there was another prom-
issory note:

Received of Mother the sum of $2.00 in return for which
I promise not to raise the subject of money again until
July 22, 1955. It is understood that I may use $1.00 of
this money for a Dinky toy, but not more than ten cents
for candy or sweets.

(Signed) Claude Bernard

No record remains of the enforcement of this contract, but
my concern for his debts continued. When he was fifteen I
was hoping that everything was going nicely with him, that
he had both his lessons and his debts well in hand. I had
reason to be concerned because I was still a creditor. Only
recently did I learn that Claude later became a banker of
sorts among the children, both David and Dorothy Lee
among his borrowers.

When the love affair with automobiles—and later trains—
had abated somewhat a new money-gobbling love sprang
up in the form of photography. Thus, writing to Dorothy
Lee when Claude was sixteen, I said that I still thought it
"fantastic for a 16-year-old to have two movie cameras,"
and reassured her that his second movie camera was not a
Christmas gift; I was taking the money it cost out of his
allowance for the next three months. Still, even when he
was nineteen there were occasional throwbacks to the

promissory-note approach from time to time. This time about a recorder which, for the moment, seemed of transcendent importance to him:

Of course, if you are sure that having the recorder would positively help you learn French—and that is the objective—perhaps we could work out a system whereby I would advance you the money and you could pay it back at the rate of $5 per month for 20 months. Or pay half at that rate. In any event, there is no more maturing experience than paying one's own way at least in part. So please think about this.

As in the case of Dorothy Lee, I descended at least once to the depths of corruption, that is, to bribery. After expressing pleasure with his grades that were so much better than I had been led to expect from the way he had talked, and hope that he would continue as well the rest of the term, I broached a shady deal, somewhat apologetically: "I don't like to emphasize grades too much but maybe we could make a deal to pay you for good grades." The details of that deal—if it ever matured—are not clear in either the letters or in my memory. In view of this episode, my reaction to Claude's attempts to manipulate me—almost a replay of my reaction to Dorothy Lee's—seems hardly warranted. In reply to a request for $100 when he was nineteen I wrote:

I can handle everything but when there is a sudden request for $100 it throws me and, in addition, I think it isn't a good idea for you to feel I have to get everything for you. As I see it, when you want something your first reaction is: how can I convince mother or how can I get this from mother or what's my best approach to mother? It never occurs to you to think how you might earn it. That's understandable so far but it can't go on too much longer. I think you ought always to think: should I ask mother to work a whole day to get this for me? (or two or three or

however many days, figuring about $50 per day). Or, do I
want this enough to work a week for it myself? I think,
that is, that you should begin to give very serious thought
to how you can earn money yourself. It wouldn't be too
early to think about the possibility of work Christmas
vacation.

Although Claude earned small amounts of money from
time to time, it was some years before he achieved financial independence, modest in scale though it was. He had
minded his dependence. He savored even the small income
from his alternate service. Despite a modest inheritance
at the age of twenty-one, he wrote to David: "I have
decided to live only off my salary and not off the [inher-
ited] monies in reserve. . . . It isn't much but it is a form
of independence from mother and other people that allows
me to be my own man."

In fact, the dependency relationship between Claude and
me was far from a one-way bond. There was a peculiarly
symbiotic tie between us. I became as dependent on him as
he on me.

Handymen were always hard to find. For major break-
downs and regular seasonal yard work there was usually
professional help available. But not always for the almost
daily nagging little maintenance and upkeep chores which
are the bane of every household. Claude was good at handling them and I came increasingly to depend on him. He
became in time, like Ezra, the kind of man who entered
the house asking if there was anything that needed tending
to—stalled appliances? fuses to be changed? pictures to
be hung? batteries to be changed? storm sash? screens?
shelves to be built? furniture to be repaired? The book-
shelves and the handsomest furniture in our home—and
now in his—were his handiwork. Hand skills were his forte.

Even after he went away to school at fourteen he was
still advising me. Thus, for example, when I mentioned the
breakdown in the television set, two things came to his

mind and he advised me to: "(1) check the extension cord and (2) monkey with the antenna. If trouble still persists," he continued tersely, "call a repair man." I'm sure he knew what monkeying with the antenna meant and supposed that I would too. In the spring of that year I wrote to tell him that "there will be lots of chores for you when you get here. I mean in the yard, getting the grass seeded, weeds killed, etc." But, I reassured him, he should not worry. "We won't overwork you." The following fall I wrote that we were saving lots of chores for him, but, lest he take this too seriously, I added, "not really." Five years later I was still calling on him. When, for example, I had locked myself out of the house one day and the police had had to break a small pane in the kitchen door to open it, "instead of calling in a glazier to replace the little pane," I wrote, "I am waiting until you return to see if you can do it." But now I was paying for his services. "Last time it happened the pane of glass cost 20¢ but the labor cost $10.00. If you can do it I would rather pay you than the glazier." I also threw in the subtle comment that "the yard is a mess" and wondered if I had told him "about the millions of nasty, brown, slimy moldy mushrooms or toadstools that have taken over?" Claude was not enthusiastic about all these chores, but he was reconciled. To David, he complained: "I can't understand why mother doesn't write more about what happens to her and less about the yard." Now, I told him, I knew what was meant when people said that something had "mushroomed." It had just sprung up, full grown, overnight. He got the hint. He helped deal with the nasty, brown, slimy, moldy things. Until he entered his alternate service at twenty-three and left home for good I continued to call on him for handyman help. Just before he left I wrote to David: "I will miss his [Claude's] services around the apartment and it is perhaps just as well that, in his shelf-happy condition, he leave before he begins to put shelves on the ceiling. The apartment has shaped up quite nicely and I think I will be able to manage without him from here on in." Just as well, indeed; the handyman services after his return were to be devoted to his own home.

It was only a step from being a handyman to being an assistant, even a surrogate. I began fairly early to turn over to him chores dealing with David. When I could not, for example, be there—anywhere—I expected Claude to take over responsibility for David. Thus to him when we were living in Princeton:

Now about Friday. I will leave a check with David. Buy whatever you need at the shopping center. I will leave at 2:50. I will be returning around 9 Sunday night. Do your homework Friday night so you can have fun on Saturday. Mabye even go in to New York. Ringling Brothers and/or boat trip around the island. Etc. If you have any questions let me know.

When he was to look after David after camp, I sent detailed instructions and ideas for him on how to spend their time: "(1) go swimming at the Vic Tanney's on K Street; (2) call Mrs. Chilman in Alexandria to meet her nephews; (3) talk to the Seymours; (4) take the barge trip up the canal; (5) revisit the museums; (6) take the Roosevelt Island walk; (7) visit congressional hearings; (8) write; (9) review your German; (10) look at exhibits at the Library of Congress. Again three days later:

Here is the daily change of plan! I received a letter from the doctor who examines the boys for football camp who had scheduled David for August 26 at 1:40 p.m. I wrote back saying David couldn't make it at that time and would he please reschedule the examination. I said David would certainly be back by the 28th. As soon as I find out when the examination is rescheduled I will let you know and we can plan from there. If the examination is rescheduled for the 27th or 28th, David will have to go directly to D.C. If it is for a later date, he might be able to make it up here

[State College] but it may not be worth the bother. By now you have looked up the transportation problems. As I see it from the bus schedule between Harrisburg and State College the problems are about insuperable. I am enclosing a check for $50 to take care of your expenses going for David and for his expenses arriving and getting back to D.C. Please keep some sort of account and if it is not enough, lend David enough money to do what he has to do. OK?

And then, three days later, having forgotten to remind him of another detail, I added: "Be sure to look after David's return. I sent him money for his ticket. Meet him at the station. Find out when to expect him. He is very homesick and anxious to see us all." Claude was meticulous and dependable about carrying out all these charges.

It was just another small step from surrogate to secretary-assistant. I began fairly early to turn over important chores for him to handle. During my long absences on trips, for example, he took over my correspondence as it accumulated. Bills, bank deposits, mortgage payments from State College, odds and ends. Thus, in 1964, when we were in the process of selling the first Washington house, he wrote:

Hold on to your hat! I just was interrupted in the middle of *Newsweek* by the doorbell. There, as I opened the door, stood the ministers of defense and finance from the Bolivian Embassy. I met them both and shook hands. After looking all around the house, they turned to me and said: "We are most interested in this house and will keep pushing it through." There is great hope in the air.

Three years later Claude was reporting my correspondence in the form of the news to me—then on a tour to the South Seas and Australia—in the form of a newspaper which he called *The 4601 Daily News.*

BOOK GOES INTO PRODUCTION

The major manuscript of the decade in the field of marriage and family among Negroes went into production this past June 30. The publishers, Prentice-Hall, were very happy to have this important work on their lists for the year. Mr. James J. Murray, III, attempted to contact the author, Dr. Bernard, but was unable to as the author was out of the country. All was not lost, however, as Dr. Bernard's personal secretary explained the circumstances to the publishing firm.

BILL ARRIVES IN THE HOUSE FOR CONSIDERATION

The bill for the successful excision of the left breast tumor of David Bernard arrived in the House for consideration today. When asked to comment on her feelings, the mother was unable to speak. The bill will now go to the banking and finance committee for consideration, and it is hoped that it will pass before autumn.

INVITATION EXTENDED FOR CONFERENCE

An invitation was extended today to Dr. Jessie Bernard, formerly of the Penn State University. Dr. L. M. Y. Nuñez extended a personal invitation to Dr. Bernard in Spanish, to attend the conference from the 22nd through the 26th of November in Veracruz, Mexico. The great popular demand for the attendance of Dr. Bernard is of little surprise as she is recognized as one of the leaders in her field, whatever it may be!

ASSETS INCREASE WITH FUNDS ARRIVING

The assets of the Bernard Corp. were enlarged today as some long-term debts were deposited for services rendered. The increase over the past balance was in the amount of 311.99 dollars. The solvency of the company is no longer threatened.

The final installment came July 30, 1965, reporting the return of the missing traveler:

DOCTOR JESSIE BERNARD FEARED MISSING

At long last the great voyage is finished and the weary traveler is returning home to recover and recoup. However, from the sound of said traveler on the phone, she is ready to tackle several problems upon arrival at home. She must be prepared to bank much cash, to sign the final contract to sell a house, to turn down many job offers, and to deal with the IRS. The latter, I fear, wishes to soak the weary of $$$. Down with capitalist devils.

Claude was, as Dorothy Lee had said, "responsible and capable of doing what has to be done." We took it for granted. We all expected him to do what had to be done—and depended on it.

chapter six

hard issues, hard answers

I was, I think, more obtuse with the boys than with Dorothy Lee. And more severe. I had no way of knowing the traumas of male adolescence. I might—and did—know *about* them. I had read any number of accounts of adolescence. But it was not until later, much later, that I learned how much anguish the male culture could inflict on its neophytes.[1] I had understood Dorothy Lee's adolescent world much better. I had not always approved of what she did; we had fought quite a bit. But we had been together, in the same world. Not so in the case of the boys. Especially in the case of Claude. Some years later I wrote that Dorothy Lee and David had noticed a matter he and I had discussed ourselves, that I was meaner to him than to them, that I had punished him for my own defects.

Explanations can be facile, their validity often questionable. Claude was vulnerable from being in the position of both dependent son and emotional support. As a son he was entitled to support from me; as himself a support to me, he felt obligated to be more than a son.[2] His feeling that I depended on him complicated his drive for independence.

In reply to Claude's first letters from boarding school, in which he had expressed his concerns, I had written:

Don't worry! It seems to me you worry all the time and then think of things to justify your worry. Of course you miss me and the pleasures of home. But natch. It's very pleasant not to have any work to do or responsibilities to meet. I have the same feelings. It's hard to get back to work and I don't look forward to it. But by now you have probably licked your feelings. But you make me worry when you worry so much. It won't be long before you are home again. What good is it if you worry all the time? Just learn to live with yourself and your problems. I'm always here ready to help you when you really need it. OK? Lots of love, my dear boy, Mother.

How different, it now occurs to me, from the letters I had written four years earlier to Dorothy Lee when she was a homesick freshman at the same school.[3]

Claude's attempts at distancing himself became noticeable early in his sophomore year. I responded: "I am a little worried about you. I don't understand why you refused to talk to me last Sunday. I have been expecting you to call me or write and explain. Were you sick? Or what? Just a word of explanation would help." Not a word of explanation was forthcoming. Three years later he noted, without explanation, that "the big problem is that you and I have lost much of the medium of communication that allowed us to speak so freely before."

Whatever demons Claude was wrestling with, his letters became less and less feeling-laden, almost stark. There was less and less self-revelation. He did not, like Dorothy Lee, in effect, shake his fist at me, declare war, throw down the gauntlet. He maintained what David, now looking back, calls his "Reichean armor." Dorothy Lee wrote from London,"I've gotten several letters from Claude who is really a charming young man, he seems content and his usually not too expressive self!" Even the salutations in his letters reflect the increasing distance he was putting between us. The third-person newspaper format quoted above was part of a pattern his letters followed from time to time as a way of depersonalizing our relationship. Even his handwritten letters, already almost illegible by 1963 when he was eighteen, became increasingly so as he grew older, a form, I gather, of self-hiding. He became, indeed, the best-defended of the children. It was not until he was on his own and independent of me that he wrote:

I am learning more about myself each month. Maybe a psychiatrist would have been a good idea a while back, and maybe in the future, but I am enjoying what insights I gain from my relationships with people on the job and in private. I have begun to open up and to be able to be more honest in discussions with others regarding personal feelings. After 24 years, I am finally opening up to myself and others.

The contents as well as the salutations of his letters from boarding school were noncommittal, informative, but studiedly impersonal. Little emotion. Courses, sports, exams, the HO train club which he and his roommate John were reviving, money, Christmas presents. . . . A typical letter might take this form:

Good to hear from you. I am in a math class that is just right for me, since all we are studying is first year concepts as a review in preparation for advancement. Tomorrow is my first math test and first English test. As of now I am ahead in assignments in biology and English. In swimming I am coming along well and shall take that part in the Physical Education tests on Wednesday. Today I bought my soccer shoes and used them in practice. I hope the back room is finished soon, and that the old TV is fixed. Tonight I and several other boys shall listen to the [Kennedy-Nixon] debates on the radio. I hope you are having fun teaching and David is learning with Mr. McClosky. How about my typing? I may go to John's aunt's house for some weekend before Thanksgiving. Saturday we decorated our room. Write quite often. Love, Claude.

The few-and-far-between letters of his junior year were much the same—formal, impersonal. Only one reveals any hint of feeling: "Do write because a letter from home is the best tonic I know to cure the Routine Blues" and "WRITE OFTEN!" scribbled across the bottom. Otherwise matter-of-fact requests for help with preparation for work camp in Germany the coming summer. At the end of April another formal, rather curt letter:

This, the long awaited letter, is coming between chapters; but that does not mean that it is written without any forethought. My purpose in this letter is to assure proper preparation for work camp. Enclosed is a list of what I will need, that is to say, all which is not crossed off. I would really appreciate it if you or David could locate a place where I can get a bergen type rucksack.

I received a letter from dl a few days ago in which she says all is well, etc., nothing special.

For English I am writing a research paper on the history of theater staging. In German we are reading *The White Rose,* about some anti-Nazis. We are into analytical geometry and in chemistry I'm in the middle of a project. I just finished working on *The Skin of Our Teeth,* a dramatics class play.

Junior privileges have come into effect. I don't know when or if I will come home before school is out. Write often. Love, Claude.

By the end of 1962 he was quite sure that he didn't want to come home. He was beginning to want out. Instead of coming home early in the Christmas holiday vacation, he was staying over at school:

I have just decided to stay here for the Work Camp weekend [reunion]. This means that I won't be home until
Friday the 21st. I hope this doesn't upset any of your
plans. If it does, I can still come home early. The reunion
is just that, a reunion of former workers, and it would be
nice if I were there, as ours was the last German work
camp.

The next year, as a senior still struggling to emancipate
himself, he again begged off from coming home for the
weekend unless there was something that had to be done.
But now he reassured me that he was not rejecting me:

They say that absence makes the heart grow fonder. By
now you should be loving me beyond all bounds. Well, as
things stand now I may be coming home this weekend
on Saturday, and then I may not. This doesn't mean that I
am rejecting you and home, but I really can't see any possible gain in coming down there for so short a time unless
there is something that I must do and/or there is something
you want me to do.

Sometimes the struggle toward emancipation took
strange and painful forms. The Christmas Claude was sixteen I was writing to Dorothy Lee:

Claude felt sick because he had not gotten me a present;
he had thought about it and worried about what to get and
planned but never got around to getting it. His unconscious
made him cry out that David and I were shutting him out
Christmas morning as I expressed my appreciation for each
of David's gifts: a bottle of Tweed cologne, a fountain pen,
a desk calendar, a picture which he had painted. So, to
protect him from his own unconscious, I brought the subject up yesterday afternoon. I told him I was going to
wound him and then proceeded to tell him that I was hurt
that he had not gotten me a present, no matter what. He

could then explain it to me, try to justify it, etc. and thus relieve his guilt feelings.

There was a similar episode the next spring in connection with Mother's Day. I had always deprecated Mother's Day for its commercialism. Yet now, sensing the growing distance between Claude and me, I rebuked him for ignoring it: "It was nice to hear from you last night. I had hoped to get a card for Mother's Day, or at least a telephone call. I think you tend to forget about little things like cards or calls on Mother's Day or Christmas cards, etc. Not serious but it would be nice to be remembered." He probably had more reasons for not remembering than for remembering me.

Claude's distancing from me meant that he fought through the harrowing moods of his adolescence alone. Only years later did documents turn up to tell the story. Not in letters, even to Dorothy Lee or David, but in poems he wrote. At seventeen, for example, a colloquy on hope, or rather, on the lack of it. "You talk of hope . . . but for me there is no hope. There never was any hope. And there never will be any hope. After a certain time, all hope dies." Hope only led one deeper into the pit. Hope might lift you from time to time but then dropped you even deeper. He wanted no one to follow him, it hurt too much. For him there was no hope nor ever had been any, or ever would be. He was bitter. A second poem replied to this *Il Penseroso*. He had once been like the author of that poem, but he had given it up. "No bitterer a man could you find in any gutter, any jail, any home." What he had suffered had been faced by many. "You are not alone, you are not unique." There was hope; "hope is you." "Another try, another chance." A hurt hurts those who love you. Remember, "it is the sad and bitter in life that makes all that is good so beautiful." I'm not sure I could have helped that boy even if I had known the anguish he endured. As it was I added to it.

Whether the insecurity of his middle position or the ambivalence of his position as husband-surrogate and male child was at the heart of his anxieties, the manifest, ostensible source was academic, centering on grades. As early as the fall of his first year at boarding school, I was commenting to Dorothy Lee on his anxieties:

Claude had a nice visit, mostly catching up on his sleep. As you know, he is a terrible worrier. We'll have to work on that; otherwise he will end up with five ulcers. His problem is that he meets all four of his academic classes both Mondays and Tuesdays, but has only three hours on Monday to do four hours of homework for Tuesday. This really bothers him. I tried to tell him just to do the best he could and not worry about it. I am somewhat disturbed to see how much he does worry. . . . Then there are all the difficulties of just growing up. I think he will lick the problems by the end of the semester.

He was working on the problem. He began the next year with some philosophical editorial words of wisdom to reassure himself: "I guess it takes a pause in our routine, when we stop and realize that where we are and what we are doing is what we want to do and like to do and all our problems will eventually be resolved and for the most part worry isn't necessary." Apparently it wasn't. He was having a good year. His grades were fine. He was eating at the German table. But once having attained a good academic record, he was now worrying about maintaining it; I commented:

You are really turning out in a most satisfactory way and I am proud. Don't feel that you have to worry about keeping up your wonderful record. As I have told you so many times, if you do the best you can that is all right even if you do not get good grades.

And, again, the next year I wrote to Dorothy Lee: "Claude seems to be doing well this year but, as usual, is fearful that he won't be able to keep it up. I never tried to set such high standards for my children; but they certainly set them for themselves."

"Never tried to set such high standards" indeed! I did even worse. I made Claude his most severe and merciless taskmaster. "Remember you are the only one who really knows if you have mastered anything. You can tell, the grades don't." He was not even to have the consolation of the good grades he was earning. Nor did he have the benefit of consistency from me. At one time when I learned from his teachers that he lacked self-confidence, I hastened to build it up. There was absolutely no reason why he should lack self-confidence. He had everything. I meant brains, looks, charm. He had wonderful natural ability. He was way up near the top. He should have no difficulty in any of the courses he wanted to take. I had so much confidence in him that it seemed strange that he didn't have that much in himself. Still, on another occasion, I was warning him against overconfidence. I was delighted that everything was going so well. When he was happy and successful his voice was loud and clear and forceful and that was fine. But "don't get overconfident about your studies and neglect them." His experience as dormitory prefect "should be as valuable as a course in psychology," and I would like to know what he learned from the work.

College reactivated the anxieties about grades—and brought on the usual deluge of advice from me:

I have never made a great issue of grades [sic!]. But when you defend yourself against a poor grade by blaming the teacher's grading system, that I make an issue of. And here you have to grant I have more experience and judgment than you have. There is no blame associated to a grade of D. If that is all you know, I can accept that. I hope,

naturally, that you will maintain at least a C average; I
mean I hope you will not get any grades lower than C.
But I am prepared for whatever grades you receive. I am
not prepared, though, to have you blame your teachers for
low grades. In order to get good grades you have to do
better than the others in the class. It is a poor examination
on which everyone gets a good grade. A good examination
has such a high ceiling that no one gets 100. If anyone
can get 100, the good students hit the ceiling and the
teacher doesn't know how much better they might have
been. I try to make my tests of such a level of difficulty
that the top students fall short by at least several points.
Then the test will discriminate among the students, telling
me where each stands with reference to the others. On
our PSU curve, 5% get A and F, 20% get B and D, and 50%
get C. What the average student does is, by definition, a
C. If your teacher says that just giving a minimum answer
rates a D, now you know. If you want more than a D you
have to do better than give a minimum reply. You have
somehow or other to show that you have appropriated this
information, that you understand it, that you can use it
in your thinking, that you can apply it, that it has such
and such implications. In other words, we—at any good
university—faculty members want what you learn to *do*
something to or for you; we don't want you just to inhale
it and exhale it on a test. We want evidence that what you
are learning has some meaning for you. That what you
learn is not just an academic past-time. That you can see
its relevance for the current news of the day or some issue.
That you can see it out of the classroom setting or textbook. College is not like high school. Of course a high
school teacher would love that kind of response, too, but
knows he can't really expect it except from the top kids.
At college, we expect it from even the average student.
Your psychology teacher was right, therefore, in giving
you a D for merely answering the question. Anything less
than that could be complete failure on both your part
and his. Just answering the question, without any evidence

that what you had learned had done anything to or for
you, isn't worth much. And this goes for all your courses
except French and German which are really memorization
and drill subjects. But for economics, psychology, and,
to a lesser extent, history, you have to really assimilate the
material, incorporate it into your thinking, talking, doing.
You have to think about them even when not in class
or studying. You have to live with them.

Then, as though one sledgehammer blow was not enough,
I continued in the same vein the following day:

About grades. I am not going to make an issue of them
[sic]. You may remember that I said last spring when you
commented on how high the college board scores were for
the freshman class that I was glad you were getting this
shock early in your career. It is one of the greatest shocks
of college students in the good colleges always. All of them
are top students in their high schools and then find that all
their classmates are also top students. It was one of the
things the kids at Princeton mentioned most often. The
competition gets very rough. I don't know where you stand
in ability in your class. I would be inclined to place you
higher than you place yourself. I think a good B would be
expectable, with a scattering of As. But that is beside the
point. I was trying to tell you that at the university level
more is expected than just knowing what the teacher or the
textbook said. That kind of studying and achievement may
be all right in science, math, and language courses which
depend on memorization. But in the humanities . . . more
creativity is expected. I would like you to show a little
more initiative in reading on your own in areas related to
your courses. Not only Karen Horney, but other books.
And, let me let you in on a secret. If you can relate one
course to another, the professor will be delighted. If you
can find something in psychology that you can use in economics, or vice versa, you will find both subjects more
interesting. Also, can you relate anything in psychology to

your own learning experience? In other words, can you
assimilate what you learn, make it part of yourself, tie it in
with the world of the newspaper, etc.? Naturally, I hope
your grades improve, but I am more interested that you
learn how to use a university to become a mature intellect
yourself rather than just a parroter. Perhaps you could
apply something you learn in psychology to help interpret
your experiences last summer? Or your own development?
Can you apply what you are learning in economics to,
let us say, the wheat deal with USSR? the chicken war
with the Common Market? your inability to get a paying
job last summer? Do you spend any time trying to see implications and ramifications of your course work?

I don't want you to substitute "trying harder" for trying
better. It isn't any harder to do things the right way. In
fact, it's easier. The hard way is just to read and try to read
the teacher's mind. Dull and uninteresting. The right way
is to find applications, implications, interrelations. The
hard way is passive, just sitting there and trying to impress
it on your mind. The easy way is to look for relationships,
to be active about the learning process, doing something
instead of just sitting there. Doing mentally, of course.
I think if you get the habit of trying to see how the material relates to other material, how it helps to explain things
for you, you will find studying not harder but easier and
much more interesting. It's too bad the teaching is so
poor at JHU. All that means is that you have to do the
teaching yourself. Ask yourself questions and find the
answers. You might be able to use some of the answers on
examinations but that is quite secondary.

Well, I suppose this is enough for now. . . . Much love,
Mother.

Claude's reponse to these dissertations showed how far beyond the mark they were. He was learning. He was beginning to understand the competitive pressures of adulthood:

Dear Mentor,

I have just finished your letter of criticism, and find most of what you say is true; . . . not because of the letter, [but] because of many hours of contemplation before I fall asleep. I recognize the fact that what you say is true. And I attempt solutions. The big problem is that you and I have lost much of the medium of communication that allowed us to speak so freely before. Now on each of the points of your letter. . . .

I still maintain that the work is not too difficult, but I will also admit that this was the major factor in deceiving me as to the methods and amount of time to be allotted to studying. I entered J.H.U. knowing full well that I was just average in relation to my peers, and that I couldn't expect that I would do as well as I had at George School; and I still hold that view. I expect the majority of my grades to be in the low B and C range for two reasons: the curve and my abilities as they relate to the standards here.

The D on my psychology test was a rude awakening because I discovered that one can't just do the assignment, one must expand on the material and interpret the ideas presented as they relate to a general theme. It has been my only D so far, and I think that I ought to be able to raise it to a C at least. But the fact remains, that I was both overcome by the type of courses and scared by the atmosphere prevalent at Hopkins. Now that I am a bit more wise to the wants of the faculty and the requirements for tests I expect to do better. But a high C average is nothing to be ashamed of at a place like this. Let's face facts. Here I am only an average student. I still feel that learning (mastering) the subject is the important thing regardless of the tests or grades. True, a test ought to reflect this, but not always.

I have now spread my work out over an evenly spaced schedule so that I can devote more time to each aspect, but the work-load is erratic from week to week. I try to compensate for this by performing a minor review during these slack periods. I feel that a constant review over a longer span of time is the best thing if one has enough time, right? After all I've said, I won't guarantee anything but the fact that I will try harder. Your son.

There were no more Ds. But the most important things he learned did not show up in grades. In any situation he saw what had to be done and did it. In the several jobs he held, for example, that proved to be one of his most valuable assets. He did not have to be told what to do.

The boy who had been distancing himself from me all through high school and thus protecting himself began, once a freshman in college, to come out swinging—gently. One weekend in November, at home with friends as guests, there was a crisis of sorts. "I was very happy to have you visit us last night and bring your friends. I meant what I said when I said I would be glad to have you bring house guests weekends, but, of course, I have to know in order to have food on hand. On second thought, it is OK to bring them unannounced if you are willing to shop for them, as you did last night. So, either way. I was sorry, though, that I had to leave and that we didn't have time to talk. Because a lot of talk has to take place between you and me." Then, in a tone of voice I do not think characteristic of me I added ominously, "since you are in rebellion I am going to give you something to rebel against"—grades, weight, smoking, hair, but especially his defensiveness.

The first thing I have to talk about is your defensiveness. I began to note and comment on it last summer. It was worse last week. It is getting serious. When you have studied enough psychology you will understand why the personality has to have defense mechanisms. (Maybe when I finish this I will see if I kept a book by Anna Freud on *The Ego and The Mechanisms of Defense* and if I did, will send it to you.) But in your case the problem is why do you have to have them? You could correct the situations that require you to protect yourself. It is getting noticeably worse that you have to fight everything I say. You never do what I suggested you try sometimes, namely, say "You're right about that. I'll try to . . ." What ever I say you have a long song and dance to show I'm wrong or that it's impossible or unimportant or not worth paying attention to, or trivial or square or what-have-you. Does it ever occur to you that maybe, just maybe, I might be right once in a while? That 60 is bigger than 18? If you did what you know you should do, you wouldn't have to be so defensive, so on guard.

After long disquisitions on other issues I concluded with: "Most of all I mind the defensiveness, the guard always up against any comment I have to make. Ask yourself, just once, does she have a point?" Three days later, again: "Once we get this habit of defensiveness licked we'll be 9/10 there. OK?" (Nine-tenths to where I did not specify.) It did not occur to me then, as it does now, that with a mother who came on so strong, how could he be anything but defensive? and survive?

These assaults may have cleared the air for me. But they did little good for our relationship and they certainly did not get rid of the defensiveness. If anything, they increased it. Everything I did or said came to be suspect in his eyes. I felt that I had to preclude suspicion of my actions by disclaiming ulterior motives in advance. Was I, for example, putting down his manual skills when I asked about a mechanical toy for Christmas?

Does this appeal to you as a Christmas present? It occurs to me that because it is a mechanical toy it might interest you since you seem to like to do things with your hands. There is nothing subtle or invidious about this query. It just occurred to me that it might appeal to you. If you feel I am trying to put something over on you—like offering you the comb the other night—you are wrong. No ulterior motive. Just, it seems to me, an interesting and

perhaps entertaining game. Let me know at once so I
can order it if you think you would like it. OK?

P.S. This would not be instead of the recorder; we may be
able to work out a deal on that also.

Academic sources of anxiety were, however, only the
manifest ones. If spelling, for example, was Dorothy Lee's
bête noire, weight was Claude's. Our struggle with this
black beast did not surface until he entered college. Until
that time, though like his father of heavy frame, he had
been able to maintain—albeit with considerable effort—
normal weight for his body build. As early as age fourteen
he was reporting to me in Hong Kong that this morning
his weight was down twelve pounds. When he was fifteen,
I wrote to Dorothy Lee that "Claude had a very good
report card for last semester. . . . He lost ten pounds and
grew .7 inches," showing at least to my own satisfaction,
that weight and success fluctuated inversely together.

A childhood marked by almost lethal attacks of asthma
and polio had precluded an active sports life. But growth
had used up all the calories. When he entered college, however, he began to gain weight. There were plenty of explanations. Dormitory food, which in boarding school had been
used up in growth, could always be attacked as responsible.
(For almost anything, in fact.) But there was more, including the eating used for allaying anxieties. And because
weight was a continuing concern of my own, I could be
especially savage:

Let's begin with your weight. It is perfectly possible for
you to get down to a neat, handsome 160. You have done
it. You did it last spring or fall, I forget. But you can do it.
You can be abstemious. But for some reason or other—
there are reasons for overweight—it is too hard. You don't
care enough. Or something. Or off-and-on-eating—which is
the worst way to control weight—suits you. So you are
overweight and it is not becoming. Why aren't you spend-

ing some of the free afternoon hours in the gym? Why did you interpret being excused from physical education courses [because of allergy attacks] as meaning that you didn't have to do anything? Before you spend all your mental energy thinking of good excuses for your physical inactivity or proof that you aren't inactive or any other defense, drop your defenses for a moment and look at yourself from my point of view. If I look like this to her, maybe, just maybe she has a point. Maybe I *ought* to take myself in hand. After all, what's it to her? Why does she go to all that trouble if she's completely wrong? At any rate, maybe I ought to take my physical condition more seriously. Why, I ask, not try it at any rate?

His reply:

I know very well that I am overweight, and the problem concerns me. I also realize that it concerns you too, but what you probably have no idea of is that I do do something about it. I have cut out such things as candy, baked goods, gravy, etc. In other words, my diet during the course of one day may consist of the following items: 3 glasses of milk, serving of meat, serving of vegetables and potatoes, and perhaps ice cream or jello. This is the main meal that I eat during the day, at about noon. Then in the evening something small and nourishing to tide me over till the next day. Is this so much? And is it too much to ask for a good meal when I can have the benefit of good home cooking [on visits home] as a departure from the drab, regulated diet we get here? I have a natural tendency to cut down a great deal on my intake of such food as is served here after I am used to it. And I am doing so.

As for exercise. I do them in my room at night or other times. And why don't I make use of the gym? It all boils down to this: at the present time there isn't anything I could do there better than I can do in my room. One can do calisthenics in the room, and one can borrow a friend's weights to use. These are the important exercises that one

should do, and, if one can do them without going over to
the gym, why shouldn't one spare himself the walk and
time consumed; besides one gets plenty of walking exercise
elsewhere.

In response to this, I came on strong:

Let's examine your statement about diet, etc. Instead of
looking at the problem as stark reality, you look at it as a
sort of matter of justice. You tell me what you have cut
out, what you eat, etc. You ask me "is this so much?" You
also ask, if it is too much to ask for a good meal when you
are at home, etc. Alas, my dear son, this is not a matter
of justice. The facts are that your present eating habits, no
matter how hard they are or how abstemious, are not taking off weight. No matter what I said—that it isn't so
much, or that you are entitled to good meals, etc.—it
wouldn't make any difference. My judgment of your eating habits wouldn't affect the fact that they do keep your
weight down. Do you get the point? No matter how good
a case you make, to yourself or to me, the reality is what
counts. If the fact of the matter is that the only way you
can keep your weight down is a diet of let us say 1200
calories a day, no matter how unfair this is, no matter how
unjust, no matter what either one of us says, this is the
reality of the matter, the fact. So the next time you defend
yourself—about anything—ask yourself if it is the defense
that is important or the fact. Many facts of life are unfair.
That all of us in our family except Dorothy Lee have
weight problems and cannot enjoy eating as much as we
like is terribly unfair. But justifying ourselves in eating by
saying it isn't fair for us to have to watch our weight is not
the answer. The same sort of thing goes for exercise. OK,
you take exercise. But is it accomplishing what it is supposed to? . . . I don't know too much about exercise. I do
know, however, that there are certain standards of fitness
that young men ought to judge themselves by.

I could speak so feelingly—or unfeelingly—on the subject of weight because I shared that incubus. Sometimes, though, as I reread the letters I wince. "Losing weight would also reduce the heaviness of the face, too, and make it handsome again. I am not a great one for vanity or too much emphasis on appearances. But when I see a boy of 18 permitting a certain grossness to creep up on him I think it is time to pay attention." Some four years later when Claude, now twenty-two, was in London, I wrote that I was glad about his weight loss and that it both looked and felt good. I suggested that he be measured for a suit by a London tailor.

As with Dorothy Lee, the issue of smoking also arose. "I mind your excessive smoking—I noticed that neither of your friends had to smoke and that you had bought a carton—also because it is another evidence, like your weight, that you are too indulgent with yourself, that you coddle yourself, that you are losing control of your appetites." Without reminding me that I was probably part of the tension-generating environment that called for relaxation, he replied that smoking was "a pacifier, much as eating or gum-chewing is with many people. To me it is a way to ease tensions and relax in the face of problems such as school work. But I realize that I can become too dependent on cigarettes, so I make an attempt to control the amount that I smoke. So far this has been of some fair amount of success. I have cut down from un- to filtered cigarettes, and have reduced the number I smoke by about a third. It was a vice that I knew about when I began, but I took the risk."

Like other mothers throughout the 1960s I brashly took on the issue of hair, only to learn that here the peers had all the advantages. "I feel less strongly about your coiffeur," I wrote to Claude. "I do think the part is too low and gives your head a lop-sided effect. Once more, I mentioned it to you only to receive the reply that you were going by the advice of your peers who said the farther down on the side the part, the better. Wrong. For your particular shaped head, farther up would be better. And much shorter." Gently, politely, I was put in my place:

When at George School last year, my roommate and several others mentioned the fact that the location of my part in my hair was not in the best location as per looks and generally prevalent styles. This criticism hit me hard at first, but I accepted the fact that they probably knew about things like this better than I. So with much consideration, I began to move my part down. To conclude: it makes little difference to me as to how my hair is parted, but I feel that my peers have a better idea about contemporary styles.

Fortunately I knew when I was licked. The issue did not arise again.

It is part of the enigma of family life that despite all the pummeling Claude received from me as my son, he never wavered in his support of me as confidant-mentor. Even at an early age he had assumed the role of mentor. Even as a small boy when I became angry he had made allowances for me, explaining to all concerned that I was tired and should be humored. When, in connection with some crisis or other in Dorothy Lee's life, "I was anxious all morning and kept yelling at the boys," I wrote to Dorothy Lee, Claude—then twelve—told me that I was "more jumpy than Dorothy Lee about it" and proceeded to "give me a lecture about not demanding too much from my children, quoting his guidance textbook to inform me how to behave."

At twenty-two he was interpreting my children to me, gently instructing me in ways to deal with their rebellion. From London, with the perspective time and distance offered, he presented what amounted to a critique of my performance as a mother: too soft, too engulfing.

Your letters sound as if you bear the burdens of the world on your shoulders. You have perhaps too much empathy with your children which sometimes may make you over-react to their problems and frustrations. In fact, there seems to be a duality of purpose going on within you. On the one hand you can't wait until we are on our own, yet your love for us makes you softer through each of our growing-up and break-away pains. This I think we three all recognize, but in a confused way. You are a too-good person in the respect that we all realize the soft cushion that is there, but wish to get off on our own. This whole problem is complicated by the fact that you had to raise us on your own and there was no other person for you to run to for comfort while we were rebelling from authority.

Perhaps we have sublimated our open (?) rebellion through our going away to school either at George School or in Europe. Always we seem to be happiest away from parental discipline, with our peers, but we would be lost without the cushion of love and security you provide.

Perhaps I am the luckiest of us three. I have lived away for eight years being able to come home for short periods of family life and then depart for my own world, always knowing of your love and concern. But I was away from any direct pressure you might exert.

The pressures of living at home, he was telling me, were oppressive. It was apparently as hard to be a son as to be a daughter of Jessie Bernard.

David is not so lucky. Like Dorothy Lee and me, he wants to please you, but [along with] the pressures of going to school at home and fearing your disapproval, real or not, he has not had the benefit of any moderating influence offered by distance. That he wants to live away from home next year is not a sign of lost love between you two, as you seemed to hint, but, I think, a hope on his part that the frightful pressures existing between you two will cease and that problems of breaking away will be less intense.

As early as the spring of 1963, when Claude was only eighteen, I caught myself in a letter expressing great anguish for Dorothy Lee—"sometimes I weep for her"—and, reproaching myself—"but why do I bother you with all this?" I knew the answer and feared it. "You are a great comfort to me and the danger is I might lean on you too heavily for support." Still, in my own rudderlessness in dealing with Dorothy Lee's dilemmas, I continued to lean on him. Four years later I was still asking the same question: "Why inflict all this on you?"[4] He replied, in effect, keep out of Dorothy Lee's way:

With Dorothy Lee, I get the feeling, as you have often expressed, that Brick was her rebellion. Yet you won't let her rebel. You are always there to give comfort, both spiritual and material. That she is quite independent and strong is evident in the way she faces up to Brick and his problems. She does a remarkable job of putting up with . . . him. . . . Yet the whole situation is confounded by your greatest weakness, your deep love for us and aversion to seeing us get hurt in any way. So the problem never comes to a head.

Then, as mentor, as gently as possible, his advice:

Perhaps what I say next is completely wrong, but I have the feeling that the best thing that could possibly happen to Dorothy Lee would be for her to bear the entire burden of Brick without any help from you. For you to accept her method of handling the whole situation, only offering advice when asked, never offering criticism no matter how much what Brick does hurts you or affronts you personally by his doing it to Dorothy Lee.
I realize that doing such a thing would hurt you deeply, to stand aside and to see Dorothy Lee suffer so. It hurts

David and me too. But, if Dorothy Lee is to reach some climax with Brick, it should be her own doing so that she will understand the situation. If Brick is wrong for her, she alone must realize the fact. No amount of advice from others will convince her of her situation. The actions of Brick must tell her.

Claude was sympathetic with Brick as well as with Dorothy Lee and me. He understood the pressures weighing on him as well as on us. According to Claude, Brick knew he was failing Dorothy Lee though he loved her and needed her strength for, Claude said, Dorothy Lee was strong like me. If Brick proved a loss to her, she could take the blow. Most important was the fact that I would be there for comforting aid.

The letter was reassuring. I expressed my appreciation in a letter which caught in a few words the essence of our relationship:

Your letter was very consoling. Both David and I agree that you are a really great guy; you hold no grudges; are always sympathetic and empathic; take almost anything (from me), etc. Both he and Dorothy Lee had noticed the matter you and I talked about before you left—that I am meaner to you than to them and that I punish you for my own defects. But still I find myself leaning on you more than on them and finding you a real support. As you have already learned, I suppose, there's no justice in human relationships. In any event I want you to know that I appreciate your support. It helps.

However legitimate any grievance Claude may have had against my treatment of him—that I had, for example, been "meaner" to him than to the other children—he harbored none.

In 1963, the summer before Claude entered college, I had written, "During the next few years you will have to

make the two most important decisions of your life—mate
and career." And four years later, when he left college, I
was writing the same letter:

You can use your inheritance for the next year or so until
you find what you really want to do. I may have told you
in previous letters, but since it is on my mind, I may tell
you often that I would like for you to have the next few
years to find yourself without hurry or rush. To take a
look at whatever might interest you. Fail whenever you have
to. Change if you get into a wrong track.[5] There are two
major decisions of a life-time that you will make in the
next few years—occupation and wife. That is why you
should have the freedom to do them right.

chapter seven

two major decisions

"What's a mother to do?" In an old television advertisement, a hassled mother turned to the audience for answers when her children refused to eat nutritious meals, or whatever. It is a good question whatever it deals with, not only nutrition. What, in the present context, is a mother to do to help the induction of her children into the adult work world?

In a poignant analysis of parental responsibility—and sense of guilt—for a non-achievement-oriented generation, Midge Decter asks young people why they have found it so hard to take their rightful place in the world? Why have the hopes of their parents come to seem so impossible to attain?[1] She concedes that these expectations were inordinately high.

As children of this peculiar enlightened class, you were expected one day to be manning a more than proportional share of the positions of power and prestige in this society; you were to be its executives, its professionals, its artists and intellectuals, among its business and political leaders; you were to think its influential thoughts, tend its major institutions, and reap its highest rewards. It was at least

partly to this end that we brought you up. That we attended so assiduously to your education, that we saw to
the cultivation of every last drop of your talents, that we
gave you to believe there would be no let or hindrance to
the forward, upward motion into which we had set you
going from the day of your birth. I don't believe that this
was actually a conscious intention for most of us. We did
not—anyway, most of us did not for most of the time—
tell ourselves of these expectations in so many words. Yet
they were unmistakably what we had in mind.[2]

I think Decter is accurate in her descriptions. And the
questions she poses for the antiestablishmentarian generation of the 1960s have puzzled a lot of people. Still, I'm
not sure the expectations she refers to were mine for my
children. If upward mobility or worldly success as defined
by Decter was the goal of good parenting I was not a successful mother. I did not train my children for the jungle.
They were not toughened for the fray. But I did take preparation for some kind of life work seriously.

Upward social mobility has been a major preoccupation
of my discipline for decades and induction of young
people into the work world one of the most researched
areas of both sociology and psychology. Knowing that, in
the case of boys, fathers are especially important in this
task, I felt myself at a great disadvantage. The two men in
Claude's life—his father and Ezra—were both skilled with
their hands, appreciated tools, found joy in working with
metal and wood. The most cherished piece of furniture in
my own home was a harvest table Claude had made in
boarding school. He was—and is—an excellent cabinet-
maker. In his spare moments, that is. But when the time
came for a lifelong career decision, cabinetmaking was out
by his own choice. OK, yes, as an avocation but not as a
life investment. Cars, trains, transportation, these had early
become his major preoccupation. Photography, not literature, his preferred art form. Our miles of home movies

were primarily his creations. Hand, more than verbal, skills were his forte. Theater lighting was his college activity and my own walls are still too small to hold the never-ending stream of pictures that emerge from his dark room. How to parlay any of these interests, talents, skills into a career was the question.

The world, Claude knew, expected him to make himself useful in some field of work, if not at the exalted level Midge Decter described, at least at some other level. As a male he was both figuratively and literally conscripted. There was no way, as there was for Dorothy Lee, to avoid that grim expectation. So far as I could tell, I was as much concerned about summer jobs and odd jobs for Dorothy Lee as for Claude. But with Claude my concerns "took" more than with Dorothy Lee. When he was a senior in boarding school I wrote: "I am going to let you have the very valuable experience [that Dorothy Lee had not had] of learning to measure yourself against the outside world by a job." Precisely what form that experience would take I did not make altogether clear.

Although I consistently reassured the children that there was no rush about selecting lifetime careers, I was eager to start the process of thinking about the subject and experimenting fairly early. Thus when Claude was seventeen, at my insistence—in fact, by my initiative—he took a Civil Service Student Trainee test. As it happened nothing came of it; he was registered for it at the wrong time. In April of that year there was more about jobs:

Both good and bad news for you. I have just forwarded the letter from Cornell which says you have been accepted there. . . . The bad news is that the papers say it will be very hard to get jobs in the government in Washington this summer. You will also be handicapped by being late on the scene. So be prepared for a lot of disappointment. You may have to look for a less attractive kind of job. But it will be a valuable lesson. OK?

A few days later I sent him five local newspaper clippings advertising jobs:

Just a few ads I ran across in the paper this A.M. to give you an idea of the job market. Problem is going to be that most jobs will ask for men who want to stay with the company. But anyway, if none of my friends in the government can find openings, there are other kinds of work. Experience is more important than pay. Hope everything is going nicely.

The ads certainly represented variety. Claude was not interested in following up on any of them. I persisted. A few days later another push:

I talked to a friend about a job and he said the son of a friend of his turned down exactly the kind of job you would like—aide to an engineer in the field (in New York). It was with the Geological Survey. At your earliest convenience, get another Form 57 from the local post office (get several since you will need one for each application and it will save time). Then fill it out and send it to the Personnel Office, Geological Survey, Old Dominion Building, Washington, D.C. I am enclosing a model kind of letter to send.

None of my—it now seems coercive—efforts succeeded. Because of his crippling allergies which had kept him almost housebound a good deal of the summer, Claude had not been able to do odd jobs during the summers of his high school years. He had had experience only remotely related to genuine work when he had served as dormitory prefect which, though it called for adolescent wisdom, had not provided the experiences of real, paid-for work. In the end, he took a volunteer job—available through the good offices of a friend—working with delinquents in a detention home in the District of Columbia.

It proved to be a disillusioning experience. He wanted more action. He had hoped to be able to *do* something for the boys. But there was no straw to build bricks with in that graveyard. After almost two months on the job he began a report which he called "The Glorified Guard." In it he described his own duties—which ranged from counseling to feeding isolation cases, from taking boys to the clinic to pulling files—and presented his own diagnosis; lack of adequately trained personnel. If an error was made, no one cared; the attitude seemed to be, "We don't care what you have done, just don't bother us . . . by a criminal act." He liked the people he met but noted that "lack of morale can ruin the best organizations." He concluded, "We simply don't care enough." Dealing adequately with juvenile delinquents "takes something that many of us are reluctant to part with, and that is our precious time." But wasn't "it worth our time to save our greatest natural resource?" He seemed to feel deeply on the subject. While he was working on this report he wrote me that "it could go on indefinitely." Could he, he asked, ever get it all down the way he wanted to? I did not know the answer to that question, the question that plagues every serious writer. We finally just chalked that job up to experience. By that time I had already begun making inquiries in the Rural Sociology Department about possible interviewing work on one of their survey projects for the following summer:

At a meeting today I talked to Professor James Coleman of the Sociology Department at JHU. He told me to tell you to come up and see him sometime. Every now and then they have research jobs and there might be work for you. I told him how well you did for me last summer and he was interested. I am not telling you to do this. It is up to you. I am just doing what he told me to do, tell you. I think you would be interested in the project, though. You are among the subjects. It is based on a questionnaire you filled out. I don't know the details but I do know that he is a top man in the field and any research he does will be interesting. In addition, he is working on a new method of teaching social studies in high schools by way of games. He has invented a game that operates much like Monopoly but instead of making money you try to get bills enacted. It involves trading votes, winning votes, etc. instead of money. It is written up in the most recent issue of the JHU magazine if you would like to learn more. Let me know if and when you talk to him. He could be very useful by way of advice, etc. also. But if you can earn money in addition that is all to the good. You will have that much more.

Nothing came of this lead.

Jobs were one thing. Career plans were something else again. Jobs meant only money and experience; a career meant a life. Claude entered college after experiencing a kind of epiphany which he interpreted as pointing to a career in some aspect of the foreign service:

Begun Monday Aug. 5, 1963

Dear Breadwinner,

About me:

As you know, I have been doing a [large] amount of thinking as to my "self" and who I am. One thing has come up about my future. I just finished watching a show about a foreign correspondent, and bang a thought hit me.

Ever since we returned from Austria, I have had a general love and fascination for the German-speaking peoples as well as world society. Then tonight all my subconscious and conscious thought hit on a sore spot that had been just below my feelings.

I know now that I have a very special place in my heart for Germans and Austrians, if not for all Europeans, and for this reason, in connection with a great love for travel I have given serious thought to some kind of job in the foreign service, for the government or a corporation.

This may sound strange after my show of wonder over the film industry, which is still as strong as ever, but for the moment and most likely for a while I want to proceed along the aforementioned topic.

You don't, of course, know what brought all of this on, and all I can say is that through the year and in Europe last summer, in getting to know the [German] people, I came to love and respect their heritage, problems, and future, and I have a strong feeling about helping and planning with the future for them and the world.

Perhaps this is the first indication of a new breed of people in my generation. We of the atomic post-war generation, or at least me, have a strong feeling about world comradeship. We (I) want to change the situation as it now stands and create a new peaceful world.

Then, suddenly aware of his strong feelings, he added self-deprecatingly: "Me and my utopian ideals." The next day there followed a humdrum page of details about his clothing needs for the coming year and then, "After thinking over last night's little essay, I have nothing to change. So if you think about anything in it send your thoughts. As for anything else, that's all. Love, Claude." And five days later: "I haven't had any extraordinary personal revelations, but I'm still in the process of thinking . . . every insomnious night."

In response to his request that I send him my thoughts, I wrote:

Now about your career plans. They sound tremendous to me. But, as you know, I don't want you to commit yourself before you have had a chance to try out a lot of things at college. You might find something you never even heard of that appeals to you. I would, of course, be proud and delighted if you really did choose a career in the foreign service. But you are still very young and may change your mind several times before you finish college. But if you do continue your interest in the foreign service, JHU is the ideal spot for you. As you know they have in Washington and Bologna, Italy, a terrific School on International Relations. It is possible, I have heard, to get a master's degree

in four years. I am not suggesting this, but if it works out
that way you could go right from Baltimore to the Washington or Bologna program. But we should wait and see. In
the meanwhile the program you have mapped out—lan-
guages, history, psychology, economic geography—sounds
perfect for what you want. It is just barely possible, too,
that you could combine your theater interest with the
foreign service interest. You can talk all this over with
your adviser.

Claude liked what I said "about a mixture between the
cinema and the foreign service." In the same letter I had
referred to the son of a State College friend who was also
in the foreign service and liked it a lot. I promised to get
his telephone number. Then, lest it seem that I was pushing too hard, a week later I gave reassurances that there
was no hurry:

In your case the problem is a plethora of talents and interests. It will be a question of selecting which one will
give you the most rewarding life. I feel sure you will be
successful in any career you choose. The difficulty will be
in eliminating any of them. But it is always possible to
make an avocation of some interests. For example, if you
select photography as a vocational interest, then psychology might be an avocation, or vice versa. At any rate you
have plenty of time to find yourself. Just continue to
think the long thoughts of youth and don't feel that you
have to hurry to commit yourself. Just so you are on your
way there is plenty of time.

The foreign service proved to be a transitory interest.
When he arrived at Johns Hopkins and learned that he
would have to decide at once if he wanted to enter the
special program designed for the foreign service, he began
to have doubts: "I am still a bit in doubt about the foreign

serivce as . . . my true goal. History still has a certain aroma in my nostrils. . . . If it weren't for the necessity of getting into this special program [immediately] I wouldn't even worry at this stage of the game. . . . We can discuss this at greater length when I start home."

Still, I kept my eyes open for possibilities. Thus, in the winter of his first year at college:

I forgot to suggest that you also write to the German Desk, State Department, as we talked about it while you were here. You might ask for a summer internship, telling them that you are almost bilingual, that you spent a summer in Germany, that you understand the political problems (fear of Germany on the part of European, as well as Communist, countries), that you understand the problems of youth in Germany, etc., etc., etc., that you like Germany and think you can be useful at the German desk. I don't suppose there's much chance, but no harm in trying. You could mention that you will be 19, a sophomore at JHU, have studied economics, sociology, history, psychology, political science. It is my opinion that your training so far would make you very useful to them.

This proved to be just one more suggestion that did not take.

Several years earlier, when Claude was only seventeen and a senior at boarding school, I had used my influence as a large shareholder in a financial corporation to suggest that he be given a summer job. I wrote directly to the top man, Mr. Hain, pointing out all of Claude's assets—he was serious, conscientious, hard-working, willing to learn, a good student. The job did not materialize until two years later. This is how he described his summer in high finance when he was nineteen:

Chapter One
(or the Iceberg Melteth)

June 15, 1964
Dear Provider,
    I am sitting here in my room while outside a much-needed
rain storm is cooling off the city. It seems to rain whenever
something good happens to me; for instance when I got
my room, or started work. But let me begin from where I
left you on that long-ago Friday.
    As you will remember, I was quite anxious to leave
Washington (not necessarily you) in order to get here as
soon as possible after noon. I thought that I would find all
sorts of complications to smooth over when I got here, my
living quarters not the least.
    Well, when I got here at three-thirty, I was hot and tired
from the long drive (three and one-half hours on the road)
so I immediately went to the "Y" and got the last room
they had. (My first break.) Then, full of apprehension, I
went on to the offices of Penn Square. In I walked full of
doubts as to what I should do. Then a man asked what I
wanted, and I replied, "To speak with Mr. Hain and let
him know I'm here."
    We exchanged greetings as Mr. Hain was busy, and this
man, Bruce, introduced me to those who were still there
on a summer's Friday afternoon. After that, when he was
free, I was introduced to Mr. Hain, who seems to be a pleasant person, although very busy at the moment. Then as my
parking meter was running out of time I left the offices
and went back to the "Y."
    That evening I drove around the city and then went to a
movie. After the movie I came back and slept till noon
Saturday.
    Friday I had checked the "rooms for rent" section of the
Reading Times and found my room only two and a half
blocks from the office. I moved in Saturday afternoon. It
was raining. Then I went for a walk and bought a James

Bond novel to read that evening as I knew not what else to do. When I returned I went about securing a parking space for my car at $10.00 a month. It is only half a block from the room and quite easy to get in and out of.

Since a picture is worth a 1000 words I have drawn a sketch of my room. I have only three things to add to my art. The closet is too narrow, the bed is wide and soft, and it (the room) is blue. As you see it is on a corner so it receives all the West and South breezes. For $8.00 a week it isn't bad. And at the present I have the bath all to myself.

A pensioner lives on the second floor who knows some of the older people at the office and has spoken to me of them, and they of him. Also on the second floor live a young married couple. It is the wife who does the cleaning in return for a rent reduction. The first floor is the Mono-son answering service. The gentleman who owns it was quite nice and didn't require me to produce any references. (Perhaps due to my handsome honest face, or the fact that I had none.)

In any event, by Saturday night I was settled in and sleeping in my new home.

Sunday I drove around Berks Courts, went to a movie, read another book, walked around the city, and went to bed wondering about the next day.

The next A.M. I was awakened by a whistle and chimes which are practically next to my window. Will have to speak to the Mayor about that, but saves me the need of an alarm in the A.M. Got up and got dressed and went to the office. First came the introductions and names, most of which I forgot right away, but have managed to pick up over the week.

My job, and this is what you have been waiting for, is a sort of file-clerk, office boy, everything. Since there is a lot of material to be filed, orders to be checked, and other duties to be performed we summer workers were hired and that is what we do. Mostly by hook, and partially by crook, I have acquired a desk in the back part of the second floor which is the accounting section in which I work. I have

To my grandmother, almost as important as God himself and obviously his wife, we went for moral guidance: was this a sin? or that a blessing?

I was the third of four children, all of whom, clearly, took life very seriously.

Inscribed on the back of this picture, January 25, 1941: "To my beloved child . . . taken when I was carrying you."

Before their father's death, both children had a parent of their own. I belonged to Claude; their father, to Dorothy Lee. We were a "balanced" family.

After five years of practice, the children had learned—in a fashion—how to share a single parent.

When we were *all* very young—clockwise Jessie, LLB, Claude, David, Dorothy Lee.

Linda and Michelle have now joined the family.

also acquired many new and fine friends there. There is
Davis who makes out certificates and is a divorcee with
two sons, one at Texas A & M, the other is a senior in high
school. I think she has taken a motherly attitude with me.
There is Peter who runs the office, Ralph a member of A.A.
Many of the orders section: Allison, newly married and expecting; Esther, the general handy-woman; and Thomas, a
Negro boy attending summer business school so as to be
more proficient at his new permanent job. He and I have
about the same general duties.

Since this letter is getting too long and it is getting late,
I'll stop now, but in my next letter I pick up with the
Chamber of Commerce Banquet, the Young Republican
Club, and how I solved the "Case of the Seven Shares."
Until then much love and XX.

I wonder what Theodore Dreiser or Cameron Hawley
could have done with all this—or with the events reported
in the promised next letter.

June 19, 1964

Dear Correspondent,

After a taxing first day on the job, I was ready for a quiet
evening at home with a book. And that is how I ended my
day.

My daily routine is pretty much constant in that I rise at
eight, dress, wash, etc. and arrive at the office at 8:45 to
read the local paper. Then at nine I go to work by checking new orders. Then it is a day of filing, or posting certificate numbers, or running errands for the other people in
the office. From 12:30–1:30 I eat lunch and read the *N.Y.
Times.* Then back to work till five. At five I come back to
my room and freshen up.

My evenings are spent walking, or reading, or sleeping. I
do and I don't miss a T.V.

My first Wednesday, Jim Yoakum [second in command
at the corporation] asked me if I would like to attend the
Chamber of Commerce Banquet in his place as he was tired.

So I accepted (the idea of a free good meal was too good to resist) and went back to my room to doze. At six-thirty I arrived at the Ballroom of the Abraham Lincoln Hotel and met five others from Penn Square. The meal was good as was the speaker, a vice-president of Westinghouse, who spoke on the Common Market. I enjoyed that evening.

Thursday night Jim invited me to dinner after I helped him address some envelopes for a concert by the Warsaw Philharmonic orchestra. For the second night in a row I had an excellent meal. Jim also took me to the Young Republican Club and then showed me around the city. It seems that he knows everyone in the city. Through him I am meeting quite a few people. Then to top things off, this past Wednesday Jim's family invited me out to dinner at another one of Reading's clubs. Again I had a good meal and a wonderful time. I think Jim has taken me under his wing.

It has occurred to me that if as a child Claude had sat around a dining table in a home in which business openings or opportunities were part of the common talk, if he had heard men discussing business deals,[3] if the nature of the market was part of his accepted lore, he might well have understood the meaning of being taken under the wing of a successful corporation executive. Especially since, as it turned out, he was so adept at the job:

The first Thursday I was at Penn Square a tape was run to check the actual number of shareholders against their filed listing. Well, there was an excess of seven shares at the end of the day, and a recheck on Friday didn't help matters.

Seven shares may sound trivial, but I assure you that they can foul up the bookkeeping. We were all upset that weekend at the prospect of a long re-recheck the next Monday.

Well, Monday rolled around and we began another check. Who do you think solved the problem? Of course, who else? A mistake had been made on one of the filing cards from a man in Washington, D.C.

Then it was back to the routine. Monday a girl, Barbara, came in, and today Mike arrived, and together we finished all the back filing from April. Next comes posting of certificate numbers from May and June.

It was not too long before the characteristic bugbears of bureaucratic organization dawned on Claude.

Dear Mother,

. . . I don't remember whether I told you about the new comptroller that was hired for the accounting department or not. Anyway, he has upset all of us up on the second floor to the extent that it isn't the same place as before. He, Meyer Weiner, was supposed to make things run more smoothly, but so far they haven't. Perhaps I am too critical of things here, but I get more so every day that I work here. I think it is that I don't like to see things get messed up to the extent that work starts to lag and pile up. You know that we summer help were supposed to get rid of this backlog, but up to now it seems that there is more work than ever to do. Of course we have gotten much accomplished in the few short weeks that we have been here, and perhaps it is only the aftermath of the dividend that is causing the tieup, but everyone seems less happy now.

Claude was apparently being tried out, if not actually groomed, for upward movement in the organization. He was given a wider berth. He observed what was going on and did not care for what he saw.

My work now takes me all over the place doing little odd but important jobs so I get the general drift of feeling that permeates the air. Everybody has their minor complaints, but the sum total of all of them is enough to get me down. I have begun to work out in my mind a more efficient method of running things around here because it seems to me that a $66,000,000 corporation should be better geared to get things done. . . . When my thoughs are clearer I will let you know them.

As it turned out, he had done well. Mr. Hain wrote to me that he had proved "to be an ideal employee, alert, responsive to any situation, and apparently very much interested in the work here." I relayed this to Claude and added that it was "reassuring to me to know that every job you have ever had (all two of them!) you have succeeded in and received high praise from your employer." However well he had done, however, this job was no more congenial to Claude than the earlier one had been. And he was too young to see his experience this time as a main chance. He wanted more—to expand his horizons, to find himself. Five years later he might have had a different perspective on the opportunities open to him at Penn Square. But not yet.

Last night I lay in bed thinking my summer over, and what I thought I had accomplished for myself. I will now confess that I have reached some realizations that have got me wondering just what kind of person I really am. For one thing I often get this feeling of wanting to know much more about life in general than I now do. I want to be able to do more than I can now do, and I get frustrated at not being able to do more than I can. For this reason I like to travel, to get out and learn first hand about new things, people, and customs. I think this is why I enjoyed Europe so much, and even why I can get to know new cities so well so quickly and am such a good navigator. At present these feelings aren't too clear either, so you will have to wait for a while. But don't get the idea that I am dissatisfied with myself because I'm not. I happen to like myself.

The last comment, I must note, was a response to a point I frequently made to the children, namely that it was important to like oneself, to have confidence in oneself, to be autonomous, "true to one's self." And, of course, as a corollary, to be the sort of person one *could* like.

My response to Claude's self-analysis was practical and matter-of-fact. I did not urge him to follow up on his summer experience; I did not try to impress on him how valuable his "in" position at a large corporation was; I did not pressure him to keep up his contacts with Mr. Yoakum who had taken him under his wing, or with Mr. Hain, who would have been happy to take him under his wing also. I wrote that I understood his "identity problems" but I also noted the importance of learning the ropes of the job market:

Your search for identity is interesting and normal. I can sympathize with your feeling of wanting to know more about life, to be able to do more, etc. But if I financed all this learning, it would still leave you dissatisfied with yourself. Suppose you started off next summer and worked your way across the country? That might be a very useful experience. Perhaps Brick could teach you how to pick up jobs here and there. It might give you a feeling of being able to land on your feet. I think partly what troubles you is your dependence on me. That is normal, too. But if you could have the experience of getting jobs and taking care of yourself while having adventures at the same time, that might be interesting. Or perhaps you could get a job on a ship. Maybe some time in Baltimore you could go down to the hiring halls and see what there might be. In any event, all this is part of growing up.

The idea seemed to be that if he saw the work world from a different perspective he might appreciate the Penn Square opportunity more. I did not, however, press him to exploit that proposal. Would a father have acted differently?

If Claude had been more worldly, if he had been reared

as an "outsider," he might have had a sharper sense of the main chance. He would have been able to see this Horatio Alger opening as a good opportunity, a foot inside the door. As it was, he did his chores, made friends with the clerks and office personnel, enjoyed the hospitality of the top brass. And took absolutely no advantage of his privileged position. I had not prepared him to know the ropes even when they were dangling before his eyes—or to seize them if he had. I have no regrets. Nor has he.

It finally dawned on me that, for whatever reasons, my efforts in Claude's behalf were not going to be productive. I might be able to open doors but I could not push him through. His rejection of all my earlier suggestions and his lack of follow-up on the Penn Square opening may have been only part of his efforts at emancipation. But they may also have been recognition that his own interests did not lie in those directions. These interests began to surface during his sophomore year. They turned out to be in an area totally foreign to me: theater arts, especially lighting. But I was amenable. I discussed the subject with a neighbor in State College whose son was also in the theater: "I talked with Mr. Schlow about his son, Steve. He has a good job making documentaries. . . . After our discussion I concluded that if you are still fascinated by theater, the thing for you would be camera, not lighting work. But you can talk to him yourself when you come."

In the summer between his sophomore and junior years, 1965, Claude worked in the Johns Hopkins summer theater. It was a happy learning experience:

The theater is going well for the moment, and I am learning several facets of technical work which I have never quite learned. I have my hand in all phases of the operation and am being helpful in all fields. Work is interesting and is really educational, but I am afraid that I will have to

do a good deal of self-education before I am ready for anything advanced.

He was following the implicit rule I followed—that experience was more important than pay at this stage of the
game.

But even as a senior Claude had not yet found himself
occupationally. By now I had learned not to exert pressure:

It may take you more or less than four years to find yourself. We can take as long as necessary. The important thing
is to find something you really like to do, regardless of
anything. I would like you to do it on your own, without
any advice or butting-in by me because I think you probably tend to be influenced by me and I do not want to influence you. DL had lots of disappointments before she
finally succeeded. You may, also, but I am sure you can
take it. As I have said so many times, I am anxious for you
to find yourself and I hope this European trip is helping. I
am still discovering things about myself after all these
years. You are just beginning to discover yourself and I
hope it is going to be an interesting experience. Mainly
one has to like oneself and have confidence in oneself and
be autonomous and "be true to oneself" to coin an expression. Well, I didn't mean for this letter to turn into a didactic sermon, but my talk with DL seemed to trigger it.
Have fun.

In any event, careers were now becoming of secondary
salience in those violent years. There was always the draft
for young men to face. On Claude's twenty-second birthday I had to write to him in Europe that the graduate
schools at Maryland as well as Michigan—bursting like graduate schools everywhere—had turned him down:

What I now worry about most is how hard all this may be
on you. As I have told you so many times, in my opinion

it is really a good thing so far as your own life is concerned, that a taste of non-academic life may be just what you need. And if, after your turn at alternate service, you still think the academic life is for you, I am sure that you will be able to get into graduate school. It is just that you have come along at a very bad time historically. Your generation has been a big wave all along the line, first inundating the lower schools and now the higher schools and, worst of all, so many have been using graduate study as an escape from military service. It is this combination of factors that you are a victim of. Catherine Chilman reports that many of the seniors at Oberlin have had the same experience, an unheard-of-thing there. So, if you can, just grin and bear it.

Now that the draft was finally staring Claude in the face, firm and final career choices had to be laid aside. In the interim, while he waited to be called up he went to a computer school and searched for suitable alternate service projects. The decade had begun to achieve some kind of coherence by 1967; the young had organized themselves to oppose the Vietnam War on campuses, and since Claude was a bona fide pacifist who had been reared as a Friend and educated in a Friends' school, we anticipated no difficulties. A week after his twenty-second birthday I wrote to Claude in London:

I wrote to the man in charge of AFSC [American Friends' Service Committee] projects in Philadelphia for information about kinds of projects that might be suitable and available for alternate service. It has occurred to me that perhaps the draft board might consider teaching school in Germany as a possibility. As non-combatant service perhaps. If you have a sympathetic draft board that might be worth asking about. Or, for that matter, teaching at any installation. But since you know German, that would be best. You can study the situation when you return.

On his own, with no input from me at all. Claude located an acceptable spot the next year with the Youth Service of an American Friends' Service Committee project in Dayton, Ohio. In July 1968, I was writing to David that:

Claude seems finally to have his alternate service bit settled, although we won't be sure until he is actually at work. He thinks now that he will be in Dayton doing youth work, although it seems to me that the job will be about what he wants to make it, just so it has to do with young people. He will have headquarters in Dayton but this work will cover four states—Kentucky, Indiana, parts of Michigan, and Ohio.

And some two weeks later, that "Claude begins his job today. . . . He found a pleasant three-room apartment . . . so if you just happen to feel like it I am sure he would appreciate a letter. He sounds lonely." Three weeks later Claude sent David his own account of his work:

I started work on the first of August. I was a blind man in a featureless room. I had no conception of what I should be doing at the time. Gradually, however, the immediate needs of my job began to resolve themselves. I went around to meet various people and see various places, a process that still goes on. Along with this mobile life, I began to fit into the routine of the office. . . . Last week I went to observe the closeout of two projects (work camps) in Indiana, and to attend the Western Yearly Meeting. . . . Now I am in the process of writing out my observations on the projects and projecting what I feel the Youth Services program should be doing in the next years.

Actually, it was to be several months before Claude was finally confirmed in his job. For there were problems with the military on the legitimacy of accepting Quakers—notorious for their long-time antiwar activities—in alternate service jobs.

Protocol required an OK from the officer in charge in an area to which conscientious objectors were assigned. The colonel overseeing Dayton had expressed opposition to having any more Quakers assigned to his jurisdiction. Everyone knew they were breeders of trouble. Wherever you found a disturbance you were sure to find a bunch of Quakers. Even one or two were enough to cause trouble. The AFSC was, as everyone knew, a subversive organization, "prime instigators of student demonstrations at the various colleges and universities . . . almost always prominently mentioned in reports of uprisings concerned with racial problems, the war in Vietnam and other social-political demonstrations." An example of the kinds of things AFSC-sponsored conscientious objectors did was a registrant from Michigan. When a student at Oberlin "he was involved in a weekly vigil to protest the war in Vietnam, and he was also a proud member of a Quaker Action Group that sent first aid supplies to all parts of Vietnam in flagrant violation of the law." Fortunately, despite the objections of the colonel, final approval of Claude's assignment to the nefarious AFSC-sponsored job was eventually forthcoming. Washington was too sophisticated and too used to Friends to try to buck them.

So Claude served as a conscientious objector for two years (1968–1970) proving the protesting colonel quite right. He recruited high school and college protesters for marches, vigils, seminars on the war, retreats; he filled my apartment with demonstrators and, in general, obeyed the edicts of conscience and the imperatives of his generation without a hitch. He did well. His mentor appreciated his work. He could enter in the middle of the act, see the lay of the land, find what needed to be done, and do it.

After all these trial-and-error experiments and experiences in the search for an entry into the world of work, Claude finally chose teaching. Not for him The Glorified Guard, not the apprentice financier, not the theatrical lighting expert, not the diplomatic service officer. Hard as it was, it suited him. I do not know how Midge Decter would evaluate a teaching career. I am not sure it would measure up to her conception of a position of power and prestige; it certainly does not reap society's highest monetary rewards. Still, I am proud of his choice. His students have given him the highest accolade: he is hard but fair. Perhaps the fact that he has seen the financial world from the inside and found it uncongenial gave him the assurance that his profession was not entered *faute de mieux*.

High-level careers were not all that Midge Decter's generation coveted for their children:

Not all our expectations were of this nature. Beneath these throbbing ambitions were all the ordinary—if you will, mundane—hopes that all parents harbor for their children: that you would grow up, come into your own, and with all due happiness and high spirit carry forward the normal human business of mating, home-building, and reproducing—replacing us, in other words, in the eternal human cycle.[4]

I am not sure that reproducing, replacing me in the eternal human cycle, seemed important to me at the time, but a good marriage did. Between high school and college, I wrote, in reply apparently to a letter that has not survived:

I think the mate-selection problem will be important because you are going to need a mate who will encourage you socially, make the programs and contacts for a good social life. In most marriages the wife is the one who does this, who makes the social life. I think you will need this since you are not aggressive socially. A wife who will make an attractive home to which you can invite your friends and who will make friends for you, who will round out your life. You will be a serious, reliable, charming husband and your contribution will be to help her.

Then, noticing that I had been somewhat carried away, that I was, after all, writing to an eighteen-year-old boy, I added: "This has turned out to be sort of irrelevant." A kind of thinking out loud—more to myself than to him. I was, to be sure, more articulate than most people on the subject. But, I am sure, the same kind of thinking goes on in all "matchmakers," whether arrangers of blind dates, hostesses making up guest lists, sorority sisters. "You'll like him. He . . . " Or "you'll like her. She . . ."

As it turned out, I was to have as little input in the second of the great major decisions in Claude's life—marriage—as in the first—career. But, somehow, I felt more comfortable about it. I did not know much from my own personal experiences about the male work world outside of academia. But I did know about girls.

There had always been little girls in Claude's life, from nursery school days on. Some, like Joanie, quite close. But the whole ritual of dating did not begin until he went away to boarding school. And even then there seemed not to be much of it. At least the letters did not have much to say about girls in them. (He was already beginning to distance himself from me.) Trains, cars, and school activities seemed to take up most of his time. In one of my first letters to him at school, however, I was "delighted that the girl you asked accepted. What is her name? I hope you have a wonderful time and I am sure you will." Then, unsolicited, I proceeded to tell him how to behave: "Remember, be attentive, let her talk (if she wants to, but not if she doesn't). What I mean is, some girls prefer to let the boys talk; others want to talk themselves. OK?" After that, complete silence for four years in the letters that have survived.[5]

Then, in the summer before he entered college, he wrote from Washington to me in State College that "Kimmy . . . said definitely that she's coming. So I will have something pleasant to do this weekend." I replied that I was glad

Kimmy was coming though I was sorry I would miss her visit. I hoped they would have a wonderful time together and supposed he had something interesting planned. Then, in case he did not, I proceeded to suggest things for them to do:

August 10 falls on a Saturday so you won't be working, I take it, and you can do a lot of interesting things. Why don't you plan an interesting program of things to do, bearing in mind her interests and letting her veto anything that doesn't appeal to her. There may be a waterside concert in the evening. The canal trip is always interesting. Perhaps an art gallery or museum. You might want to rent a canoe? The naturalist walk on Roosevelt Island is interesting. Why don't you look in the paper for the program for that day; there is always a pleasant choice. Before she comes why don't you become familiar with how to get places so you won't waste time getting lost. You might take a cab if it takes too much time transferring, etc. to get places. She will probably want some time just to sit and talk. The little park back of our street is pleasant. Or she might want to walk along the river. You know her better than I do so you can make plans she would like. And remember, with her or any other girl, be yourself.

Then, not being one to miss an opportunity to make a point, I entered into a long harangue on how to relate to girls in general:

Girls may not be able to say what it is about you that attracts them, but you do have something that girls like. Don't be embarrassed if something goes wrong. Have a sense of humor and perspective. No one starts out being experienced. Experience takes time. It is much more appealing for young people to admit they are young, just learning. It is also less embarrassing than a false front of sophistication. When you finish college you will be more experienced, less afraid of girls. But right now you are only a freshman. And don't be intimidated by the greater experience and sophistication of others. Don't be afraid of being yourself. Like yourself—everyone else does—and be convinced of the fact that the way you are is OK. Now that you have discovered girls you will find a wonderful new dimension of life and I hope you learn to make the most of it. Don't make contacts with girls a duel or battle. Don't put them on the defensive. Bring them out. Look for the pleasant differences. Show them that you like them. I suppose George School taught you the amenities, how to treat girls on a superficial level (opening doors, standing, holding chairs, etc.). What I am talking about includes that but goes beyond that. Use your good looks and your very ingratiating smile. If I have said all this before, please excuse me. I am very anxious for you to be a happy man, a good husband, and a successful human being. And being at ease and comfortable with women is part of all this.

It so happened that I was working on a book on communication between the sexes—titled by the publishers *The Sex Game*—and so was full of the subject. I went on:

As you may know, in this book, I made a big point of men and women liking one another as well as loving one another. The sexual side of the relationship is important and I am not running that down. But the social side is important too. And it is not too early to learn how to cultivate the social side.

Then, somewhat tangentially:

I wonder if you have any regrets about having chosen a man's school? You commented on the value of a coeducational school in your letter. Do you think Cornell would have been better? I'm told that Baltimore is a social city and you may receive many invitations to parties. And, of course, Goucher. You will meet a lot of girls through Kimmy.

I returned then to the major theme:

I want you to be as good emotionally as you are intellectually. It is important to be a whole man, with the ability
to be happy and relaxed with women, as well as able to
love them wholeheartedly. I send out oceans and mountains of love and wish the very best for you in every way.
You are especially dear to me and I want everything good
for you, including a happy marriage when the time comes.

When Claude reported on Kimmy's visit, the program
did not sound at all like the one I had suggested. Except
that they had talked and ridden in cabs:

I suppose that you want to know about last night, so here
is a minute (no not quite)-by-minute account of last night.
Kimmy arrived with her brother who brought her in to
town, and went to Georgetown. We walked for a time,
then went in for a cup of coffee and talked. Then we got
into a cab and came back home and talked for quite a
while about all sorts of things. Then we took a long cab
ride until it was time for her to go home to Virginia. She
could come in only this once because of a wedding yesterday and an early departure today. However, that one night
was worth it.

I never pressed for more details. I was pleased if he was.
And, obviously, he was.
    Whether in anticipation of Kimmy's visit or in response
to some other incident, I had written about two weeks
earlier a brief *vade mecum* for the young-man-on-a-date:

One thing I would like to say is that no one should feel he
has to be someone else. Be yourself. If you don't have
anything to say, don't be embarrassed. You have a very
wise smile and you look as though you understand and
silence is nothing to be afraid of. As I said yesterday, your
talent for appreciative listening is a rare one and people

love it. And here is something to remember. Other people are far more scared than you are. Be kind to them, help them. Ask friendly (but *not* prying) questions. Lead them on to talk about things they can talk about well. But if you run up against someone who wants to lead *you* on, wants *you* to do the talking, why then oblige them. But I can't emphasize enough that you are a very attractive person; people will be prejudiced in your favor; you have a lot going for you with girls, peers, and adults. Remember they like you. Put them at ease, build them up, make them feel appreciated. You can do it. And you don't have a thing to worry about so far as social maturity is concerned.

I note now, many years later, that I was prescribing for my son the behavior expected of women, the basic rules for the traditional feminine role. Be kind, help, lead others on to talk. . . . But also of my conception of the masculine role:

Don't feel you have to seem sexually more blasé and sophisticated than you are. Admit that you are young, not a man-about-town or a roué. But be sure of your masculinity. Girls like masculine men, but not brutes. And being masculine means you don't have to put on a blustering act. Masculine men can enjoy the company of women because they are sure of themselves. Women like to feel like women and masculine men do this for them. Don't act as though girls were just like boys. They are different and the differences should be enjoyed. Not by running down the feminine approach but by playing it up in an appreciative way. I may overdo this because, as you know, I am writing a book on the subject. But there is a lot of truth in it anyway. Most of all I want to reassure you about your social maturity. It's way above par. And don't feel you have to work at being social. Just cultivate your natural talents. That will do the trick.

Thus, at least for the time being, ended the Polonius-like homily.

Despite my heroic attempts to build up his self-confidence in relation to girls, Claude felt woefully inadequate. Less than two weeks after the delightful date with Kimmy he was brooding over his "social immaturity." He was carefully assessing his situation, tracing the cause of his "social immaturity" to a parent who, unlike "parents who want [their children] to be like all the others," had provided less social training for him.

In college there was little if any discussion of girls. Claude brought home young women from time to time, but by now the distance between us precluded confidences. I had the feeling that Claude was sometimes overawed by the experiences and adventures of his peers. One young woman especially—lover of the young man Claude was sharing an apartment with—fascinated him. Earthy and ethnic, she wove a potent spell over both the young men. Claude was apparently not ready for her; his housemate later married her. The young women Claude brought home were more vanilla-flavored.

I occasionally made passing comments about girls. To London in the summer of 1967 I wrote asking "by the way, have you talked to any interesting girls?" To Dayton I wrote soon after his arrival: "Why aren't you chasing the girls?" I needn't have concerned myself. He was soon living in a cooperative household:

The house is . . . in a pleasant residential area in the north part of the city. We live in half a duplex about a mile (maybe a bit more) from center city. The house has six rooms and bath with a full basement and an unlit and unheated attic. Linda, Johanna, and I live upstairs in the three bedrooms. Remember what my rooms have looked like since I have lived in apartments and elsewhere? With the same material I have little else I can do with the room. (See drawing.) Downstairs is the big kitchen with both girls' implements. They are good cooks and I have to be

careful. There is a big living room—about the size of yours
without the TV nook—and what used to be the parlor.
That is Jay's room, separated by a sliding door. It has become home for all of us and makes living in Dayton that
much better. I have some pictures which I will try to get
to you when I come to D.C. next month. Will call on Sunday, I think. . . . Things are going well and I feel at home
in the house, the first time really, since moving to Dayton.

In June, Linda wrote, addressing me as "future Mother-
in-law," and described the plans for the wedding, scheduled four months later. The marriage was to be under the
sponsorship of the Yellow Springs Meeting:

We will get married in my folks' church (Church of the
Brethren) in Brookville, but with a Quaker service. It will
have a few traditional touches, but still simple. My mother
is making my dress . . . which is ivory colored but will be
of simple design. . . . I have never been to a Quaker wedding but like the ideas, as Claude has described them to me.

Dorothy Lee and I returned from Japan—where we had
arrived after a trans-Siberian railroad trip taken to help her
get over the end of her own marriage—just in time to
attend the beautiful wedding which went off just as Linda
had planned it. She and Claude have been living happily
ever since.

part III

Danik

and I

autobiographical introduction

Autumn that year—1949—had seemed especially beautiful in central Pennsylvania. I had never felt better. If this was menopause why did women dread it so? The alleged syndrome was just another old wives' tale. I was emerging from my postwar trauma occasioned by learning of the Holocaust. I was becoming buoyant and I was pleased with my world. My work was going well; my last book was being well received. The children were doing well. LLB seemed to be doing well. The symptoms of the dread disease had not yet become alarmingly apparent.

It was a long time before it occurred to me that this was not menopause. I had been able to tell very soon after I had conceived Claude. Not so in the case of this totally unexpected child. This time—at forty-six—I did not know until three months later, at the end of November. The news came as a devastating shock to LLB. He never, literally, recovered psychologically from it, as he was never to recover physically from cancer, now beginning its ravaging course. There was never any hesitation in his mind that the birth of this child must be averted. He was fighting his illness heroically, but this was too much. Even I could see that. So I concurred.

My serene well-being of the early autumn gave way to
anxiety. How did one go about this sort of thing? At a
later time, when the liberalization of abortion laws was
becoming a public issue, a roster of about a hundred names
of distinguished women—including Steinem, Hellman,
Tuchman, Beauvoir among others—appeared in the public
print, all of whom had had, or said they had had, an abortion. In some cases it may have been a gesture like that of
the good Danes who appeared with the Star of David on
their sleeves when the Nazis ordered all Jews to do so. But
no doubt many of these women had, indeed, had abortions.
I wondered how they had all been so successful in securing
them. I was not.

Many years later there were Cuban doctors available, and
trips to Scandinavia, or to other liberal countries, and
alternate resources in our society less costly if more dan-
gerous. When Dorothy Lee was in college she asked me
from time to time to extend weekend hospitality to some
young woman or other. I never asked questions and it was
only later that it dawned on me why they were there. In
the case of another young woman, a friend of Dorothy
Lee, I paid the cost myself. Not in such a network myself,
my knowledge of how to go about the matter was
minuscule.

I wrote to my sister in New York and she said she would
make inquiries. I went there during the Christmas holidays,
well into my second trimester. To no avail. We did not
know the ropes. We did get the names of doctors by way
of the female grapevine and pursued every lead. All in vain.
No one would undertake the procedure. It was, in any
event, too late—too hazardous outside of a hospital and
too mine-seeded inside of one. Nor would any of the
psychiatrists validate a request. "You are the most stable
pesonality I have ever examined," said one, and the others,
one way or another, agreed. If not to save *my* life or
sanity, then my husband's? Not a chance. . . .

At home the utter banality of family life even in a crisis
was reflected in the letters to me from Dorothy Lee, eight,

and Claude, four, dictated to their father and written by him:

                              December 24, 1949
Dear Mother,
   We have just finished building the fire. We got your letter and we want to know your street address. Yesterday we weren't too good, but today we are being better. I dry the dishes and Daddy washes them and Claude puts the silver away. I ironed some clothes yesterday morning. I put Claude to bed. In the morning when he wakes up he says he is too tired. This morning I scrubbed the floor around the kitty's sand box, because Daddy said that must be what is smelling so. Claude and I were worried because we hadn't heard from you until your card came. Claude and I are using the davenport and the love seat for a couch and we use the pillows for beds for the animals and we cover them with coats and sweaters. Claude lets me play with Pinky, the dog. We gave the kitty a bath this morning. We warmed the water on the stove and then took it up-stairs and put it in the basin. Then we put the kitty in the water and he went szzz and scratched. So we put him on the edge of the basin and poured the water over him. Claude was afraid to hold him. We dried him as much as we could and put him beside the radio and then he licked himself trying to get dry. Then he purred because he likes to be dry. He smells like the soap now. The man from the Children's Shop called up and said they couldn't get the doll. Claude and I are trying to be good for Daddy.

                     Love from Dorothy Lee XXX
[Drawings of two smiling faces, one labeled JB and one DL.]

Dear Mother,
   I am glad you are at the hospital so you can get well. Tonight is Christmas eve. Tomorrow morning I am going to find my [toy] gas station [promised before I left].

I hope you will be better pretty soon. If you don't get
better you would better stay at the hospital. Dear Mother,
will you write some letters very often? . . . We got another
camel for our [crèche] stable from the Sunday School
teacher, Mrs. Johnson. I hope you will be home soon. We
miss you very, very much.

With love from Claude

(Drawing of me in bed with XXXX and of him.)
(Drawings of all members of the family, again with XXXX.)
(Printed by Claude himself): We love you.

December 26, 1949

Dear Mother,
   We gave the kitty another bath today—Laura and I—and
the kitty is getting to like the bath. He licks himself to get
dry. He sleeps in my doll crib. I washed the sink and the
kitchen table tonight. Claude and I help Daddy wash the
dishes. I dry them and Claude puts the silver away. I set
the table and carry in the milk, after I have been told
several times. I washed Claude's sweater, shirt, and blue
jeans this morning and got him some clean pajamas. Last
night I gave him a bath. Claude's bed broke and we fixed
him a bed on his mattress on the floor and he likes it.
Daddy hurt his back and when it is better he will fix the
bed again. Claude and I are trying to be good and Daddy
says I am helpful. Claude has been marking up books and
Daddy had to spank him. I mopped the floor where the
kitty's sand box stands and scrubbed the tile on which it
stands. I cleaned the salamander's bowl. Claude picks the
salamander out and isn't afraid that it is a ghost any more.
We found out what was so precious about the green ginger
jar [in the story being read to them]. It was a ruby.

Dorothy [signed in her own handwriting]

Dear Mother,

I am over the mumps. We appreciate your buying the gas station for me. I take a nap very often on my bed on the floor.

Claude

All our lives were being profoundly—and inexorably—influenced. Still, silver must be put away, dogs taken care of.

A Catholic doctor did finally say he would undertake the procedure. He took me to a Catholic hospital. I was on the operating table when the nun who ran the hospital called the doctor aside. A suspicious nurse had alerted her. I was returned to my room and discharged the next day.

In a letter I wrote many years later to explain to David why I had loved Ezra so much, I told him:

When the plans for the abortion in New York fell through I went to Ezra. When I told him I was pregnant his face showed great joy; he had never had a child and the idea delighted him. There was a well-known physician in Central Pennsylvania with a reputation for having great skill, wasn't there? Yes, there was. Would he take me to him? His face darkened. Why, yes, of course he would if I insisted. But why should I want him to? Why not have the baby? Did I really want the abortion? Well, not really. It was more for LLB's sake than for my own. And wouldn't he [Ezra] object? Wouldn't it embarrass him? Of course not. And who would take over my courses? Why should anyone take them over? Wouldn't he want me to take maternity leave? No, not at all. If I wanted to go on teaching that was OK with him. I could stay right on as long as I felt like it. He seemed even to like the idea of a member of his faculty pregnant and carrying on as though nothing unusual was going on. Schools, libraries, supermarkets, offices were all

filled with pregnant girls and women that year. They were
everywhere. Why not at the professorial lectern also?
Carrying her full [academic] load? The idea seemed to
appeal to him. He said he would talk to your father. He
did. He tried, valiantly though unsuccessfully, to reassure
him. No way.

Ezra loved you who were, in effect, his own child in the
sense that though he may not have contributed to your
conception had contributed to your rescue. Whatever male
presence there was in the first two or three years of your
life was his.[1]

The students—in my coeducational university, like my
students earlier in a women's college—took my pregnancy
in stride. Once it became evident, there was not a second
thought given to it. This was, after all, the era of the
feminine mystique and having babies was no big deal;
everyone was doing it—even, in the case of students who
were veterans, their own wives. So why, after all, not their
professor also? So at the end of the spring term I completed my grades, cleared by desk, went to the hospital
and had David. His father had to leave the next day for a
teaching engagement in the West arranged a year earlier.
Ezra took over a lot of the chores—transportation, arrangements for services, and the like—usually performed by
fathers.

When the department met the next day to square away
for the summer school where I was scheduled to teach, one
of my colleagues came in, looked around, and asked,
"Where's Jessie?" Didn't he know, came the answer. "She
had her baby yesterday." Yes, he knew, but "that was
yesterday. Where is she?" I had long been known on
campus as Jet Bernard. I resumed my teaching duties on
schedule when the summer term began.

chapter eight

family and friends

David's father was a long time dying. Only in the last three months did that iron-willed, mind-over-matter, indomitable man concede. It was only then, when he had become bed-ridden, under almost constant sedation (though, for fear of addiction he never knowingly allowed himself anything stronger than what one might ordinarily take for a bad toothache) that he admitted the truth. Not that he accepted it. He did not go gently into that night.

The doctor had said in the fall that it might take six months. I was relieved when it turned out to be three. On that January day I had been sitting alone all afternoon in the room across the hall from where he lay quietly, breathing just audibly. Outside the snow had been falling all day. The window in my room looked out over Nittany Valley, quietly screened off by the falling snow as the silent hours passed. The nurse was out. The two older children were not yet home from school. I was alone except for the infant who lay peacefully in his crib on the other side of the room. I knew that this was to be the day. The struggle in the room across the hall was subsiding. The iron will that had triumphed over so many obstacles for almost seventy years was visibly weakening. It could not be much longer now.

When the older children came home they seemed more subdued than usual. Dinner was uneventful, muted. The nurse returned, checked her patient; and presently everyone was asleep. I waited. From time to time I tiptoed in to listen. It was not long before it happened. The silence became permanent. I was glad the vigil was over. There was no grief. A great sadness, yes. But mainly a need to put it all together. To add it all up, the past, the present, the immediate future. I lay awake all night with the thick snow still falling, still hugging me in. A moment of solitude —utter and complete. In the morning I called the children in to say good-bye to their father before the matter-of-fact world burst in. This was his last moment as a human being. When the world did burst in he would be merely a dead body. Only half understanding, solemnly, they paid their last respects and were off to school—the infant in his crib still endearingly undemanding.

With the pall of slow death lifted, the household fell into a new pattern. A thousand family details had to be taken care of—he had left no will—and university duties to be resumed, the first far harder than the second. And an infant to rear who would never have known his father.

The juxtaposition of birth and death had profound ramifications on all our relationships, especially on David's, as I tried some eighteen and a half years later (March 1969) to explain to him, for it was he who bore the brunt of his father's lingering death and the family asymmetry that followed it:

Infants need almost a satiety of physical body contact, cuddling. Just as they have to have their fill of sucking— breast, bottle, or thumb. But when you were an infant your father was very sick and demanding. For the last three months of his life—when you were five to eight months old—I had a dying man in one room and an infant son in another, both needing me. Then when he died and I should have been able to make up to you the attention you needed, I was confronted with the painful readjustment we all had to make to his loss. While he was alive he belonged to DL and I belonged to Claude. Each child had a parent and there was an equilibrium. When he died, DL horned in on Claude's property and for almost six months there was continual competition for my attention. It was terribly painful for all of us, including, I now see, you. Because it kept me from giving you more attention.

To abate the struggle between Dorothy Lee and Claude I took the family to Bermuda. The tensions were relaxed for all of us, even for David, infant though he was, and he remembered forever that "sunny place" and "the sailboat race," as so delightful that he hoped they were true and not just a dream.

David, in brief, was born into a family already structured. For five years Dorothy Lee and Claude had been learning to live with one another, competitively and hence intensely. Now they were having to learn how to share a single parent. Many years later I learned from David that there were times when he felt like an outsider, an intruder in an ongoing set of relationships, a feeling made even more threatening by the teasing he was subjected to by Dorothy Lee to the effect that he was an adopted child. Serious and solemn, he believed it—at least enough to cause him to worry about the security of his position in the family. He felt, in effect, like a tagalong, surrounded by so many others who were bigger than he.[1]

Perhaps as a result of this, David became extremely family-minded, strongly attached to all of us. He needed to be near me in a way I did not completely understand until later. He was—I see now—like a child running after a mother who seemed to elude him. He was attached not only to me but to the whole family, to the idea of family as much as to each of us individually. He was more attached to Dorothy Lee and Claude than they to him. There were more letters from him to them than from them to him. Family gatherings seemed to be more precious to him. In a document called for to accompany David's application for admission to a program run by Andover in Spain (when he was sixteen) I had written—but deleted at his request—this paragraph:

David has taken charge of family holiday celebrations, trimming the Christmas tree, dismantling it, coloring Easter eggs, supervising the Easter-egg hunt, etc. He has made the birthday celebrations. He has a very close family-sense and makes a big point of doing things as a family.

When he was eleven I wrote to Dorothy:

Now we are getting ready for Thanksgiving. We are going to have two. We have been invited out for dinner, but David thinks this is sacrilegious because Thanksgiving is a family affair, so we will have our private, family Thanksgiving dinner at noon and the formal one in the evening. We will set a place for you (figuratively speaking) at the table and think of you. (Perhaps at the very moment that you read this letter.)

The next February, David was talking of a trip to Puerto Rico next Christmas, "all of us, as a family." From camp when he was thirteen he wrote that it was "nice to have a family that cares." From Spain when he was sixteen: "Last week I thought of my whole family and how much I love them; I am truly thankful that they are my family. I hope everyone is happy and that everything works out if there are any complications. . . . XXX." When he was eighteen he wrote, in response to a suggestion broached by Claude: "Oh, I think it is a nice idea for a reunion [at father's grave] on Memorial Day. We haven't done this as a family since the year we came back from Austria."

David's clinging to family ties may have been, in part, compensation for the trauma he suffered from frequent loss of friends, for he was a victim of the mobility characteristic of professional families. "For the most part they [children] have had to be passive passengers in the moves made for the survival and ambitious needs of a parent or parents. In the process children have seen their own existence battered by loss of friends, credentials, and those ballasts of community life that are needed for feelings of security and well-being."[2] Dorothy Lee had first complained of it as a freshman at boarding school, she said that there was a limit to the number of times a child could be transplanted. And some years later when she wrote nostalgically about the house on West Fairmount in State College I wrote back that her comments "gave me a little pang." David had attended six schools by the time he was twelve. It was hard to make and leave friends so often. At Princeton he was especially lonely; it was the first time he and I had lived alone without either Dorothy Lee or Claude and he was suffering the severance of ties with his State College friends. In November of that year I had written to Dorothy Lee.

The best news yet is that David has finally found a friend, an English boy in his room. . . . He is the son of someone from Oxford; he has been here only a few more months than we have and until now has not had any friends either, although he has two brothers, which helps. David was so happy about finding a friend that he couldn't even fall asleep. It is good for him to have the friend. He still loves Bobby, though, and calls him up almost every week.

The year at Princeton was not, therefore, a good one for him. It was a Civil-War-Abraham-Lincoln year for David. For bedtime reading we went through all three volumes of Sandberg's life of Lincoln. We visited sites. From time to time we went in to New York to see plays, including *Andersonville.* But Princeton was not State College.

Uprooted again two years later when we moved to Washington, David was once more missing his old friends. I expressed my concern in my letters to Dorothy Lee:

Another problem is friends. David is very lonely. Unlike
you, he doesn't make friends easily; I don't know why. He
seems to be shy and diffident with other children. He talks
and plays with them, but never invites them home. Maybe I haven't given him enough time [to make friends].

A few days later I wrote that although David seemed to be
content, I felt "terribly guilty about his not having any
friends." To the ever-present though not necessarily always
articulated question that so many parents face some time
or other—"What did I do wrong?"—I replied: "I should
either have postponed my sabbatical until he was in George
School or else made living arrangements in a neighborhood
where he could meet children naturally. . . . I think he will
survive, although it would have been pleasanter for him in
a more child-centered neighborhood." And, still again, a
week or so later: "David still hasn't made friends, but he is
sensitive about any efforts on my part so I just say nothing
any more." Then, again the same mea culpa: "I sometimes
wonder if I broke ties in State College two years too soon,
that perhaps I should have waited until he was ready for
George School. . . . Well, it's too late to worry about that
now." There were brief respites when we returned to State
College during the summer when he could resume his old
friendships. "David swims, rides his bike, has arts and
crafts at the park, goes on picnics, to movies, etc., and has a
generally good time with his friends." These visits re-
plenished him for the return to Washington.
    It was not only David's unwilling mobility that affected
him, but also my own willing mobility. For I was increasingly off to professional meetings of one kind or another.
Knowledge was growing at such a fast pace that one had to
run fast to keep up with it, and that meant going to conferences, workshops, conventions to hear papers that
would not be published for months. David as a child had
an extremely peripatetic mother.

David first showed up in the letters at the age of three when I reported almost daily to Dorothy Lee from Graz to Geneva. He appeared first as the obstreperous child who became more and more boisterous as he became more and more tired on the way from Zurich to Graz and drove one man out of our train compartment. He appeared as the little boy who didn't want to go to kindergarten when I took him in the morning, though he seemed happy enough once he got there. As the child who, while I was on a trip to Spain, was left at kindergarten until six in the evening, thus developing a horror of kindergarten. Who left the school one day and was found only much later in a store, crying because no one understood what he wanted, namely, candy. Who fell in the mud two or three times a day, leaving us quite desperate for clean clothes to replenish him with since laundry was done so infrequently in that household. Who insisted on wearing under his overalls the little suit, both pants and bolero, his sister had made, telling everyone proudly that his adored sister, Dorsy Lee, had made them for him. And who, as if to exacerbate every fiber of guilt in my own mind, hit his head against a marble tabletop in play during my absence in Scandinavia and had to be rushed to the hospital to have stitches taken on a gash over his eye. . . . No wonder he had talked so much about his friends at home and about our house there, the house with the two screen doors.[3]

The first bona-fide letters from David himself were from State College and Princeton to me on my trip to Stresa, Italy, when he was nine. The fourth meeting of the International Sociological Association was scheduled for Stresa in the late summer of 1959 and my own paper, for September 10. The timing coincided with the renewal of long-standing invitations from two friends—Ralph Lewis and Wolf Ladijinsky—to visit them in Seoul and Saigon respectively. I decided to accept both invitations and go

to Stresa by way of the Orient. I left a package of envelopes addressed to me at the several hotels I was scheduled
to be staying at along the route to assure at least periodic
reports. Some reached me, some never did, and some
were "returned to sender," including several of David's. I
wrote the children almost every day: sixty-five letters plus
two cables survive. Some were to them individually, some
to them as a group. The letters from Seoul gave a fair
enough account of those parts of my visit there that might
interest them. Ralph Lewis, whom they would remember
from Graz, was now a cultural officer. He booked me solid
for talks and events where I could meet and talk to stra-
tegic Koreans and be seen and talked to by as many people in the countryside as possible. Best of all, I told them,
he took me to the northern provinces where I was feted,
wined, dined, and flattered in the Oriental manner that
makes even simple courtesy look like genuine love. I wrote
August 3: "My trip to the country . . . was a wonderful
experience. I spoke to a women's club in Chonan. Then
there was a party at which I wore a Korean costume and it
was given to me. Two little girls danced for us. I was given
two large bouquets of flowers and a little silk bag." The
letters from Saigon, still a very French city in 1959, were
noncommittal. Only Dorothy Lee had ever met my host,
Wolf Ladijinsky, and her memories of him were vague. He
lived in a charming French-style villa complete with
French-trained servants. He was an agricultural-economist
well known throughout the Orient for his brilliant land-
reform work as a member of General MacArthur's advisory
staff in postwar Japan. On the basis of that success he had
been invited by President Diem to advise him on land reform in his country. That was what he was doing there in
1959. There was not much to write home about, certainly
not to children. Wolf was punctiliously noncommunicative,
never talked of his work, took me sight-seeing through the
countryside, showed me the villages, even those protected
by barbed wire. Never a hint of trouble brewing; it looked
peaceful. Too much has occurred on that scene since then.

But at that time I was able to write, August 11: "This morning I went to a tea at the house of the wife of the Chinese ambassador. There were women of many countries there—France, Thailand, Switzerland, etc. I met one woman, Mrs. Li (pronounced Lee) who has a daughter (Dorothy) at Vassar and one at Alfred University. I took their names and perhaps we can invite them to our home. Another woman who studied pharmacy and cosmetics at the University of Michigan, is opening up the cosmetics industry in this country." How gentle, how *feminine* it sounds now, like the calm before a storm.[4]

Not all the letters to or from David reached me and usually there was a considerable hiatus between a letter and a response. To a letter dated July 31—"Dear Mother, Nobody reads your letters so I don't know what you are doing," to which Dorothy Lee had added parenthetically "(did read)" and Claude, also parenthetically "(True)"—I replied from Hong Kong, "David dear, please insist that both Claude and Dorothy Lee read my letters to you. I want you to hear them because I want you to get your great big share of the love I send each time. OK?" In the same letter David had said: "The more you are gone the more I miss you," and proceeded to fill me in on his activities: "At the park we are getting points and I have the most. So at the end of the year the first 3 people get prizes and that will be on August the 3, 1959. I'm hoping that I will be first. Claude and I sleep together some nights because my room is too hot and then I cough. Claude does not mind it. I hope you liked the last letter. What Washington died of old age?" In that letter Claude had also written reporting that since David now had control of his sleeping habits he was often grouchy, so in my August 7 reply I chided him gently: "David, my darling, why don't you go to bed early so you won't be tired?" and added that I was proud that he was doing so well at the park. When I wrote the children of a package containing gifts they would be receiving, David was concerned that they might not arrive in State College in time. Also he had learned how to float on his back and dive. "It was fun." "I miss you very much. I wish you would come home. But not everything can come true." He had learned a lot. Then he added: "Thank you for you." I wrote that I was proud David had won a prize; and a week later, I was happy that David had done so well at the pool. "It was fine to come in second place and I am awfully proud of you. I will want to hear all about it when I get back." The next day I wrote that I was counting the days till my return; David seemed to be weighing on my mind. "David, I worry about you quite a bit. Will you write and tell me you are fine?" Two days later I wrote that I had "told a 4th-grade class at a government school about David"; three days later I was expressing concern about David's first day of school at Princeton: "Look into David's school, Dorothy Lee, and see that he gets there the first day. Take him and explain why I am not there." The next day from Tashkent, Uzbek S.R.: "David, my guide said she liked you best of all when I showed her my pictures." From Tbilisi: "Nelly, my guide, liked the pictures of David also. He would make quite a hit here. Nelly says he looks like a Russian boy." David's first day of school at Princeton was on my mind—August 29: "Maybe David will be in school by the time you get this"; August 30: "I hope . . . that David's school is OK"; September 1: "As soon as I get to Milan I am going to have my ticket changed to skip Lisbon and fly directly home. . . . I have been separated from you too long."

David's reactions to Princeton were evident quite quickly. The day I was writing my last letter from Stalingrad, David was writing from Princeton to me in Zurich, a letter that was "returned to sender" weeks later since by then I had cut Zurich out of my itinerary.

Dear Mother,
    I'm fine. I often wonder how much fun it is to take a trip around the world. I suppose it is fun. I wish I was with you. Thank you for the trade dollar, belt, tie, wooden carvings, and scarf. That makes 5 things that you have

bought me. The mover won't take my bike because it has
to be wrapped. Dodo and Bill took the hi-fi to the Hutchison's. Nancy's wedding went OK. She looked beautiful.
The Hutchison's are on a trip. The train [here] was late by
2 hours so we had to wait. We came a day early so we had
to stay at Cindy's house for the night. There is nothing
to do. I don't like Princeton. I wish I was in State College.
Today is Monday. We are going to pick up Claude and
Stella. I miss you very much.

P.S. I love you [43 Xs.] All for you.

The next day another letter, this time to Lisbon, also "returned to sender" weeks later:

Today it is raining. It has been raining every day since the
day we came. I packed all of my things and Claude did
not send it to Princeton so I don't have anything to do but
watch TV. Dorothy Lee got us a tv for $2.00 for 10
months. We can get over 7 channels. Claude and I sleep in
the same bed. I wish you were here. We got Claude new
clothes, but teachers get 10% off of cars. We opened a
charge account. There is a shopping center in back of our
house. It has everything but a movie. Claude is bothering
me. It has been fun for us 3. The day you come is the day
I start school. I found a golf ball. Love, David.

P.S. I love you [half a page of Xs]. All for you.

With so much mobility in his background and with such a
peripatetic mother, it was perhaps little wonder that David
clung so lovingly to his family.

Nor was school to provide a source of friends. David was
in the sixth grade when we first came to Washington after
an intervening year in State College. I had anticipated little
difficulty. Schooling in my middle-western childhood had
been such a simple, straightforward matter that the complexities confronting parents in the '50s and '60s came as
something of a surprise to me. I had walked a mile to

school, played with my classmates, and returned home to play with neighborhood children. Race was, of course, now becoming one of the major issues parents were having to face. So far as I knew, my children had had little if any contact with racism. And race had played no part in the school decisions I had had to make for Dorothy Lee and Claude. I accepted the 1954 Supreme Court decision—rendered the year before Dorothy Lee entered boarding school—in good faith. When I once asked her why she had never mentioned the fact that her chemistry teacher—the one she later remembered as among her favorites—was black, she couldn't understand why she should. At Sarah Lawrence her first suitemate had been black. As had Claude's first roommate at George School. Desegregation had seemed simple and easy in those early post-Brown days. Not so seven years later when I confronted it with David.

The Washington school system had only recently been desegregated when we moved there and it was still in the throes of coming to terms with the process. The school David was assigned to was almost all black. I assured myself that it made no difference and he was duly enrolled. I wrote to Dorothy Lee: "The public school David will go to . . . —Adams School—is three-quarters Negro. Think what an experience that will be for David." And, a week later, not quite so reassured but still positive: "Tomorrow David starts to school. If his school is too crowded, I understand he may change to a less crowded school. We'll see. . . . I feel a year in a Negro school will be a very worthwhile educational experience." Forgive the patronizing stance; my consciousness had not yet been raised—at least not far enough.

My enthusiasm was short-lived. It wavered when I actually saw the school. Crowded, with scarcely enough room for the teacher to move about—not enough textbooks and those that there were so old that railroads were still new and interesting subjects to read about. Children sent on to junior high still—many of them—not able to read. After a week or so of soul-searching and conscience-assuaging I wrote to Dorothy Lee that I was trying to have David transferred "to a less crowded school." I did finally succeed and by early October I could write that David seemed "at least satisfied with his school" and so was I. "Since he has some written work to do I guess it is an adequate school. As you know, one of the criteria I apply in judging schools is how much written work they require." I urged her to continue writing to him. "He told me to tell you that it was my idea that he change schools because he doesn't want you to think he's a brat. Which, indeed, he is not." I felt bad, I continued, that David didn't like school but I didn't know what to do. I was apparently applying inappropriate criteria in judging schools. David did good work but he said his teacher yelled a lot.[5]

The next year, when David was twelve, he left the public school system to enter a private school. But however adequate its academic program may have been—and it was —it was no place for a boy like David to find friends. Sidwell Friends' was a school where competitive, out-to-win men—presidents and cabinet members and media stars— sent their children and it reproduced a kind of grotesque parody of the Washington social status structure. Though nominally a Quaker school, its football style was as violent as any professional team's. The boys were exhorted to "hit hard," "kill!" Not a place where gentle, loving boys would find much congenial companionship.

In the spring before David became thirteen I broached the subject of camp. I had found one that I considered "to be perfectly lovely for David in Switzerland for the summer, where he could learn French and German also," I wrote to Claude. But David did not agree. He did not want to go. "And after my experience with you," I continued to Claude, "when I thought the camp was a lovely idea and you thought it horrible, I'm not pushing it." David wanted us to go to Nevis, an island in the Caribbean, but what would he do there? Apparently, despite my disclaimer to Claude, I was pushing camp. For, quite aside from the

usual reasons parents have for sending children to camp, I
had the urgent one of giving him more contacts with adult
males. He remained reluctant. He would have preferred to
join his friends in State College where I was to teach that
summer and remain with me. But he did finally consent to
go to camp.

As it turned out, he loved it. And, once having learned
that he could survive without me or Claude or Dorothy
Lee, his psychological distancing took the form of actual—
though often apologetic—physical distancing. After that he
was never again to spend a summer with me, in Washington
or anywhere else. But it was not always to be easy, on
either him or me.

True to form, I could not see him off to camp. I had to
leave for State College before camp opened, thus:

Dear Claude and David (in alphabetical order),
    I haven't had any letters from you and don't feel I really
know what is going on. . . . I am . . . especially concerned
that David get safely off to camp. Is that all provided for?
Is the money holding up? . . . I ought to know what the
financial situation is. David will need a little pocket money
when he leaves. He should have a box lunch for the train.
That means sandwiches, fruit, cookies, carrot sticks or
celery stalks, or tomato or some vegetable. Can you manage that? Please let me know.

David responded reassuringly, bringing me up to date:

Dear glorious mother,
    Everything is just fine. Claude and I get along alright.
Any differences we have we work out. At least we don't
hit each other. We eat very well and wisely. Saturday you
got a letter from the camp. I took the liberty to open it
since it would concern me more than it would you. . . . Be
sure to keep well and go to the doctor. . . . Have a good
summer. At least try.

Camp proved to be a great experience for David. Still, for some reason or other I seemed to demand an exorbitant amount of reassurances. I made it a point to send him at least a daily card and he replied that it was "the most pleasant thing to get a letter [from me] every day." It is hard to understand why since my letters sounded like research questionnaires. For example:

Do you like your cabinmates? How many cabins are there? Are there any other children from Washington? . . . Do you have enough to read? What do you do 1:30 to 5 in the afternoon? Can you do all that is required of you? Do you get enough to eat? enough sleep? How is your swimming? has your endurance improved? did you get the rowboat fixed up?

Dutifully he replied. "I'm glad to get questions, so here I'm answering them." He proceeded to give me far more information than I needed to know. Everyone in the cabin was wonderful. There were four cabins: Killington, Okemo, Shrewsbury, and Pico. He was busy, as was everyone else. He didn't have much time to read; so far only the Sunday *New York Times* and a chapter in a book. They did their planning during rest time. The food was plentiful; breakfast especially was huge.

Even the most meticulous researchers would have had to concede that my informant was conscientious in replying to my questions. Still the gnawing guilt demanded reassurances. So I drew up another questionnaire that sounds quite bizarre as I read it now: "Are you really having fun or do you say so in order not to worry me? Is the camp too rugged for a city-bred boy? You make it sound like great fun and you act as though you enjoy it a lot. But you are such a thoughtful boy you would act as though you liked it even if you didn't." The anxiety sounded a bit much: "Did you like the other camps [in the complex] better? Would you have preferred to go to one of them?

If so, could you still be transferred?" And, relentlessly, two days later: "Why not tell me more about the counselors, about the other boys, about what you think."

Now his reply showed a bit of—understandable—irritation. "I don't see why you don't think I'm having any fun. I'm having a great time. I didn't think I was going to but as you see I like it a lot. . . . What do you mean I act as if I'm not having fun? I'm having fun. I think that I've told you about the other boys." But, patiently, he repeated himself and mapped the cabin and spelled out his cabinmates: Jon, Estey, Charley, Paul, Joe, Dick, Will, Mike, Sam. A six-day hiatus in the correspondence during a five-day hike called forth a complaint from me about the mails and a suggestion that perhaps I should send a telegram. Once more there was a request from me for even more news, "a *long* letter with all kinds of details about" —for heaven's sake!—"your room, food, friends, activities, etc., etc." This time David was resigned but appreciative: "It was nice to get back from the hike and get all the mail I got. I got your postcards and letters, one from Dorothy and comics from Claude. It is nice to have a family that cares." He reminded me that he had already told me about the kids in the cabin, the counselors, and all, but he is indulgent: "I guess you would like to hear more about them; after all they take care of me." After that I accepted his statements that he was having fun and stopped insisting on reassurances myself. Many years later he said "I *did love* camp. Perhaps the reason you found it difficult to believe me when I said so was because you knew that (up to then) I would say I was happy when I really wasn't." He was probably right in his interpretation, but probably wrong in protecting me.

The rest of the letters from camp were filled with accounts of twelve-mile hikes, of canoe trips, of swimming feats, of caving expeditions, of picture-taking, of work, of learning how to handle a knife or axe, of food, of bouts of illnesses in the camp, of the weather extremes, of reading material—and especially with complaints about the mail that always seemed to take too long. Standard, I suppose, for letters from children everywhere to parents everywhere. Not perhaps so standard were the concerns expressed for my own health, a concern that seemed to trouble all the children. "I'm glad that the doctor in a routine check-up so far hasn't found anything wrong with you. Remember: *a mother healthy, wealthy & wise, never dies.* I'm glad that you are getting a chest x-ray. I wouldn't want you to have T.B."

The most stabbing letter from camp that summer was his reminder of the looming threat that lurked in the minds of even children in those days, the threat of the Bomb:

One of the nicest things that happened to me today was the headlines in the *New York Times* telling about the good chance of a test ban. Sometimes I think that if they ever drop the bomb while I'm up here in the wilderness that everybody in the family but me gets it.

Then, lest it seem that he was more concerned than the others, he added: "Oh, well, half of the other kids in the cabin feel that way so I'm not any different than they are." That night he and two other boys talked about the test ban. It was important to them. They did not want to survive the loss of their families. In a few years the Vietnam War came to overshadow the nuclear war we had all feared so intensely in the early 1960s. Modes of delivering the Bomb seemed to take precedence over the Bomb itself. I'm not sure whether to be cheerful about that or fearful. I wonder if children still worry about it. And I ponder over a world in which children experience such anxieties. Far worse than those evoked by the Grimms' grim monsters and ogres. At least they could be exorcised.

chapter nine

lengthening tether

The unexpected pleasure David had experienced at camp had the effect of showing him that separation from me did not necessarily mean being miserable. He could be happy away from me. Happier, in fact. He was now "deserting" me rather than I, seemingly, him. He was now the one having the adventures to write home about. He liked the idea of spending summers away from home. Summers, yes, but not whole school years. He did not want to go away to school. It had never occurred to me that David would not follow his sister and brother at George School. But he did not want to. Not to that school or any other boarding school—not even to Valle Verde with its fabulous curriculum including anthropological and archeological field trips which, with his interests, should have appealed to him.[1] No, he just wanted to stay home.

But summers, yes. That was something else again. He liked the idea of summers away from home so well that when he saw in the *Saturday Review* an advertisement by a French family that took in American boys and girls for the summer he asked if he could apply. Of course. By March arrangements were completed, Madame Thévenin accepted him. She loved my letters, she wrote, and "both

my husband and I love David's photo." She was "sure we
shall be as happy with him at home as he will be with us."
And, in fact, he was happy with them.

I was teaching—my last stint—that summer and also experiencing some uncertainty about David. Going to camp
was one thing; to France, quite another. Although I could
not see him off, I followed him hour by hour on his way:

I said, now he has reached home. Now he has gone to bed.
Now he has . . . gone to the bus station, now he is on his
way. . . . I was sitting at the telephone when you called
even though it was an hour earlier than I really expected it.
Last night . . . I stayed awake until 1 o'clock when I told
myself that you had just arrived at Orly. All morning I
have been telling myself what you were doing and by now
(2 o'clock) perhaps you are settled in your room and have
had a chance to rest up.

We were quite close during the summer. David made a
point of writing a long and informative letter at least once
every week. "After all, you are my mother (and good
friend) and have top priority over others." Nanou, as
Madame Thévenin was called, had, he wrote, fallen "'in
love with your charming letters.' Thus you are a charming
lady." He wrote of the anticipated "joy of seeing [me] on
the 10th."

For the most part the letters on both sides were about the
trivia and banalities of daily life—his lessons, his activities,
his reading. In addition he told me about his travels, his
adventures, his concerns, including fear that the war would
be escalated into North Vietnam but, hopefully, not into
a world war. I told him about my work, my social life,
theater, trips. In a certain way the correspondence repli-
cated, though in a minor key, the same guilt-generated call
for reassurance as that of the previous summer at camp.
Was he *really* enjoying himself? Did he *really* like it?

I am glad you seem to be having fun. Don't the other boys and girls seem too old for you? Do you like them? Do you enjoy the things you are doing? You are such a thought-ful boy that even if you weren't enjoying yourself you wouldn't want to trouble me. So I will just take it for granted that you really think it is wonderful and that you really enjoy it.

I wrote this despite the fact that even before I asked he had reassured me that the first week had been wonderful, that it was beautiful and wonderful there, that he loved it very much "and would like to come back next summer. You can't imagine, it is perfect freedom."

I had not been able to see David off to France; I was not going to be able to meet him on his return. So the ever-recurring apologies:

You will return from football camp September 10, while I am in New York, so it will be the 11th before I see you. But I hope you won't mind. I was asked to attend this meeting before I knew when you would return from foot-ball camp. I thought you were going the 29th and would be back the 8th. But you are used to having a mother who is away at meetings all the time. I hope you don't mind. I love you very much. Oceans of love, dear son.

And then his loving reassurances:

You ask what I must think of a mother who is always off at meetings? Well, I like it. I don't like it when you are off for more than a week. I do dislike it when you make me feel very bad when you center your life around me like that. Sure I love you very much but you yourself said that it is bad for us to be together all the time. Then you start making a fuss. "Oh, I'll be gone for a week, leaving you all alone with the Seymours." Or "I'll leave you all alone for 3 days." But I don't mind. Don't think I am trying to hurt you by saying this but I think it should be out before you

start turning down other things. Remember I love and love
and love you very much.

The letters from David during his second summer with
the Thévenin family were from an evidently more mature
boy. He could now go three weeks without hearing from
me, as was sometimes the case since I was on a cruise
around the world myself and mail infrequent. In two
letters he wrote that he was having the best time of his life,
nothing could be better. This year, thank heaven, there
were three girls his age. He had met a distant relative
whose great-grandfather was a Willson, as was his own
paternal grandmother. He hoped his letter was not a disappointment, he was trying to be independent as I had so
often told him to be. He was ready—he wanted to know,
was I?

You say be independent and I'm trying, but of course that
is not why. . . . I've been thinking about next year. My
first objective will be to get a job abroad. That is next to
impossible because I'll be only 16 but there is always my
Red Cross volunteer work to fall back on. In September
I'm going to start looking. I want so much to get away
from Washington etc. I love it there but I'd like to be on
my own. Anyways I spend 9 months there working for
school etc. The pressure would be there with you around.
Don't get me wrong. I think the world of you and at my
age Dorothy and Claude were away most of the time and
didn't build up little animosities. Absence makes the heart
fonder: the reverse can be true. That's why I want to go
away in the summer, not because I don't love you. I hope
you understand.

He hoped I agreed with his strategy. I did, of course.
He was a more self-possessed boy than he had been the
year before. He wrote calmly about his plans if I could
not meet him at Kennedy on his return. Throughout all his
letters he responded to mine, commented on the sights I

had described, hoped I had not been lonely, was not embarrassed to learn that I was taking dancing lessons on the ship; he only became embarrassed when I talked about him. He asked about the "withdrawal symptoms" I always complained of when away from my typewriter too long. He hoped my getting back from my trip would not be too much of a letdown.

Still a loving boy, he was so excited by my telephone call that Nanou had to hold him down to calm him. It was too bad that the women outnumbered the men on the ship so I could not dance as much as I would like. "You're such a scincillating partner; if I were there I would make sure you got enough dancing." He loved Nanou; she was a French version of me. He hoped I was having a wonderful time but also resting a lot. He was indignant at a *New York Times* editorial on Project Camelot[2] with which I had been associated. He had read it so many times he knew it by heart. Sight unseen he defended me. He was sure he did not have all the facts and that I would tell him the real facts. "I'll be at home as soon as I see you."

The next year his letters from Barcelona—where David was participating in an Andover-run junior year abroad program—Schoolboys Abroad—were informative, interesting, upbeat. He wrote about the trials and tribulations of his "family," about the marriage of the son in that family, about the festivities of the country, about the political scene, about runaway boys, about trips, about courses, about grades, about lessons, about school for next year, about gifts, about money. . . . When, or if, he was depressed he did not write at all.

Increasingly David was coming to want a longer and longer tether. Still he wanted the stake of the tether firmly anchored. He wanted to be bodily away from me but at the same time sure of the knot of the tether to the stake.

No summer was spent together after he was twelve. It was not lack of love we suffered from but too much closeness, too much togetherness. David came to find his ties to me increasingly chafing. As early as 1961, still in State College, I had written to Dorothy Lee that David—then eleven—and I were "getting on each other's nerves, what with the heat, the house in turmoil, etc."

Still, when we were separated, mail became an exceedingly urgent concern to him. From camp, from France, from Spain, his letters were filled with capital letters and exclamation points bemoaning the delays in the mail which cut him off from contact with us.

David had written to us every day from camp except when on an extended hike or canoe trips, and he was as concerned that we receive all his letters as that he receive all of ours:

How long does it take my letters to reach you? . . . I'm worried that you don't get all my letters. This worries me very much. Maybe you could write me and tell me if you haven't gotten any of my letters. . . . Please write and tell me if you've been getting a letter daily from me for about 5 days. . . . I hope you got my letter about the cave trip. If you haven't please tell me and I'll tell you about it. . . . I'm worried about the letters. I spend most of my spare time writing to you, Claude, and Dorothy. It makes me sad if you aren't getting my letters. So please tell me; if you aren't I'll inquire.

PS I think maybe one reason that my letters may not reach you is State College is very unknown and the post office up here is old fashioned and they pick up the mail a day after it is mailed. In all it might even take a week to reach you at the most. I don't know if I'm worried about nothing or not.

Two days later he reported that he had just got my letters, but he feared his letter had been lost. Had I been getting the rest of his letters? Then, a week later, relief. "I'm glad that you have been getting my letters. I've been worried for awhile." In anticipation of seeing us all again soon:

"I'll see you in about three weeks or at the end of August. It will have been more than two months since I've seen anybody from the family. Boy, will I be glad to see everyone." He kept a strict account of letters written and letters received and showed great concern when there was no acknowledgment of his letters or when none was received for him to acknowledge.

The next year, perhaps because the distance from France was greater than the distance from camp, the anxiety about mail escalated: "As of today *I have not received one piece of mail!* and I have written faithfully." And my usual reply: "I am sure that mail has been lost. I have sent several letters and you have not received them. This makes me unhappy because I am sure you want to hear from us often." There were times of near-panic when mail did not come. "I have got very exasperated by the mail . . . Oh! This mail business makes me mad. I seem to go through it every year." Three days later:

Dear folks,

I am very mad at the Postal System. This is my 5th letter. I sent my first one on the 10th and still by the 22nd you haven't gotten it! Furthermore, it makes me sad, all the letters were important and I don't know what I'll do!!!

He had described his life there, asked for money, told me about his field trips and other activities, and about his friends at the pool. Then:

MAD MAD MAD MAD

Also will you ever be able to get any mail? Did the same thing happen to others? Gosh, will you ever get this letter? Oh I am just MAD MAD MAD. Maybe I'll wire you. I don't know. . . . MAD! MAD!

The next day he did, indeed, send a cablegram. "I don't know why but I felt very uneasy, and hurt a bit. I don't know why but I want just to tell you that I had written. So yesterday . . . I went into Limoges . . . to send the cablegram."

When he finally received two letters, "what great joy!" Then apprehension: "Were you mad at me and trying to stress a point?" After reading them, relief. I was not mad at him. He greatly enjoyed both of my letters. "I just hope you won't be mad about the letter I wrote before this, though I was writing it in good faith."[3]

The second summer David was in France I was on a trip around the world and mail from me therefore was erratic. He could now take it easily in stride. "So far for the last 3 weeks I've received [only] 3 letters, but I don't mind." Still, a month later: "Did you get all my letters? I must have asked this question a thousand times. Haven't gotten a letter from you for about three weeks but that's OK. Maybe they got lost or you were too busy." When I called him, he was "very excited [and] was shaking. Nanou was beside me trying to calm me down." Five days later he had "entered the third week without a letter from you. However I think it is the mail system so I'm not worried." He was trying to be independent; he could even talk about his little "animosities" toward me. By then our contacts were becoming almost touch-and-go. "We hardly had a chance to get acquainted between your return from France and my leaving. But I hope you are still the charming, lovely, intelligent, thoughtful boy I have known all his life."

From Barcelona the following year there was to be a real basis for alarm; the mail was, indeed, erratic. "I was a bit worried that the mail wasn't coming through since it's been exactly two weeks since I got your last letter. Sometimes we don't get mail at the Institute for days because the mailman gets sick—last week it was the flu." A week later I telephoned him and he was delighted. "*Just talked to you* and it was very pleasant! matter of fact, wonderful, and I was glad to talk with you after 2 months." He still enjoyed close—postal—contact with me: "I'll try to write more because I enjoy telling you my experiences and do not find letter writing a chore (though reading them may be)."

Still, I should have been alerted when the hiatus between letters became long from time to time. Sometimes he wrote every few days; sometimes once a week or even every two weeks. If I had known of the depression I was only later to learn about I would have realized that the long periods of silence must have meant anxiety. Thus, late in November, after three weeks, he wrote: "I am sorry that I have not written in such a long time. However I shall try to make up for my long silence with a long, interesting, and well written letter." Then, buried among the many activities that had made this the busiest week of the year, a clue to this anxiety, an item on math. He had dropped calculus and substituted trig. And a postscript: "It's also been a long time since I got a letter from you— maybe the mail?"

At the beginning of the postholiday session, the mail once more became a real cause for concern. A number of packages had been sent, weeks earlier, and not yet received.

The first day of school went very well except I did not receive the letter or package. This makes it more than a month since I got your last letter. I am very mad, not at you, of course, since I know you have written, but because I was expecting something. I would like to know what has happened, especially to my winter coat and the books Claude sent me, just to know what titles. The only thing to do is go to the post office and put a tracer on both things and collect the insurance that the packages were insured for. Also if I don't get any word of your (plural) whereabouts I shall call, for all I know you may be dead in 4601 and no one knows since you live alone. Have you been getting my mail? My last letter was from Madrid.

One last note. He had run out of money and needed some, especially to buy a winter coat. Could I please send it at my earliest convenience. The next day he had received my letter and felt "much better and less worried." Three days later, "the mail has finally begun to arrive, the average time for air mail is 2 *weeks*." Four days later the telephone once more bailed us out: he was not wholly reassured. After we hung up he wrote: "Just talked with you. You seemed to be a bit sad. Nevertheless it was very nice hearing your voice. . . . I repeat, I hope you are all right. You sound tired or sad if not both. I am VERY happy and all goes well. Please take care of yourself. Don't stay alone if you are lonely." Then, in a somewhat different key, three months later:

I got your letter of April 12, the first one since March 22 except for the one from Puerto Rico. It looks as if we both have been quite silent and I am sorry on my part. . . . I have tried not to write about the unpleasant things about the program, preferring to discuss them in person. One thing I can tell you, no one is all good or all bad. . . . Well, I'll (or we'll) talk a lot when I get home.

The struggle between the desire to be independent and the lingering need to remain in close touch with me went on for a long time. It was painful, as always, to cut the umbilical cord.

Dorothy Lee had had her ups and down; there were letters of considerable exuberance, but also of depression. She had not hesitated to ask for "cheering" or "praising" letters when she was low. Claude had managed to present an equable exterior, whatever his inner despair. David's moods were either sky-high or intolerably low. He reported the ups; he did not report the downs. He wanted to protect me from them. He never asked for "praising" letters. He withdrew; he did not write. But the highs were always superlative. From camp, from France, from Spain extravagant superlatives: "best time of my life," "nothing could be better," "I'm very happy," "everything is great," "one of my best days in Spain," "I am *very happy*," the

ski trip to Andorra was "the best time I've had," the last
nine months in Spain had "been the best in my life."
(Though he was glad he was going to see us all soon, especially me, whom he had not seen for ten whole months.)
The summer he was at Andover his exuberance was more
muted, but still upbeat; everything was "very pleasant
and successful" and he was pretty happy.

This was the boy I knew. But there was another David.
It was to take us a long time to learn to understand one
another.

chapter ten

will the real david
please stand up?

When David in 1966 had applied for admission to the
Andover-sponsored program for high school juniors in
Barcelona—Schoolboys Abroad—I had been asked to send
in a brief sketch of his background. This is what I wrote:

David is the youngest of three children. The oldest is a
sister (25), Dorothy Lee, a graduate of Sarah Lawrence,
now married to a man receiving his A.B. at Harvard this
month. The second is a brother (21), now finishing his
junior year at Johns Hopkins, a history major. David was
born June 2, 1950, in Pennsylvania. He lost his father,
Luther Lee Bernard, when he was an infant, in January,
1951. Both of his parents were professors of sociology.
(His father kept a copy of *Don Quixote* at his bedside for
years, for reading when he could not sleep; he also trans-
lated Spanish poetry as a hobby.) Although David enjoys
reading, he is not a bookish type. He enjoys sports, dancing, camping, and social activities. He is socially adept,
cheerful, and assumes a friendly world. He is well-read and
shows great interest in current events. His career plans as
of now seem to lie in the direction of public life, perhaps
the diplomatic corps or state or national politics. He is not

as orderly as he might be and his bedroom is not kept at
a very high level of tidiness. Still I anticipate that he will
go out of his way to ask how he can help in his Spanish
family and that he will gladly assume any responsibilities
reposed in him. He does not apply himself with much
dedication in things he is not interested in.

David gets on well with his sister and brother; he and I
have our differences. We do not always interpret events in
the same way. Like all of his generation, he takes his blessings for granted. Affluence is taken as a matter of course.
He is not, however, materialistic and would not feel at
home in a materialistic setting.

David has traveled a great deal. In the United States,
from Canada to Florida and to the Middle West as far as
Minneapolis. He spent the year he was three in Austria. He
visited Bermuda when an infant. He took a banana-boat
trip through the Panama Canal to Ecuador. He spent the
summer of 1963 camping in New England and visiting
Canada by way of canoe and the summers of 1964 and
1965 with a French family near Limoges, France. He has a
cosmopolitan outlook on the world and is comfortable
with members of other races and cultures. He seems to
have no prejudices.

He is meticulous about his person, not at all beatnik, and
does not smoke.

Finally, may I say that David has been reared as a Friend.
He has not, however, become a member of the Society of
Friends on his own. His affiliation is through me. He will
probably wish to attend Catholic services from time to time
while in Barcelona, especially if this is the wish of his
family. There would be no objection to this on my part.

I was not dissembling. That was my view of David. I
thought this an accurate picture of him as he approached
sixteen. And all the letters I had ever received from him—
and was to receive from him in Barcelona—seemed to
corroborate what I had said about him. But the perceptual
moat dividing parents and children was never wider than

the one between David and me. Whereas, for example, I was seeing him at sixteen as enjoying sports, dancing, and social activities, he saw this picture of him as a fantasy. He did not, he later told me, enjoy sports, nor had he ever said he did. He had simply seen participation in sports as a vehicle for making friends. This after all that rowing, swimming, horseback riding, soccer, bullfighting, skiing, mountain-climbing, even football? Whereas I saw him as socially adept—he seemed to be with my friends, and reports from his teachers seemed to confirm my own judgment—he had not *felt* adept. He had been "socially paralyzed." It was to be more than ten years later that the growing literature on male liberation clarified for me the harsh jock culture that pressed on boys.[1]

Adolescent depression was, I knew, an old phenomenon in Western society. In the form of *Weltschmertz* it had been the hallmark of the romantic young hero of the early nineteenth century. The crisis of adolescence in the twentieth century had been adumbrated by G. Stanley Hall early in the century.[2] But the cohort of young men born in the late forties and early fifties seemed to me to have suffered more developmental traumas than those who were either younger or older than they.[3] The Bomb, for one thing, hung menacingly over the years of their adolescence, 1962–1970. There was much talk of bomb shelters and how to stock them. The times were violent.[4] There were shattering assassinations. Everyone's adolescence became more painful in those explosive sixties. We will be a long time paying for that decade.

David had a more personal explanation for his own adolescent unhappiness. "*All* teenagers are unhappy," he had once said, his own teen years along with those of his peers, but his own may have been even more painful than those of others his age. "Perhaps my unhappiness was deeper and exacerbated by not having a father and the subtle societal prejudices aimed at boys growing up without fathers."[5] Of the three children, David most keenly felt this deprivation.

He, in effect, appropriated Dorothy Lee's. That is, the father who had written to Dorothy Lee before she was born and when she was an infant. In a letter dated two weeks before she was born he had written to his "dear Son," telling him how great his love was and his hope that "he" would "study and think and acquire the good and useful skills, both physical and intellectual, and to learn to be a man of importance." And on December 16, a week after Pearl Harbor, more somberly: "I feel very apologetic for bringing you into such a world as this, a world which will probably grow so bad before you are grown up that it will be painful to live in. . . . You must be brave and develop efficiency and responsibility and make a way for yourself. At the same time you must try to make a bad world better, so that other babies like you, who are not responsible for the badness, may live in it happily and grow up normally and usefully." Both letters were suffused with great tenderness despite their gloomy outlook for the future. David came to love the man who had written them—and miss him. I understand why his father's absence added to David's unhappiness. Still, the impressive corpus of research on the effects of "father-absence" on boys yields equivocal results. Present or absent, fathers make adolescent sons unhappy; and, of course, vice versa as well. So, also, do mothers and adolescent sons.

From camp when he was thirteen David had written that the past two years had been the best of his life, hence the happiest, and he was thinking that the coming year would also be a wonderful one. The prediction was to be proved wrong. But I was not to know how wrong for many years. Little by little the obstreperous, emotional, loving child was to become a depressed and unhappy teenager. I never realized until years later just how miserable he was in those years. Even then, only by chance. In fragments from a journal I discovered only when I sat down to collate the letters I learned, so many—ten—years later, that I had sometimes driven him to suicidal anger. In an entry dated

February 6, 1964, he wrote: "We got our report cards to-day. I went up in English and down in four things. Mother was sort of mad. I felt like killing myself.[6] I really did." The other items in the journal were for the most part quite matter-of-fact, with little of the emotion that had spilled all over the letters of the thirteen-year-old camper of the preceding summer. Emotionally uncharged comments about school, girls, sports. The picture that came through was of a boy who spent a good deal of time in libraries and book stores, a lot of time reading and studying. What emotion there was was attached to me: "Mother gave me a little lecture about she is always right because she is the oldest." There was hurt when I was not home and had left no word of my whereabouts: "Mother wasn't here when I got home from school. I was a little disappointed that she didn't even leave a note. I went to see 'Four for Texas' and 'Straight Jacket' with Joan Crawford. Both were ok." (And a noncommittal reference to a homosexual advance made at the movie: "A young man in the theater tried to pick me up but I wouldn't let him. I feel sorry for that sort of people."[7]) Even today, so many years later, his words reach me. I still grieve for that unhappy boy, I am still overwhelmed by the inadequacy of one parent—certainly a mother—in helping a young man live through adolescence, in this or in any other age.

To this day I do not know all that was involved in producing so much misery in him. Separation from his friends? School? Absence of a father? The beginning of the separation trauma characteristic of parent-child relations in our society? The "times"? All these factors, no doubt, and many more—including me. Early in the period that David had judged the happiest of his life, even before we had left State College, I had written to Dorothy Lee that David and I were "getting on each other's nerves, what with the heat, the house in turmoil [in preparation for the move to Washington], etc." And some four emotionally crowded years after David had predicted a happy year, I wrote Claude we were "talking very seriously of his finding some

place else to live this coming year." It was not that we
didn't love one another very dearly, I continued, but "I
agreed that adult children should not have to live with
their parents; they get along better when they don't." If
Claude did his alternate service in Washington perhaps he
and David could share an apartment. Then, to lighten the
somewhat somber implications, I threw in "an apartment
that had maid service available!"

David and I had had our own pattern of togetherness. He
sometimes reminded me of our hikes in State College over
hill and dale to Shingletown Gap when he was quite small,
of our shopping trips to the A & P when we ran to see who
was faster, and how I used to read to him when he went to
bed—Carl Sandberg's *Life of Lincoln,* Kipling, *Charlotte's
Web,* among other books—as well as of the almost ritualistic
bedtime playing of the record, *The King and I,* which he
loved. The word games we played together—Scrabble,
Twenty Questions, Geography, among them—filled hours
and hours. In small-town State College, no special arrangements were needed for play and recreation. Life could be
more spontaneous. But in a large city that was not feasible.
So when we first moved to Washington I had made a point
of arranging activities that we could enjoy together. I reported them to Dorothy Lee: "David and I plan to have at
least one historical and one scientific jaunt every weekend"; "David is taking art lessons there [Corcoran Art
Gallery] "; "I don't know what we will do today; we usually
try to do something interesting every weekend"; "David
enjoys his art lessons a lot"; "David is now studying flute
in school, as well as art on Saturdays"; "Yesterday David
and I went to see an exhibit of Egyptian art at the National
Art Gallery but it was so crowded he had to leave. (David
gets sick in a crowd.) So we went to the National Archives
and looked at pictures and documents about American history"; "Yesterday we went to see *Fiorello;* I enjoyed it a
lot but fear David was a little bored."
The first year in Washington, then, when David was

eleven, started off well. We liked the house we had bought. "Last night David and I had a fire in the fireplace in my room. . . . David also loves his room, which is directly above mine and he has fixed it up very attractively." But the second year in Washington was to be less auspicious than the first. I had to return to State College once a week to resume my post-sabbatical teaching and arrangements for David, now twelve, were difficult. Although the university was more than generous in arranging my schedule to call for a minimum of time on campus, I wrote Dorothy Lee, I didn't quite know how to handle the situation. "I'll have to work out some sort of commuting system maybe. I just can't ask David to transplant himself so often. Maybe all together we can work something out." A week later, I wrote, "I may advertise in *Saturday Review* for a pleasant couple to live in the house to take care of him for the ten weeks involved [and I would move up to State College]. Then you and Claude and I could take turns being here on weekends. Problems!"

My forebodings were validated. In the fall I was writing to Dorothy Lee that David had come to hate the Washington house and I was looking for something else. "The trouble in part is that he is alone once a week which is very hard on his morale." His school work was suffering. "David and I had a set-to about arithmetic last night. It appears that teachers have so downgraded parents that he won't take anything I say as correct and we had quite a hassle about adding and subtracting negative numbers." I was hoping that when Ralph Lewis came to visit us he would play chess with David while I was gone, thus lifting his spirits.

Although my weekly absences had a depressing effect on him and though he came to hate the house, David tried to put up a good front. He did not want to cause me pain.[8] But we could no longer talk freely and joyously as we once had. We had to carry on polite conversation at meals, or I felt we did. But the usual pattern came to consist of stilted questions on my part and monosyllabic replies on his. He wanted me to express interest in his problems, to make inquiries about them, but also to accept his angry refusal to talk about them. When he was quite young, he cried out "Don't pry!" When he was older, it became a polite, "I don't mind your asking. I hope you won't mind my refusal to talk about it." There were occasional outbursts that only hinted at the volcanic emotion underneath the effort to protect me.

David's college years at Haverford—1968 to 1972—were convulsive years for the country as a whole. College campuses had become front-line battle scenes. Less volcanic at Quaker Haverford than at some others, but no less real. And now the anti-war forces had about turned the country around. Although David was to remember his college years with customary alumni nostalgia, they were, actually, painful for both of us. Frequent confrontations; frequent "reconciliations." On the occasion of one such "reconciliation" in the spring of his freshman year I wrote:

My trip was very pleasant. There was hardly anyone on the bus, the weather was beautiful, and I had lots of time to think. Like you I was pleased by our conversations and I felt happy to learn that you really wanted me to love you, to be close, to share a little of your life. I had been misreading the signals so long that it came as a surprise. I had read them as "keep away!" "don't pry!" "leave me alone!" I should have known if that was your real message it wouldn't have been so direct. It would have taken the form of superficial pleasantness and real withdrawal. But hindsight is always so clear. I can now re-interpret the past and understand you—and me—much better. First of all I can now see how very deprived you were as an infant.

There followed the story of his infancy and of my professional preoccupations when he was a small child.

I had reached the point in my professional career when recognition comes in the form of lots of invitations and I was off on trips. I used to laugh at myself saying that I deserted my own family to talk to other people about families. And I remember how heartstricken I was to see the joy in your face—you were about 3—when I returned from a trip.

Then, expectably, an apologia: "It seemed to me that I did give you attention when I put you to bed, that I read to you, sang to you, lay with you, played records for you. But it was probably too off-hand, too casual, not engrossing enough. . . . I suppose about this time you had given up on ever getting love from me so, in effect, you began to say—in acts, not words—OK, if you won't love me I won't *let* you love me and began the rejection of me. I suppose your refusal to go away to prep school was a sort of blind clutching to the hope that if you stayed home you could win my love." Finally, I attempted an interpretation of my own behavior:

Those years were as painful for me as for you. I think, too, I was doctrinaire in my fear of being a devouring mother. The intellectual world during those years was strongly anti-momism. The "good Jewish mother" who forces her children to feed her emotional needs was a universal cliché. And I was determined not to make my children my entire life. I overdid that bit. I love you very dearly and though I don't think words can make up for years of deprivation I think that if we dig deep enough long enough it will finally get through to your gut that I do love you and want you to love me and that just the talking we have done so far has added a new dimension to my life. I guess I had sort of read you out of my life on the assumption that you wanted it that way. And it is very nice to think that I have not lost you.

This letter signaled only a reprieve, an interlude of open communication which continued to be episodic.

Four months later there was another crisis. Now he was

in Innsbruck to learn German in preparation for archaeo-
logical work on a dig in Italy. Inadvertently, through a
letter from him to Dorothy Lee, I had learned of his involvement with marijuana. To my letter pointing out the
danger for American college students in Europe caught
with drugs, he replied angrily that my letter was "insulting,
destructive, and just obscene." This was the first letter in
quite some time which was not impersonal, noncommunicative, though full of information. I replied that I disagreed.
I thought it meant we were approaching a real—meaning
open—relationship. He did not:

In reply to your last letters I have little to say. I have never
felt that our relationship was false or unreal. I take it that
you think we should fight or something similar. I refuse
to do this, thinking that this is wrong and only succeeds in
hurting the other person unnecessarily. I feel that I have
learned well how to handle my emotions towards you and
am able to realize why I am angry at you and channel this
anger in a way that does not hurt you; therefore I will not
argue. I suggest that you sort out your feelings towards me.

Reading—wrongly as it turned out—his message as "keep
off!" I planned a trip to Israel for the Christmas holiday of
his sophomore year. In November, sending him my ad-
dresses during my visit to Israel, I added that I wished he
had told me what it was that was depressing him so much.

I guess I shouldn't have planned the trip during the holidays. If I had thought it made any difference to you, I
wouldn't have. But it seemed to me that you didn't really
care one way or another and Christmas was a good time to
visit Israel. I will leave my itinerary on your bed so you
will always know where I am. I wonder if there is some
anxiety about not knowing where I will be that is part of
your depression?

Still the bruising confrontations, so painful on both sides, continued—and, at the same time, the reconciliations. "It was nice talking to you last week," he wrote the next summer, "I feel a great deal of relief that we aren't fighting things out."

Among the letters I found a handwritten, unaddressed, undated note by me on a slip of paper which listed David's telephone number and his courses—sculpture, art, history, Greek—with this frantic appeal, apparently never sent:

Is there even a remote possibility that you can do something—I don't know what—but I have such confidence in you—to help David? He was seeing a psychiatrist twice a week last spring; this year the psychiatrist suggests three times a week. He had mononucleosis last spring and he is still tired all the time this year. He is quite hostile to me, suggesting that I do not visit campus Parents' Day.[9] I have not seen him since June; he spent the summer in Europe and I was in London when he returned to college. He planned it that way. He needs a father. Can you give him just a tiny part of one via mail? *Please?* Not, of course, mentioning me.

It may have been intended for Ezra. I do not know. I am quite amnesiac with respect to it.

"He needs a father." Despite the equivocal nature of the research on father-absence, I sometimes explained anything that went wrong in my relations with Claude or David in terms of their lack of a father. One parent was just not enough, rearing children was just too hard for one parent. Or, perhaps, it later occurred to me, even for two parents. Substitute my name for Pat Brown's and David's for Jerry Brown's and the following interview rings true for us as well as for them:

Pat Brown is confused. And a little hurt too. He picks up
a clipping from his desk and waves it. It's a story about
how his son Jerry is treating him badly. It is one of many
similar stories surfacing these days. He stand up from behind his desk in his paneled law office here and paces back
and forth.

"Of course I'm upset," he says. "I never thought about
how Jerry and I got along before. He'd call me up from
time to time but I lead a busy full life of my own. Now
they're writing about it. And you worry about it. It's like
somebody said 'what's that defect on your face?' You'd
never noticed it before. Then you start worrying about it.
Do my kids love me? I don't know. I love them. . . ."

Pat Brown is like all the fathers in the world. A little too
loving perhaps, maybe sometimes embarrassing his children, maybe getting a little blustery at times, maybe trying
to interfere in their lives a little too much. "I was probably
far more dominant than I thought I was," he says. . . .

We've done many things together, hiked the High Sierras.
. . . He and I have always been very close, like a secret
love affair. You don't manifest it, you don't express it,
but there's a very, very strong bond there. But he feels very
strongly that he has to be on his own. . . ."

Jerry Brown seems a bit exasperated—but philosophical—
by this sudden publicity about his relationship with his
father. . . . "I don't know what the general standard is for
relations to your parents. . . ."[10]

Who, in fact does?

In the 1970s, researchers were talking of an "epidemic"
of adolescent suicides. There had been an increase of 250
percent between 1954 and 1973, from 4.9 per 100,000 in
1964 to 10.9 in 1974. In the newspaper report of a work-
shop on adolescent suicides a profile of the typical suicidal
adolescent was sketched like this:

. . . the typical suicidal adolescent 15–24 . . . is one who is
likely to be white and male, who has suffered a major
loss of some kind in his life, who has moved frequently
during his lifetime, comes from a broken home and rarely
lives alone. He comes from a middle-upper-income, well-
educated family.[11]

The picture fit David almost exactly. He was white, male,
had suffered a major loss, had moved frequently, came
from a broken home, did not live alone, came from an
upper-middle-income, well-educated family. But so did the
picture fit Claude. The one difference was that David had
moved more frequently. The report was, of course, only
statistical in nature, there must be hundreds of thousands
of young white males who qualify for that grim population.
Still it is frightening to me to realize how close David may
have come to the final solution of so many troubled
youngsters.

I had long since forgotten the whole abortion episode.
Now, in the 1970s, abortion was becoming a major political issue. Arguments pro and con were preempting time
and space in the media. In stating their case the advocates
were making the legitimate point that every child should
be a wanted child. No one could cavil with that. But now
they were drawing on even more gut-level arguments, the
possibly destructive effects on children of refusal of abortion to women. This letter to the editor of the *New York
Times,* June 11, 1976, for example:

I was one of the children that did not get aborted because my mother was too late to have a successful abortion.
I was one of the children who were born despite my parents' desire not to have any more children. And though
there was never the abuse of which we hear so much,

never the broken bones or the vicious beatings, my parents' not wanting me was brutal and crushing.

I spent many years frightened and futilely trying to understand why my parents didn't care enough to discipline me. There was always food and a bed but no warmth or emotional support for years. No kind, wise mother to guide and encourage. Just emptiness and loneliness and bitterness. Only years later as I trained to try to cure lonely and desolate feelings in people such as I had been did I recognize the patterns of obsessive behavior which I showed. Years later I saw my overwhelming fear of sights and sounds of fury and abuse as evidence of the constant intense degree of anxiety which was my daily experience. I sometimes cry for the terrified little girl that I was.

David was not one of those children who remained unwanted. So far as I could tell I gave him as much love as I gave the other children, and, in addition, I had given him a father he could love and admire. His psychiatrist had, in fact, once told him that I had done one of the best possible things I could have done for him by giving him a wonderful image of his father. His father had been part of his intense family consciousness. He had treasured whatever scraps of information he had acquired. When he was nineteen he sent me a story he had written for one of his college courses, about his father—beautifully nostalgic, telling the story of the move his father's family had made from Kentucky in the 1880s when his father was a small boy. I was deeply moved:

I was fascinated by the story. It sounds just great to me. I was dumbfounded that you had such a vivid picture of the events. Who ever told them to you? One little item might be interesting. The little mug that Cora and John used were left in the house. I don't know what the significance of that was. But it always stayed in my picture [of the family story]. Two little mugs standing forlornly on the shelf as the family moved away. Also, did you know that they went down the Ohio in a boat on their way to Texas? Also that it was one of the major treks in US history, from Kentucky and Tennessee. I don't know if you plan to carry on. But if you do, one of the starkest things in your father's memory was the contrast between the lush green of Kentucky where everyone had a garden and the aridity of Texas, where even Kentucky green thumbs could make no headway against the dryness. I may have told you that your father finally learned that onions grew well and when he was still a young boy he planted acres of them so they would have any fresh vegetables at all, etc., etc. Much love.

David was pleased and wanted me to share the rewards: "I'm glad you liked my story. You're the one who told me all the things that I know about my father and I'm very grateful for that."[12]

The unhappy boy who had sometimes felt like killing himself had never shown up in the letters; he had chivalrously protected me. Neither his letters, therefore, nor those of any of the others who had had occasion to report on him had alerted me. The director of the summer session at Andover had forewarned parents about to receive reports on their sons that they need expect no mincing of words. Teachers and housemasters, we had been told, were asked to make their reports "as straightforward and uncompromising as possible." We were warned that we might well be disturbed by the frankness of the reports, we were told that if we did feel that way we should "be comforted by the thought that the teachers and housemasters . . . [were] trying to give parents, the students, and the summer session administration an accurate and full report of the student's progress, attitude, effort, adjustment, and prospects." We had been told that the competition was rough, the standards high, and that the boys were "being judged in the context of a group of bright, energetic, and highly motivated students." We braced ourselves for the promised and anticipated blows.

As it turned out, the "straightforward," "uncompromising," "accurate," and "full" report of David's progress, attitude, effort, adjustment, and prospects which we had been so carefully warned to expect, proved to be of a boy any mother would be delighted to receive. For example:

From his teachers ". . . very successful . . . thoughtful leader of discussion . . . a pleasure having him in class . . . contributions to class most perceptive and helpful . . . a bright, courteous, and good-humored boy." And from the housemaster: "David seems to have had a great summer here, both socially and intellectually. The reports from his teachers are most enthusiastic. He has a wide group of friends, and has hit it off especially well with the girls. . . . He is very courteous and friendly, and gets along well with the other boys in the dormitory."

I was, of course, "delighted and overwhelmed by these reports," I wrote to David. "Is this my boy David? Gee, I'm impressed!"

It occurred to me as I mulled over the letters that the reason the unhappy boy had not shown up in them was not only that he had tried to protect me from his unhappiness but also that he really did not feel all that depressed when we were separated from one another. Absence—as both Claude and David had reminded me—may actually have dissipated the misery of proximity.

chapter eleven

girls and jobs

Most of the talk about girls in David's letters was in those to Claude, though he raised the subject with me. In August of his first year in France, he was already planning his return. He was going to "take a Dutch Liner to Rotterdam with another girl from Chicago who is also returning. Visit a girl in the The Hague who is here now, and then take a train here! I really don't know because Janice, the girl, could change her mind within a year." On the boat returning the next year, Janice was, indeed, going back:

I got on the ship fine and at first I just hated it. It was crowded with people everywhere. But after I discovered that Janice and Lou were ten feet (physically, their cabin is, as the crow flies) away from me things began to brighten up. Now I love the whole thing. . . . My cabin is very nice. Not as large as Janice's but much better. You see it has windows while even though Janice has a bathroom, it can't compare to windows.

The three of them—David, Janice, and Lou—had a lot of fun but still they "were glad to get off the boat."

This summer was even better than last, for "there are

(thank heaven) three girls my age—Cindy, Nancy, Kate. Jan is 18, Lise 16, Linda 18, Janice 17, Tucker 17. The rest of the boys are 15 except for David who is 18. Yesterday I borrowed a racket and bought some balls and played tennis with Cindy, 15, Nancy, 15, and Tucker. A lot of fun." The next week Nanou's daughter, Noelle, and David were teasing one another during the Bastille Day celebration and "eventually I chased her and we both broke a window." Later, when the summer was over, the remaining girls and boys had greater freedom. "Now one can get up any time he wants to and do anything he wants to, even going up to the girls' floor. I did go up to the girls' floor and it was a mess beyond all belief. 38 towels in one bathroom. The boys were so much cleaner compared to the girls."

In Barcelona there had been an American girl in the same apartment building; together she and David prepared an American Thanksgiving meal for David's "family." His best friends were the son and daughter of the math teacher. "The reason she is so interesting is she's the only girl in the program." David was to serve as the escort of one of the guests at the marriage of his "foster" brother, José.[1] "The story goes this way: a friend of the family is trying to match me up with the girl. We've met once but found each other disinterested in the other, so at least it will be amusing."

At home, Robbie and David had been longtime friends, from childhood on. There were few occasions therefore for her to appear in the letters. There was a casual reference to her when David visited her during a stay with her relatives in Austria, but not much more. She was a student at Swarthmore and they saw one another either there or at Haverford. Wendy began to appear in the letters at the end of David's freshman year. I never met her. I heard her voice over the phone from time to time but otherwise I knew only that David was incensed when her family refused to let him visit her in their absence:

Wendy has been having a bad time with her parents. They
had become absolutely tyrannical. They told her that they
had to have a written invitation if she wanted to spend a
night at another person's house and were attacking her for
everything from wearing too short skirts to not going out
enough. Finally her sister came home and I suppose she
felt she had an ally or a supporter. Anyway, one night at
dinner she told her parents how she resented being treated
like a 15-or 16-year-old and that they should be more open-
minded about what she wanted. Her sister then got up and
said that she resented their nasty remarks about her marriage. It ended up, she says, in an "encounter group," with
everyone, except the father, getting out their pent-up hos-
tilities, then agreeing with each other, and then crying. At
one point I thought it interesting because their "fight"
turned into an "encounter" group type experience and
Wendy had once said that they never raised their voices
in their home.

To which I replied:

The story of Wendy's family sounds interesting. I suppose
you told her we live in a perpetual Encounter group? Do
you want me to send her a written invitation to visit us?
Regardless of what may or may not happen at college, I
could not in good conscience let you sleep together if she
visited us. I would have to respect her family's wishes.

Apparently there were plans for a visit from Wendy when
David returned from the dig in Italy:

I take it that you are hoping to have a house guest here
when you come back. That made me think that perhaps
Wendy was expecting to come then. And that made me
think that it may be rather complex with both Robbie and
Wendy at Swarthmore and that Wendy, being a very intense young woman, might, just might, become pregnant

in order to win and also to overcome the kind of problem
her sister had with their father. A *fait accompli* sort of
thing. If that would be OK with you, fine. But your generation is always complaining about having no control over
the important decisions in their lives. Here is one decision
you can have control over. As you know I am very much
of a theory-of-games woman and though I know very few
decisions are actually rational, I think as many as possible
should be.

Wendy never came. I never got to know her.

Vicki was a fellow student at Bryn Mawr when David, in
his junior year, lived on that campus. They later lived
together in an apartment for a year and a half and even
after they separated they remained good friends. No hard
feelings on either side.[2]

Like countless other children across the country, David
and his friends in State College sold lemonade on the golf
course in the summer. And, like thousands of other boys
from time immemorial, he wanted to go down to the sea
in ships:

As you know the kind of job I want next summer is either
on a ship or in a mental hospital. Well, by coincidence one
girl's brother is working on a boat. I rather prefer the job
on the boat if I could get one at 16. The girl's brother
is 17. I hope I can start working on it soon, apparently
there's a lot of work to be done.

No more than in the case of Claude did I know how to
induct David into the world of work. But from the age of
sixteen on he was highly motivated to escape from home
and was active in finding his own way in. In Barcelona he
had hoped to find a job on the Costa Brava for the summer.
It was to prove an on-again-off-again will-of-the-wisp all
year. "Lolito, a Spanish university student," he wrote in

the fall, "says that it will be very easy for me to get a job at a resort on the Costa Brava since I know or will know three langauges. The job would be to check people in and out." Two and a half months later he was following through in all seriousness. "A friend and I are beginning to probe the summer job situation; my friend's foster family's father owns a restaurant which is next to a restaurant of a man who owns a large resort on the Costa Brava. The prospects are good and I have no doubts about getting a job before March. My friend's foster father says that tips amount to $35 daily. This does not sound reasonable." It all sounded rather convoluted to me, but not to optimistic David. Thus, in February: "The job situation is looking up; the friend's foster family which is getting the job for us says we will know by the end of the month." Two weeks later, however, David and his friend were becoming impatient: "The people, the foster-parents of Jeff, keep saying they will tell us at the end of the week about the job and they don't. If they don't tell us by Tuesday we are going to another person who said he could help us. The new contact is the principal of the Common School and, I am sure, is more dependable. I am sure that we will get a job, but I wish I could know as soon as possible. I would be very happy if you would come and visit me. Claude could come down also and we could do something together." The uncertainty persisted. Three days later: "The foster-parents of Jeff, the boy who is going to work with me, are hopelessly vague about our job and keep telling us they will know more next week. Luckily the principal of the American School has offered to help us and seems more dependable." In response to my own doubts, he added: "I just got your letter of the 23rd. No, I do not have a job positively. . . . I will try to find out definitely by the 18th (on spring trip). I would return by student flight, hopefully with money I earn during the summer." Two and a half weeks later he came to terms with the inevitable. The job on the Costa Brava had been a mirage, an impossible dream.

"As you see I have found no work on the Costa Brava. This has been a rather unpleasant experience with Spaniards who kept saying they would know for sure whether or not we had this or that job. They never told us anything definite while keeping us on a string. I realize they had good intentions and Jeff and I were a bit naive to put all of our trust in them. So that's it." As I picture it the friendly family told the boys what they wanted to hear. They probably expected the boys to understand that it was just a lovely fantasy. Fun to talk and dream about. But implement? That was quite another matter.

Among the many kinds of work that appeared in David's letters as possibilities was teaching or tutoring. In France at fourteen, for example, he wanted to return the next year and after that "to return . . . and be a teacher or tutor . . . for a family since the only jobs foreigners can get over here are teaching positions." The next year he was less sanguine. Getting a job would be "next to impossible because I'll be only sixteen." Another possible alternative when he was sixteen was "to work in a kibbutz in Israel. To work in one all that one has to do is show up at the kibbutz and work. They will feed and board you." Still another possibility, one friend told him, was work on Cape Cod, where there were lots of jobs. As it turned out, he went to the Andover summer school instead where he worked in the mail room. In the summer of 1970 he wrote of driving a cab if nothing better turned up. At college he became paymaster in the Bryn Mawr dormitory where he was living that term and took another job as waiter at the same time. He had a job lined up as camp counselor in the Poconos for the summer of 1971 but it fell through. One that did go through delighted him: "The best news of all is I got a job on a horse-breeding farm and riding school near here. . . . It's the ideal job for me—being out in the country and being around horses."[3] It was the kind of job history that could probably fit thousands of other boys and young men—jobs to earn money, of course, but also and perhaps mainly, to have fun on, to learn by, to have experiences. To explore their own world. To escape from mothers. Not intended in any way to serve as career stepping-stones.

Less typical were some of David's other interests. At fifteen, for example, one alternative he had in mind was working in a mental hospital; he could use his Red Cross voluntary training. Four years later he was still interested in working in a mental hospital and actually did do field work there when he was a freshman at college. Dorothy Lee had had her CND; Claude had had his alternate service. David had no such macrosociological cause. Instead he served by helping patients. He "danced" with quasi-senile women and felt good about bringing pleasure into their lives. It seemed to me that his career would be in people-oriented fields.

After a freshman year heavily accented on the humanities—his best course was one on Cervantes—the influence of his psychiatrist began to turn him toward the sciences, especially psychology and biology. I had never learned the course his dealings with the psychiatrist was taking nor what kinds of insights David was experiencing. He did not volunteer information and I never asked. Only in the letters from Innsbruck did I get any inkling. From there, when he was nineteen, he wrote:

I've been reading *On Aggression* and find it very interesting as well as your comments on it. I understand now why the shrink suggested that I read it. Lorenz claims that animals and humans have four basic instincts and at any one time one of them can dominate over the others, nullifying them. The shrink probably wants me to see what part fear plays in my life and how it dominates me. In any case I find that book and *Territorial Imperative* very interesting. . . . Of course there is my father-projection on the shrink that plays a large part. But if I'm genuinely interested in it I see nothing wrong with the motive.

This letter was the first I ever knew of the fear that David's psychiatrist had convinced him "dominated" him. *Now*, my reaction was, *now* he tells me! That, then, was why he sought challenges: mountain-climbing, bullfighting, scuba diving, skiing. Not the challenge of tennis or competitive sports—(except soccer, which he loved)—but the challenge to his fears. But fear of what? What did a "golden boy" have to fear—a boy who had been everywhere? I was not convinced. There was something ironic, I might add, in the fact that a man who apparently believed strongly in human instincts, as David's psychiatrist did, was a "father-projection" for David whose own father had been one of the most insistent critics of the instinct hypothesis in explaining human behavior.[4] Ironic, too, that when he followed up his interest in psychology it was not in the Lorenz tradition but in one as far from that tradition as imaginable, the computer model. He was finding data processing interesting and hoped to be a qualified programmer at the end of the course. And he was applying mathematical theories to his psychological research:

Surprisingly everything has been going extremely well. Remember that psychology paper I had to do? I did it using mainly exchange and game theories and applying my own hypothesis of the analogy of how people react to others' behavior and how a computer solves a program. After I handed in the paper I couldn't stop thinking about my own analysis of my group and have since been forming my own hypothesis of interaction. It is not a system to analyze behavior but a hypothesis to analyze the processes of behavior. Anyway, I'm very much into developing this hypothesis hoping that I could possibly publish it as a scientific paper. This is the last thing I would have thought could materialize from this psychology course I'm now taking.[5]

But he had already decided on a medical career. A month earlier in one of his near-"manic" moods, he announced that he had decided on a medical career and he was elated:

There are several things that I want to tell you. There are a few things that I would like to discuss with you mainly because you will be extremely interested. What I would like to talk about is my decision to start a pre-med program next semester and the events that led up to this surprising decision. I made the decision just in the last week and nothing else has excited me more that I can remember—well anyways I am riding on a crest of good spirits and just wanted to tell you why.

In what seems to me a case of almost monumental perceptual differences, David reported to Dorothy Lee that he felt I was displeased by his decision:

Mother is not excited by my doctor plans. She was very happy when most of my energies were spent towards sociology and I think she's a little disappointed that I seem to be so firmly decided on medicine. This is all understandable. I have this great job as a research assistant for this research team at Haverford which is studying militant nonviolence. . . . So in a way I'm a professional sociologist.

I was not aware of any disappointment on my part in David's decision, nor of any pressure on him to become a sociologist. I was, to be sure, interested in his work in sociology. But if I was less than exuberant as he was himself about medicine as a career it was related to the difficulties involved in getting into medical school in the first place. However, the following spring he was deeply involved in a sociological research project:

I'm getting busy on a sociology project for a term paper—
it is semi-original research on the spread of scientific information through journals. I hope to have an original
angle—in any case my sociology of science course is turning out to be one of my best.

And two months later:

My sociology project is showing extraordinary results—a
graph shows about eight years of approximately the same
number of articles each year, then in the 9–10 years a
slight dip and then a 300 percent rise in number of articles
before another 8-year period of constant number of articles each year. [A graph accompanied this statement.] I
may try some economic (supply and demand) theory—but
have not really decided as of yet since I must organize my
data more completely.

The title of the paper turned out to be "Elucidating the
Patterns of Change in Bacteriophage Research Reporting
by Journals 1920–1970" and he could recite it in his
dreams, and did. He had done "a very empirical paper,
proving everything with data" which he had "coming out
of his ears." I thought it was a good paper myself, in fact,
quite publishable and urged him to try to get it published.
But, no. That was not the direction he was set on.
    Despite his genuine enthusiasm for his work in the social
sciences he persisted in the "harder" sciences. He was even
writing of taking a fifth year to complete a major in
biology. He all but made the grade into medical school,
getting as far as the final interview, but not all the way. He
was, to be sure, disappointed, but settled for a next-best—
environmental health.
    As I have reread the letters it has occurred to me that
perhaps David's turn toward the "harder" sciences was
part of his attempt to distance himself from me. It may
have been another way to lengthen the tether.

part IV

Home and Career

chapter twelve

woman's work

In the nineteenth century homemaking and housekeeping were viewed as intrinsically related. Catherine Beecher, the great proponent of the "cult of domesticity," saw both as part of "women's sphere." She wrote of both as contributing to nation building and as productive enterprises, not at all banal. Toward the end of the century the housekeeping component became, in effect, an engineering activity subjected to the same kind of thinking as industrial engineering was, even to the degree of importing Taylor's time-and-motion studies. At the present time there is a reexamination of both homemaking and housekeeping; the effect of technology on both is now engaging the research attention of women historians and social scientists, with interesting insights. There is among economists, under pressure from feminists, an attempt to evaluate the contribution of housekeeping to the gross national product and among social psychologists an attempt to evaluate the costs (loss) in terms of homemaking, if any, of allocating women's time to the outside labor force. No matter how conceived, however, homemaking was always viewed as woman's work. When men have done it it has had a different job description—and paid considerably more.

As, for example, in the case of Secretary Joseph Califano's cook. Art Buchwald has shown how closely the job description of this position paralleled the job description of a homemaker. He emphasized the correspondence between the role of wife and Califano's cook:

1. Incumbent . . . is responsible for anticipating and meeting the necessary logistic requirements to facilitate appropriate recognition and well-being of the family and visitors.
2. Incumbent . . . is responsible for supervising and arranging for whatever provisions are required to accommodate small formal groups of outside visitors.
3. Incumbent . . . is responsible for operating family discretionary fund and special services fund, and she provides the . . . children with a fund proposal together with appropriate justification.
4. She maintains records of supplies and all financial transactions. She receives and deposits monies in accordance with approved instruction.
5. She is responsible for managing, supervising, and performing work involved in the food supply service of the family's private dining room.
6. Incumbent is required to operate a family vehicle.
7. She performs other duties of a confidential nature as assigned. . . .
8. She performs duties independently, recognizing the need for assistance from children. Is depended upon to handle all duties in a timely and discreet manner. . . . The nature of the assignment requires a continuing day-to-day association with the . . . children. She must be continually in their presence in carrying out their services. This fact demands the utmost in personal discretion on the part of the incumbent . . .[1]

It is true that all the functions specified here—budgeting, procurement, record-keeping, storing, filing—are fundamental and basic operations involved in any ongoing enterprise whether in industry, the military, government, school, church—even home. Still, they are essentially banal. There is room for inefficiency in carrying them out, even crime. But not heroism. Comedy, perhaps, from time to time, and occasionally drama, but rarely, if ever, tragedy. Kingdoms are not often lost for want of a nail. But careers may well be. In fact, for either a woman or a man, without such help when children are small a career is all but impossible.

Household help and child care were almost universally available to the Twelve Women at the conference on successful women in the sciences[2] whose stories had so intrigued me and led me to review my own: "To manage my home, I have had the same baby sitter for nearly 11 years to care for the needs of the children while I am gone. . . . When I must work on a lecture or on a paper, my children always offer a helping hand in getting the household chores done quickly"; "when I was married, the depression made it easy to find such help. We had a wonderful Scottish couple who filled in all the gaps and stayed with us for ten years. . . . The use of students where these are available can be expensive, but works well"; "I got ahead fast enough at work to afford expensive child care"; "I had adequate help"; "I always employed housekeepers until the last child entered school." I had been lucky too. For many years Stella provided me with household help, staying with us through the week and returning home for the weekend. She had been recently widowed, in her middle fifties, when she came to us and remained with us until we moved to Washington. I still feel gratitude for the enormous service she provided by just being there.

Several of the Twelve Women comment on their lack of concern with household management and maintenance. "We realized that our homes were not as well kept and beautiful as they might have been, but at least we were not bowed down with housekeeping details and absorbed in minutiae"; "I never did get things organized"; "the place is generally a mess . . . our housing and life style are well below the expectations in our income level." My own major inadequacy in household management had to do with the handling of money, Buchwald's third and fourth responsibilities.

The letters are full of tight spots for which no adequate provision had been made. Money had not arrived—I was stranded without money—I left David with not enough money even for food—I must buy wine at the liquor store in order to cash a check over the weekend—I sometimes paid bills twice or forgot to pay them at all. Although there was always enough money available, there were frequent "cash-flow" problems. I preferred to make do rather than take the time to shop around. When I did have to shop I took what was near and handy. Sometimes it was a good bargain; sometimes it was not. Managing an estate required effort and attention I was reluctant to give.[3] Nor was household maintenance any more congenial to me.

"Household maintenance" covers a multitude of activities from the more-or-less simple, routine "straightening up" of at least the living quarters, to weekly cleaning, to great seasonal chores like screens and storm sash, to rare remodeling or heavy repair work. Then, also, for millions of households there is yard work which, again, can vary from routine lawn mowing, to weeding, to crab-grass fighting, to watering, to leaf-raking, to snow-shoveling, to ice-sanding, to seeding. . . . They are perennial, ongoing, never-ending. And equally difficult whether one does them one's self or sees to it that someone else does, family member or outsider.

There are several accepted ways to write about the banalities of homemaking. One is the coldly impersonal, scientific approach in which each activity is given a prestigious name—procurement, management, budgeting—and duly analyzed. At the other end of the gamut is the please-don't-eat-the-daisies or the cheaper-by-the-dozen or eight-is-enough approach which looks at the always-expectable slips in the cogs as occasions for hilarious, or just-short-of-grim, laughter. Although there was a considerable amount of space devoted to household maintenance in the letters, I did not think any of it either funny or grim, just run-of-the-mill kinds of things that could happen in any household and that most probably did—some more routinely than others.

I might report to Dorothy Lee that we burned the leaves; a university boy had come and cleaned up one of the back corners of the yard and it looked much improved; or that the electrician was working to triple the amount of power coming into the house, also inserting baseboard outlets; or that the newly painted walls looked nice and fresh but that by the time she came home they would be soiled again; or that the sun was shining brightly and the snow was melting, also *leaking* into Claude's window.

A relatively larger proportion of the maintenance-type letters were addressed to Claude. As my right-hand man and yardman he shared a lot of the hassles. When he was fifteen, for example, I wrote: "It snowed last night and is windy this morning which makes me wish I had reminded you to put the storm sash on the doors. David and I will have to do it tomorrow." After having asked his advice about the television set and finding it did not help, I had, as he suggested, called the repair man who had found some unit had become unplugged, which he fixed, so now we had two working sets, one in the back room and one in the sun room. So far this winter there hadn't been a flood in his room but the contraption we had put up to control the leak stayed there ready just in case. There would be lots of chores for him when he got home: in the yard, getting the grass seeded, the weeds killed. But he was not to worry; we wouldn't overwork him. By April it was getting warm and pleasant and David actually picked flowers in the yard today. We could all work on the grass on the weekend. It looked pretty awful.

In July I wrote to Dorothy Lee that we had finally conceded that the roof had to be replaced. "When it rained the water poured in like a flood. When the workers tore off the shingles they saw why—great foot-square gaping holes in several places." But that was not the worst of it. "The night of the very worst storm of the year, in which sheets of rain pounded down, we were without a roof. The man who is putting on the roof left us quite exposed and it just poured into Claude's room, my room, the play room, drenching furniture and books. Well, we survived that, but we'll never be the same again." Next year in Washington:

Only the usual daily emergencies, like Edna couldn't get here yesterday . . .; like the Bendix shook itself free from the floor and had to be re-inserted; like the plumber—the second—comes and can't find out why the second-floor bathroom ceiling leaks sometimes but not all the time; like —well, the usual.

No wonder that a year after we had moved to Washington I was explaining to Dorothy Lee why my voice so often sounded edgy. It is a humorous bon mot among professional women that they wish they had a wife. Holding down the fort on so many fronts could become—well, taxing.

You were right about the state of affairs which my voice registered and I am sorry I was so edgy. I can explain if not excuse it. I have so many roles to perform, no one of which is all that hard, but all of which, bearing down at once, can make terrific demands on one lone woman. There are professional chores. Then there are both the masculine and the feminine management chores. Unlike a woman who has a husband to help with such management jobs as business problems, money, investments, selling the house, maintenance problems, I have to tend to all of them myself. They are practically full-time jobs themselves. An estate has to be taken care of, at least thought about. Then there are the feminine management jobs, such as seeing that there are clean things in closets and drawers, food in the refrigerator, let alone on the table. Not hard, as I said above, but demanding. That leaves not much left for the maternal role, especially when all three children have to be prepared for school at the same time with, again, all the management involved here too. I'm afraid Brick was probably among the casualties of this concentration of demands piling up at the same time. It would have been much better if I had not had dozens of other distractions to stand in the way of our finding the right relationship between us now that you are an adult.[4]

Among the dozens of distractions was the interminable yard work. I kept David duly posted when he was in Spain: I was giving up on grass and planning to use just any ground cover, perhaps ivy; the retaining wall leaked and had to be repaired; two of the trees had to have broken branches cut off; the flagstones had to be restored; Claude was clearing the snow; we had had to plant new rhododendrum to replace those that had died; I had planted new shoots from the forsythia; and so on, almost endlessly. No wonder Claude, in one of his letters, wished I would tell him more about myself and less about the grass.

Elise Boulding, in a perceptive observation on "human services" in the family pays quite a bit of attention to waiting. She sees waiting-for as "a gift of 'free time' to another, in that the contract to be ready at a certain time is waived, with more or less graciousness, for the delinquent partner, giving that partner more flexibility."[5] There was not much such waiting-for service on my part—except waiting for Claude to wake up when there was work to do, perhaps, or the usual waiting for arrivals. But otherwise not much, and what there was, less rather than more gracious. It was not Elise Boulding's family-style human-service kind of waiting-for that filled my life. In the family I could exert some influence. The kind of waiting-for that plagued my life—like that of every other housewife's—was the service I performed for the outside world by giving it more flexibility in its scheduling. Ellen Goodman has caught its essence:

The Working Mother . . . knew . . . that she had willfully
violated a cardinal rule of American life: No Working Person Must Ever Need Anything Serviced. Or Repaired,
Delivered, Picked Up or Otherwise Touched at Home. . . .
There was absolutely no coincidence between the times
they delivered and the times she was at home. . . . The
entire service industry was geared to the myth that every
house had its housewife and that this housewife's patriotic
duty was to be thrilled at the idea of hanging around scrap-
ing her yellow, waxy, buildup off the linoleum while she
waited for deliverers, installers, and fixers.[6]

It was this kind of waiting-for that was one of the most gall-
ing, not to say grueling, aspects of the home-maintenance
job. "For a person of my temperament," I wrote to
Dorothy Lee, "there aren't many things worse than waiting." At that particular moment I was waiting for the
unending legal red tape involved in buying the Washington
house: "I haven't got a bank here yet, but will get one as
soon as 'the settlement' is made. I don't know exactly
what a 'settlement' is, but until it takes place we are hung
in the air waiting. It is a most disagreeable experience."
Ordinarily I did not burden my letters with such complaints. Only when it became intolerable as when yesterday
I had had "to spend [the day] waiting around for service
people of one kind and another—Salvation Army to haul
off the accumulated newspapers, Edna, to clean the house,
a man to measure the radiators for covers, and a plumber
to investigate a leak in the third-floor bathroom."
    Less frustrating but equally time consuming is another
human service thrust upon the homemaker, doing dozens
of little chores for others. On one occasion, after several
items from Claude I had apparently had it. So: "I hope
you don't make a habit . . . of asking me to do a lot of
errands and chores for you. It took almost all morning to
get the packages off and to get the theater tickets (running
from one box office to another). Especially since Dorothy

Lee also has a quota of chores for me, including locating
her trunk which has not yet arrived."

Actually, both to spare myself and to develop coping
skills in the children I had early shifted as many household
management chores and "human services" to them as I
could. Not included in the letters was the first "human-
service" responsibility I had given to Dorothy Lee when I
had left her, at twelve, in charge of the boys at Ostende
while I went to a professional meeting at Liège. Another
job taken on by Dorothy Lee and Claude when they were
eighteen and fourteen—managing the logistics of the mini-
move the summer I went to Stresa by way of the Orient—
was heavily recorded in the letters. Since I was to teach
at Princeton during the academic year 1959–1960, a considerable operation was involved in moving books, clothes,
and odds and ends. While I was traveling the children
stayed in State College and managed themselves and the
household; Clare Hutchison was to keep her eye on the
boys. They all agreed to take charge of the actual moving.
From wherever I happened to be I followed the log I had
laid out for them and, like a general, fired off staff orders:

Dorothy Lee, are the plans firm and well laid? Will there
be bedding for everyone at Princeton? Be sure the details
are all worked out. The Hall Motor Transfer should take all
the boxes. Records should be carefully packed in closely,
etc. Claude, will you see to that? The hi-fi should go to
Hutchison's unless better arrangements can be made. Be
sure to show them how it operates and tell them to call
Shadle Associates if anything goes wrong.

Again, a few days later: "I hope everything is going all
right. . . . Please see that Claude's clothes are all properly
labeled. Look into David's school, Dorothy Lee, and see
that he gets there the first day. Take him and explain why
I am not there." My conscience gnawed from time to time,
knowing that I had burdened the children with the drudgery

of packing and moving–and deprived David of my reassuring presence the first day at a new school.

I hope everything is going nicely there. . . . I hope the strain is not too great. Remember I have placed my bets on your intelligence, responsibility, and ability to meet crises calmly. There will be plenty of problems but you are as smart as I am and should be able to solve them. Please love one another and be good to one another. . . . By the time you get this maybe David will be in school. I will be extremely interested to hear from him how it goes.

There were also words of appreciation. "I told my guide all about you," I wrote from Stalingrad, September 1, "and she thinks you are wonderful to take care of things at home. I told her that was the only kind of children I could afford to have." As it turned out, my confidence in the children's "intelligence, responsibility, and ability to meet crises calmly" proved well founded. All went well. Except that the movers had refused to take David's bicycle unboxed.

Four years later, from me at State College to the boys in Washington:

Dear Claude and David (in alphabetical order),
. . . I am . . . especially concerned that David get safely off to camp. Is that all provided for? Is the money holding up? . . . David will need a little pocket money when he leaves. . . . Also please leave $8 plus two tokens for Edna if she is coming next week. If you want her only every other week let her know in time. There should also be food in the refrigerator for her lunch. By the way, it is about time to defrost the refrigerator. Turn it off and put a pan of hot water in the freezing compartment. In about half an hour it will be defrosted. OK?

When I could not meet David's plane when he came back from France in the summer of 1964 nor return to Wash-

ington from State College where I was teaching in time to
help him prepare for football camp there was no lack of
instructions:

Please figure out what chores will have to be done before
you go to football camp. Will there be a lot of laundry?
shopping? What kind of gear will you need for football
camp? Did you get any instructions? We ought to plan out
very carefully what you should do when and where. The
main thing I can think of is laundry. In that case, you
ought to do it in Reading where you are to be visiting with
Claude because our wash machine is not connected.

The next day, having now heard from school about football camp, I knew what had to be done. The field general
to her staff:

So now hear this, now hear this: Claude will pick David up
at Kennedy. If it is too hard to return to Reading August
25, stay at Jenny's apartment overnight and return to
Reading. Let David rest up at Reading and do whatever
laundry and shopping he has to do. If he needs heavy sweat
socks or sneakers or shoes, let him get what he needs there.
I will send money to Claude to take care of these items.
I think David should stay with Claude until Friday and then
both of you can go to D.C. Find the sheets, pillow cases,
and blankets in the boxes in the basement. Get everything
ready for Monday. David, be sure you take lunch with
you since it won't be served at school. Claude, if you have
to take time off to pick David up, return to Reading to
make up any time you lose. But if you finish the week out
that should be satisfactory. . . . Please discuss this with
your boss and let me know at once what the decision is.

Whew! So what does a mother do? Tending to these endless details is what mothers do. Unless they can get others
to do it for them.
    One "human service" I was spared. Since I do not drive[7]

I was never caught up in the mother-chauffeur trap so many housewives fall into. Further, while the children were small we lived in a town in which feet and bicycles could get you almost any place you had to go. The children could walk to school; I walked the mile or so to and from my office several times a day. Ezra took care of transportation to and from camp, hospitals, crosstown evening events. When we moved to the city there was public transportation available until the children had cars of their own.

chapter thirteen

what is mother doing?

Hitchhiking on a trip back to eastern Kentucky in search of *temps perdu* LLB had once been picked up by a mountaineer. In the course of the conversation the driver had asked, "Are you a professor?" and LLB, though somewhat taken aback (were the academic stigmata all that obvious?) until it occurred to him that he was being asked not about his academic profession but about his faith, replied yes, he was. I was a professor in the same way. Like him, I professed my discipline.

One can, in this sense, profess in many ways: anywhere, in any circumstances, in any situation, not just standing at the lectern teaching or sitting at a typewriter writing. My letters are full of such professing in the form of pedantic and didactic discourses or rules of behavior, as was also our home life. And whether or not I professed to the children in words, I was, like parents everywhere and always, professing by deed. My profession, whether I would or no, did seep into them. However, it may not have been all that functional for them. David once commented that he had had to learn for himself a lot of thing others seemed to know without having to learn them. Perhaps they were ill prepared for a world less idealistic than the world they were prepared for by my professing.

But the professing I was hired and paid to do was in the classroom and lecture hall.

When in the 1950s the townspeople heard academics complain about twelve-hour weeks it sounded unreasonable to them. How could anyone think twelve hours a week a heavy teaching load? Actually, even when I did a lot of work at home, it *was* heavy. For classroom work was only the top of the iceberg. The hours of preparation required to teach that many hours far outweighed the classroom hours, and the additional hours of library work, paper reading, exam grading, not to mention meeting with the students to discuss their work, could easily add up to at least a sixty-hour week for conscientious academics. In addition to institutional chores, committee work, and help with registration, there were always innumerable calls on the academic's time.

The children intuited early that my work was at least as much a part of my life as they were; they became reconciled to the fact that it was their major competitor for my time and attention. They were remarkably tolerant of its demands—especially of the aspects of it that they could see and understand, like teaching. They occasionally visited my classes when they were old enough but they were not impressed. Interesting perhaps but after all not all that impressive. I had a peripatetic style in the classroom. I walked around a good deal. I went up to the student I addressed questions to. I sought contact. The children could see that all this moving around might be called work, but it was not really all that hard. There were few references to teaching in the letters, though some did begin to appear in letters to Dorothy Lee when she was a boarding school freshman.

The beginning and the ending of the term were bad. I wrote: large classes were hard; I dreaded the stacks of finals and term papers waiting to be read; my teaching went well one day, not so well the next so I suppose it averaged out; the teaching went on apace; I didn't think I was doing very well, but I did the best I could. Sometimes the reports were more cheerful. My work was pleasant and the classes enjoyable; my classes seemed very sympathetic and I was going to like them; I hoped they would remain small enough to sit around the table, that made it more interesting.

Occasionally the scene was enlivened by novel projects, such as teaching Peace Corps trainees. My university was a staging area for volunteers going to the Philippines; everyone who worked with them said they were terrific. "This batch—more women than men—is going to the Philippines to teach English and science." There were also occasional lectures at summer institutes for the steelworkers or for Malaysians or for the media or for the scores of other special-interest groups that a great, publicly supported university served. These were fun. No responsibilities. Just the cream of the experience.

My decision to leave academia, which came during the 1961–1962 sabbatical year, was not sudden. A host of great sociological forces were transforming the campus.[1] Teaching was losing its appeal. Grades were coming to mean too much; everyone was beginning to look at student transcripts—industry, the military, graduate schools. A low grade did not yet almost literally make the difference between life and death as it came to later. But emphasis on grades was already getting in the way of teaching, at least of my style of teaching. I did not lecture. I wrote what would ordinarily constitute a series of lectures in book form and hoped the students would read them, leaving us time in class to play with the ideas and engage in intellectual give-and-take. I liked the Socratic method, asking a question and letting the students see how many different ways it could be approached. Facts are ephemeral; they soon come to have mainly historical interest. I did not ask for memorization; all I asked for was grounding in some kind of factual material. Personal observation would do—

or experience—seen, of course, through the theoretical or conceptual lens the course supplied. But with the increasing size of the student body and larger classes, my style of teaching became a casualty. And with the advent of television teaching, I gave up. I was too dependent on personal relations with the students, on the feedback they supplied, to relish the showmanship called for by television.

But I was not retiring; I was just changing my profession.[2] I wrote to Claude: "I find that not having a regular job means that I get less accomplished in the free time. I just read and look around and have fun instead of doing what has to be done." When I read the letters logging all the work I was doing that sabbatical year I wonder when I had time even to look around.

It had not always been easy to profess sociology. It had had a hard time gaining acceptance in the academic temple and a lingering defensiveness remained even after it had. Sometimes the very term was used as a dirty word. Although economics was admittedly a dismal science, sociology was not only dismal but also disagreeable, dealing with losers as well as with winners, with the powerless as well as with the powerful. Certain economists might be arrogant, certainly proud, professors, even though they were professing differing beliefs. One could win a Nobel prize either way. Political scientists, dealing with important events having to do with power, partook of the grandeur of their data and could also profess their faith in world-encompassing doctrines; occasionally they even impacted on national policy. Historians in scholarly fashion could profess conflict and consensual theories of history; either way winning kudos. In a class by itself was anthropology. Romantic in its reports of distant times and places, especially cultural anthropology could profess condescendingly, the professors aware that no matter what argument was being made it could be refuted by reference to the way it was on a small island in the Pacific. Even on the subject of race they could profess equality knowing that the profession of any other point of view was anathema. But sociology was as likely to deal with the inability to achieve power as with the ability to achieve it. Its data were far less picturesque than the data of history, and far less glamorous than those of anthropology. It rubbed our noses in crime, poverty, injustice, in deviance, in divorce, in our failures rather than touting our successes.[3]

But by the late 1950s it had become not only easy but sometimes even profitable to profess sociology. We were now coming to be in great demand to present the sociological point of view on everything and anything whether we had expertise or not. There was a burgeoning public pressure for sociological input into public thinking and policymaking. We were swamped with requests to talk to groups everywhere. What is going on in our society? What does all this protest mean? And, especially in the late '60s and '70s, what is happening to women? to the family? Why are the women so angry?

Sociologists profess not only to the outside world but also to, and among, themselves—and increasingly so in the '60s and '70s. For the nature of all professions was changing before our very eyes. Travel, as my letters show, was becoming an increasing part of an active professional career. Indeed, meetings constitute a major index of the changes in all the professions then taking place. An active academic career was calling for attendance and participation in annual meetings, conventions, conferences, workshops, institutes, committee meetings, board meetings, seminars, colloquia. Participation was intrinsic to one's work. Knowledge was growing at a rate that left one breathless in an—often vain—effort to keep up with it. And a growing proportion of that knowledge was available only by way of unpublished papers and reports given at such meetings by one's colleagues[4]—even in the form of informal talk at cocktail parties. A great network of relationships kept the knowledge circulating and if one dropped out it took time to catch up.

A considerable part of my professing was done locally.

To a political science class; to the agronomists; to the
Hillel Foundation; to the local sociological society—"talk
on family reactions to defective children Tuesday; talk to
students Thursday night on any old thing"; to a music
seminar on place of music in the leisure of the 1970s.

The pace accelerated as the decade wore on, and as the
distances grew I became more selective. "I got a call today
from Philadelphia asking me to talk at a luncheon in November that wasn't particularly interesting. But I learned
that their originally invited speaker was [Senator] Ribicoff
and when he couldn't come they decided to invite me."
Sometimes the challenges became more urgent. "I just got
back from a two-day trip to Cleveland and was so keyed
up I couldn't fall asleep. . . . I was in California for several
days last week and it was very exciting." Two years later
in 1966: "Last night I was so excited and stimulated by
the meetings I was at yesterday that I slept only two
hours." Referring to several conferences that month I said
that they would "be prosaic, like New York," then added,
for my own benefit more than for David's, "Imagine being
so blasé that New York is considered prosaic!" And the
next year, again to David:

I was in New York Friday and yesterday at a meeting of
Church Women United, talking about a "ministry to
women." . . . Wednesday I talk to a group at one of the
synagogues around here, I'm not sure just where. . . . Next
week Dallas and after that Tuskegee. Another talk in Washington, to city officials, at the end of the month and then
Puerto Rico. New York once more in April. . . . So you
can see this is an extraordinarily busy time this year.

In the summer of the same year:

Monday I go to New York on another assignment and at
the end of the month, to San Francisco. . . . I hadn't done
much of my own work because I get requests to do papers

for other people and that takes all my time. Now in process are papers for meetings in October.

And, again to David, two years later:

Yesterday I was asked to give a talk in Milwaukee on
March 14 and today a talk next September in Hartford,
Connecticut. I turned the Connecticut one down because
maybe I will be in Varna, Bulgaria, attending the International Sociological Association meetings. I will be in New
York again at the end of March to be on a panel of meetings of the psychoanalytic association. . . . In May I will
give a talk to the psychoanalysts in Miami on the 6th and
to the American Association of University Women in State
College on the 8th. . . . So life is very busy.

Sometimes I tried to share the talks with the children.
Thus, on one talk I was to give, I wrote to Dorothy Lee:

I am going to talk . . . on the complex woman. Some of
the material would interest you. It is based on a study by
Nevitt Sanford comparing Vassar seniors with Vassar fresh-
men to see what college has done to them. It has done
plenty. Made them more disturbed. Prepared them for the
best of all nonexistent worlds, etc. . . . Well, so much for
now. David and I are going marketing.

And to David: "I am supposed to talk on sexual behavior
of upper-middle-class kids and I am going to emphasize its
casualness, egalitarianism, etc. Any pointers?" These are
typical examples of literally dozens of letters. Chicago,
New York, New Orleans, San Francisco, on and on. Sometimes it sounded like an accelerated movie.

My image of myself, I had once written, though not in a
letter to the children, was one of almost reclusive self-
containment:

My ideal of a happy life is one of reading, studying, con-
templating, mulling, musing, observing, interpreting. My
natural habitat would have been a convent in a contempla-
tive order and my preferred period to live in the late eigh-
teenth century. It would have been an ideal life for me,
to sit in the library of an abbey and read Adam Smith,
Malthus. (My mother would have loved such a life also,
but her preferred reading would have been court intrigue
and history.) And writing. Especially writing. . . . I have
felt little desire to go forth to conquer worlds. I think of
the forces that have pulled me away from the quiet of my
study as distractions, as diversionary, as inevitable but
temporary interruptions in my real life.

Which was, of course, among books.
   How little I knew myself. Writing to Dorothy Lee in
London I was saying: "I find that when I am in the house
all day long it becomes quite depressing. I am an action
person and like to get out and move around," and several
years later, to David: ". . . having been away from my desk
for so many days now I am having to work especially hard
to catch up. But it is very refreshing to take part in all
these enterprises because it helps me to keep au courant
and I learn so much."
   The earlier letters show that I was endlessly involved in
diversionary distractions. Except those from Graz, they
document my involvement with local community chores
such as soliciting for the hospital: "Yesterday was so
crammed with chores that I didn't get a chance to
write. . . . I have to canvass our street for the hospital
before the end of the month." The next day, I had "a
committee meeting of the adult First-day class at noon."
Helping with refreshments at Meeting, working on a
committee of mothers to reduce class size in the lower
grades, getting language instruction into the schools, and
making other arrangements when the school board refused:
"David, Jay, and half a dozen other kids are going to have
their German lessons after school at the homes of the kids

rather than in school." PTA again and also League of Women Voters, not without the usual apologies and guilt-allaying explanations: "The usual apologies for not having written the last two days and the usual reasons." I specified the "usual reasons," this time including work with other first-grade mothers trying to reduce the teacher's load—and then the plea for exoneration: "You must have to get along with less mothering than other children. I feel plenty guilty about this but console myself with the thought that I have wonderful enough children so that they can get along with less." Again, the following spring: "I know you pooh-pooh the thought, but it seems to me I neglect you."

But the pace did not slacken. I look through all the letters at the kaleidoscope of activities that filled my days and wonder—I did not at the time—why my male colleagues were not recruited also for these chores or why they did not volunteer. No one excused me from them because of my academic obligations. Someone had to take care of the school, hospital, and miscellaneous community chores. I was a mother; I took my turn.

Fortunately, other diversions and distractions were more related to my academic responsibilities, such as serving as rapporteur at a rehabilitation conference, or going to Altoona "to hear about the new legislation for children," or a faculty dinner for the Board of Trustees, or a Penn Foundation meeting, or a trip to Oberlin to serve as an outside examiner for their honor students. One nonacademic diversion that might have been fun if I had felt able to accept it was "to serve as a judge in a search for an all-American family. I would spend a week at the Biltmore-Terrace Hotel at Miami Beach, etc. But I turned it down. I don't think I can neglect my family that much, however much fun it would be."

In the fall of 1957 "I was nominated but not elected to the University Senate. I just couldn't care less." My colleagues reassured me and sympathized, assuming that I must feel as disappointed as they might have felt. It was not a case of sour grapes when I told them that I did not want the honor. I knew I was not an organization person. The endless hours invested in organization business left me befuddled; my judgment was poor; I never understood the hidden agenda. And when the issues encompassed such matter-of-fact and ultimately most important problems as parking privileges, dining hall hours, and the like, I faded out. I was glad not to have to deal with that "diversion and distraction."[5]

But with so many activities, so many engagements, so many responsibilities, so many obligations no wonder I had a hard time keeping my calendar straight and began quite early to complain of my senility. But, Mother, the children reassured (?) me, you've always been that way.

I found it hard to justify my frequent absences. So the letters to the children—from Chicago, New York, New Orleans, San Francisco, Boston, wherever—included pleas for forgiveness to allay my guilt. I demanded a great deal of reassurance from them and they supplied it.

All through the letters apologies thread their way. I'll try to make it for Parents' Day, but I'm not sure I can. Sorry I can't make it this weekend. Too bad, but I have to cancel the trip. Sorry I won't be able to see you off because I have a commitment made long ago. Sorry I can't meet you at the airport, I have a meeting in Chicago. And so on endlessly.[6] Occasionally I gave defensive explanations to outsiders, as in a letter to the director of the Andover program for boys in Barcelona: "I regret very much that I will not be able to go to New York for the sailing on September 8. I will be attending an International Sociological conference at Evian, France, a commitment which I made long ago. But there will be some family member there, either his sister or his brother, or both." I added that David understood why I could not be there.

And, along with explanations, also apologies. To Claude: "I am concerned because it seems so unmotherly to have so little time to spend with you." He did not complain to me but to David he wrote: "When I got in last night [Mother] was not here, but at another meeting. Oh, does she like meetings, especially this one because of all the interesting and intelligent people." I was especially sensitive about David, whose infancy had coincided with the burgeoning mobility of professors of all kinds. In the earliest letters the children were open about minding my absences. They missed me and told me so. But when they were adolescents they were willing to assuage my guilt. "I guess you were busy all the time in New York, so don't worry about not calling," wrote Dorothy Lee.

How did the professional mother in the '50s and '60s deal with conflicting pressures? We dealt with them in different ways. One of the Twelve Women, during the school year, "restricted travel to one conference, in order not to be absent from home for too long a time. During the summers, as soon as the children reached the age of five, they . . . accompanied . . . me to conferences" both in this country and abroad. Another taught the children that they had to make some sacrifices. Another raised the children "to enjoy the benefits of a working mother." I think I "bought" my children off. But it was a solution not without its own peculiar psychological hazards.

Not until I reread the letters one after another in concentrated doses did the salience of money jump out of the pages at me. I was flabbergasted by the almost compulsive preoccupation with money they showed, from Claude's early IOUs to later matter-of-fact banking problems. Scarcely a letter came or went either way that did not deal with money one way or another. I was always wracked by the temptation to buy the children off, often against my better judgment. It was easier to concede than to fight any request for money.

In a book based on family documents supplied by students, there was one by a father who had retired early in order to have less income to spoil his children with:

When we had a lot of money coming in my children expected everything. . . . It never occurred to them that they
should be deprived of anything. There was always enough
money. I could never legitimately deny them anything on
the grounds that we couldn't afford it. That isn't good for
kids. . . . When I finally told them that I was retiring . . .
they groaned at the "hardships" my reduced income
would inflict on the family. I think it was quite a shock to
them. Land-grant colleges instead of Ivy League; two cars
instead of three (four, counting a hot-rod); no yard man;
no boat; no long trips at frequent intervals. . . . For me . . .
it was also a real sacrifice. Not the kind my parents made
for me. But just as real. I gave things up in order to deprive
my children, just as my parents gave things up so as not
to deprive me. . . .[7]

I could understand that father—others expressed incredulity. Still, some sixteen years later, a woman wrote to Ann
Landers with the same kind of story:

How can parents say no to their children when money
isn't a problem? Our kids see us buying luxury items for
ourselves and naturally they feel that they have a right to
them, too. . . . It was easy for our parents to say no because we knew darned well we couldn't afford anything
often. . . . What's the answer for the members of the affluent society?[8]

So on the other hand, like these parents, I did not want
my children to think they must have whatever they
wanted.

The result of my money hang-up was the worst of all
possible worlds for the children. They felt poor but at the
same time they were never deprived of money. They had
little sense of its value. David as a teenager felt out of
things because he felt poor surrounded by affluent classmates. Claude felt put upon because, after the sight-
seeing trip with which I always began a visit to a new city,

I walked the streets as the best way to get the feel of the place. In his eyes we were walking because I was stingy. It has occurred to me that the money the boys *felt* deprived of was a symbol of the father they were, in truth, deprived of. Other boys had something precious that they did not have.[9] It must be money.

Some years later Dorothy Lee caught me up on my "guilt trips." She commented that they reflected a kind of arrogance, implying that I had godlike powers. "If I had only done this instead of that or not done this or that, my children would have been perfect human beings. If I had given up my work, if I had stayed home more, if I had not gone to so many meetings, if I had given them more time . . ." She asked, was my guilt an expression of disappointment in them? Or in myself? And David echoed the same theme. Had I piled so much guilt upon myself because I had thought there was something about them that was bad, wrong, undesirable? I had, he suggested, fallen into the stereotype of the guilty mother. Perhaps so.

chapter fourteen

the other child

The children learned quite early that their most serious competitor for my time and attention was my typewriter. Even when I was not flying hither and yon to meetings a large part of my time was given over to my writing. Descartes knew he existed because he thought. I knew I existed because I wrote.[1] Anne Morrow Lindbergh expressed this state of mind for what must be a large company of us: "If I could write out moods which could be admitted to no one, they became manageable. . . . I felt I must know what had been happening to me, and couldn't know without writing it."[2] Like her, I did not know anything until I put it into words. The world filtered in and I shaped it into words. Then I could read and try to understand it.[3]

I do not find adequate such terms as *career, achievement, drive, self-actualization,* or *self-realization.* They have become almost dirty words with some people, especially when used in relation to married women. And they fail to convey the profundity of the phenomenon they refer to. The assumption is that self-actualization is a selfish luxury, an egocentric indulgence, something extraneous that one could take or leave. The real things are duty, obligation, responsibility. Granted, the words are not well chosen. They do have a connotation of rejection of obligations to others. In fact, the need to actualize one's self can be as intrinsic as the need to eat. Millions of people, I am convinced, have wasted away and died from lack of the opportunity to actualize themselves, as truly as infants have wasted away and died from marasmus or lack of tender loving care—or limped through half-lives.[4] I could no more have survived without my work than fly. It was as essential for me to read, research, study, mull, meditate, write, as to breathe. I was as much a sociologist or writer as I was a woman; my work was as much a part of me as my sex.[5]

"What makes Jessie run?" a friend of mine was once asked. "She's got tenure, so why does she work so hard? why does she keep on running?" I ran because I could not help myself. In psychological terms I was, I suppose, compulsive. In folk terms, it was in my blood. In literary terms, I had a daemon, as do other scientists, artists—even tycoons and politicians. A ballet teacher on a television program put it succinctly: a dancing career was not something those suffering pupils had chosen; it had chosen them.

To speak, therefore, as though a career were something one could take or leave, as though it were something one had to choose or reject is, or was in my case, to misrepresent the situation. I read and thought and wrote sociology whether I was on the road or at home. My research and writing were as much a part of me as my children.

The academic world understood. It knew my type. They recognized it even though it was housed in a female body. I was "Type A," the type of personality that pursued careers with compulsive intensity. Fast-paced—the students called me "Jet Bernard"—I had a hard time slowing down to the pace of others. Arrival times, departure times, traffic lights, deadlines. I raced to get there—wherever—ahead of the specified time.[6] My work habits became legendary at the university. I could, so the story went, be pounding away at the typewriter in my office, look at my watch and

jump up—midsentence—to rush off to class, return afterwards, finish the sentence, and proceed to polish off a
chapter. The picture was, of course, just an amusing and
affectionate caricature. But there was a grain of truth in it.

The academic community could accept all this. But
families are different. A distinguished sociologist had, in
fact, made the point that the qualities called for in the
work world were precisely those not called for in the family, and vice versa; certain personality characteristics, important in the work world, did not serve well in families. I
infuriated my husband by completing his sentences, long
after I knew how angry it made him; I found it difficult to
be patient when my children could not keep up with me.
In this respect I was not at all "motherly," any more than
I was in my absorption in my work. For it was not only
the time away from home—in the classroom, at conferences, at meetings—that my work took but also the time
it took even when I was physically there.

Some careers require a whole world of support before
they can be pursued. Actresses have to have theaters, a
ramifying complex of personnel and creative authors, even
security guards. Scientists have to have laboratories,
libraries, computers, and a wide range of support personnel. These careers cannot be pursued at home. Authors,
composers, and handicraft workers are almost the only
workers who do not need a great bureaucratic structure
and can therefore work at home. When women first began
to combine motherhood with jobs and careers, these were
the kinds of—home—work they did. They wrote or com-
posed or took in boarders or laundry, sold the jams, jellies,
cookies, and other goodies they could make at home. They
made doilies and quilts and did dressmaking in their homes,
or gave music lessons.

Still, even the careers that could be pursued at home did
have some requirements that competed with children's.
Jane Austen may have been able to write on her lap in the
living room, but she had no children to keep in tow—or to

respond to . The mother of children is not likely to be that free. I could do a great deal of my work at home, and did. My children often fell asleep to the sound of my clicking typewriter. But merely being physically present is not enough. The absent mind may be even worse than the absent body. The mother busily engaged doing physical things—cooking, vacuuming, gardening—is reassuring to children: they can go about their business without demanding attention. But the mother who is just sitting there reading, her mind clearly not present, is a different matter. What is she *doing* anyway, just sitting there pouring over all those papers and books? What is she so preoccupied with as she pounds the typewriter so intently? Why is she *frowning* over all those journals? What is she so absent-mindedly *busy* about? She is constantly being called back to the world of the child. Her intellectual concentration is seen as a threat, and rightly so. Sometimes when I sat transfixed at my typewriter my children came to my desk to demand "time off," to call me back for a few minutes, to reestablish connections. It did not take much, just a smile, perhaps, or a hug. Just some acknowledgment that they counted as much as the typewriter did.

If an idea were gestating in my mind, everything that could be pushed aside had to be pushed aside until I had licked it, imprisoned it in the right words, and told myself what it added up to. The ideas themselves seemed to churn incoherently around in my body, vaguely in my muscles somewhere, causing a mild malaise or restlessness. I could not call this process "thinking." Not, at least, in any way a psychologist could recognize. I was aware of the kinesthetic sensations in my body, but nothing as clear-cut as thinking. Presently, though, whatever it was that was going on in my muscles and viscera became focused and the words to harness and clarify it rushed up at me pell mell. I had to write it down. Preferably at the typewriter because it was fast enough to keep up with me. Otherwise in longhand on whatever scrap of paper I had about me. I was not always prepared for the rush of words that welled up.[7] It was not until I had, in effect, added up the bits and pieces that produced these ideas that I discovered the logic in them.[8]

I am sure my own concentration was often interpreted by the children as rejection, as, indeed, it might well have been. Even in playtime I may not always have been there mentally. And if I were working on an engrossing piece of research or writing, trying to make sense out of a batch of data, figuring out the best approach to a problem, I may have been only remotely present. Mathematicians have been described showing "a pleasant vacuity of expression that means that in some warm corner of the brain, complex ideas are being arranged and rearranged."[9] Marie Curie was seen by her daughter as distantly absorbed at the breakfast table. For a career of any kind is a demanding thing, especially an intellectual one. The wife of a university professor once said she hoped her daughter would not marry a professor; other men worked regular hours but professors worked round the clock. To the question commonly asked of authors, how long did it take you to write the book, my answer is not only "all my life" but also "all my life while I was writing it." The children of the Twelve Women were well aware of their mothers' absence. Says one, "In an angry outburst . . . my son charged that I had never been more than a 'distant figure' in his life"; and another says of her second two children that "they claim . . . that 'Mother was always away.' Maybe I was, psychologically, but *my* memory is of my very intense and caring feeling for them."[10] As mine, indeed, is also.

In a book I had published in 1942 I reviewed the research up to that time on maternal rejection and overprotection, including the findings reported for both the motivation of the mother and the consequences for the child. Eight years later, the year David was born, in fact, the World Health Organization published a report by a British psychologist which emphasized the importance of infant-mother relationships, including physical contact, and the separation trauma an infant suffered if deprived of it. The report was to have considerable impact on child care theory all over the western world. Mothers became fearful that if they left the crib for half an hour fateful consequences could ensue. At the same time in the United States the horrors of momism were also being widely bruited. How to supply the tender loving care which the WHO report called for and at the same time avoid momism became a serious balancing act, especially for working or professional women.

A great deal has been made by—defensive?—professional women of the quality of time spent with children as opposed to the mere quantity. But what does "quality" mean? How to measure it? What form does it take? Beyond infancy, just what is tender loving care? I found some insights from laboratory scientists. In a series of laboratory studies on human interaction in small task-oriented groups in the 1950s, they had delineated what they called the "expressive role" in terms of such kinds of behavior as: "showing solidarity, raising the status of others, giving help, rewarding, agreeing, concurring, complying, understanding."[11] In quite a different context, another scientist was showing how powerful "positive re-inforcement" could be in both animals and humans. I borrowed Eric Berne's term *stroking*[12] to refer to all the many kinds of supportive and reinforcing behavior that constituted the "expressive" role.[13] It was at least one way to judge "quality."

If I overdid the money motif, so did I, in a way, overdo the stroking, the support, the appreciation, the acceptance. In the letters I was always "bursting with pride" over report cards. The kinds of schools my children went to looked at anyone with an IQ under 120 as dull. The young people my children went to school with were among the brightest in the country. If mine could hold their own in that fast-paced world, that was enough for me.[14] Say, then, that I was overcompensating for the guilt I felt over my obsession with my own work. Still, I thought I was building the children up, giving them self-confidence. I

may have been excessive. Midge Decter, who believes that
the generation she belongs to deprived their children of the
sand of discipline, tells them that their comforters "may
have praised you, but they have not really respected you."
Dorothy Lee had the same insight. She commented, many
years later, that perhaps my extravagant reassurances meant
actually that I did not really think they were so great.[15]
Was I convincing myself as well as them? Was all that
praise for my own benefit? Did it, in fact, have the opposite effect to that intended? Did it make them fearful that
they really could not live up to it? Did my constantly
reiterated insistence, for example, that grades were not all
that important really mean that they were, actually, all
that important? Did my reassurances that Bs were OK with
me really mean exactly what my own parents had meant
when, noting a B among the As, they had asked why hadn't
I got all As? Instead of building toward independence did
my stroking have precisely the opposite effect? Did
Dorothy Lee's asking for a "praising letter," for example,
reflect a kind of "addiction"? The reassurances in my letters may, indeed, have had the same "mood-altering"
effect as a "fix." Still, I cannot, as in the case of money,
say I regret the mistake, if mistake it was, of overdoing the
supportive role, even if it were—as it may have been—
prompted by the desire to assuage the guilt I felt for not
paying more attention to them. The children have inner
security. They suffer. They fail. They make mistakes. But
they can take it. They recover. They have resilience. Would
giving them more time have done more?

The worst thing my work may have done to my children
might be not the time and attention it deprived them of
but the misconception it gave them of work. They were de-
ceived by the comparative ease of my career. I loved my
work, hence loving one's work became a basic criterion in
selecting a job. I had been able to pick and choose among
job offers. Hence choice seemed built into one's work life.
By the time they came along I was free from bureaucratic

constraints. They thought all careers could be. This was a misconception hard to overcome.

It took me much longer to gestate a book than a baby. My first two books appeared about the time my first child was born. One, which appeared in 1942, was written originally as a doctoral dissertation; it had been in process for many years during which I had been free to travel widely and examine hundreds of college catalogs.[16] The other, which also appeared in 1942, similarly, had taken many months of research to write.[17] There was recognition of my first child in the dedication of my first book: "To Dorothy Lee and her father, my best teachers."

During the years when Dorothy Lee and Claude were small—1942-1949—I did not write any books. These were war and postwar years; there were hardships; I had some help but not enough to release me for the hours of study needed for creative work. Part of the time I was commuting between home and the college where I was teaching. I could not write; but I was thinking. And by the end of the decade I was once more busy at the typewriter.

During David's infancy, 1949-1956, there was another hiatus in book productivity[18] so not until 1956 were there any references to my writing in the letters. But early in that year (January 17) I was writing to Dorothy Lee, then a sophomore at boarding school, that I had begun to read proof for my next book *(Remarriage, A Study of Marriage),* and there was a chance it would appear in March. I hoped it would; I believe it did. After that, references to most of the books did appear more or less casually in the letters.

When I did take a sabbatical—1961-1962—I was extraordinarily busy, editing one volume, gestating three others, working on a high school sociology project, and a sixty-four page chapter for a handbook. The letters log all these contributions. They also trace the final stages of another, the

revision of *American Community Behavior,* originally published in 1949.

The first edition had been well received and a revision
asked for. In a letter dated February 18, 1957, I had added
the pleasant fact that I had "been asked for permission to
have *American Community Behavior* recorded for the
blind" and I thought that was very nice. I was glad to give
permission, of course. But between the request for a new
edition and the publication of the book Stanley Burnshaw
had sold his Dryden Press to Holt, Rinehart and Winston, a
far more bureaucratic and impersonal establishment and
one far less congenial to work with. The first reference to
the revision in the letters was dated July 6, 1961: I was
working my head off on it. I was now on Chapter 4; there
were to be twenty-eight all told; I had an August 1 dead-
line. About two weeks later my work was proceeding
apace. I was stymied on two of the chapters, which annoyed me and kept me from making headway; I hoped to
solve the problem soon; I now knew why they were called
deadlines: "You are dead when you reach the line." I had
had to turn down a lot of interesting assignments in order
to finish. "One was to work with Peace Corpsmen, teaching them about American society. Another to work with
alumni, ditto." I did accept another little job, "to make a
recording for radio broadcasting on my experiences with
the Russians," a reference to my adventures in Amsterdam
at the International Sociological Association meetings in
1956 and in Russia on my way to the 1959 meetings at
Stresa. I was still being held up by annoying little chores—
writing letters for students for jobs, exams, meetings, reports. But it looked as though if I could keep glued to the
typewriter until the middle of August, the hump would be
behind me. A week later I had finished all I could do on
the manuscript. There would be months of work left on it,
but for now I couldn't do any more. I was finding it different working with Holt than it had been with Dryden.
"Dryden really gave your work a thorough going-over," and
I had come to sort of depend on it. I felt a bit uncom-

fortable that Holt took the manuscript without discussion. In about a month I would get galleys. The "months of work left" kept me busy until January "mopping up small chores . . . such as writing for permission to quote." I had hoped the revision would be out in the spring, in time for teachers to examine it for fall adoption. But it wouldn't be out until summer, the very worst time—too late for fall adoptions, too early for winter adoptions. I wasn't expecting many adoptions, though, because it was too unconventional for a text. A month later, when the publishers asked me to spend a day with them in New York shortening the manuscript, I was apparently fed up and I felt, I wrote to Dorothy Lee, like telling "them to shorten it themselves." The book appeared in due course and was well received.

Although I always give each of the children a copy of every book I write when it appears I doubt if they ever read any one of them. But my next publication, an issue of the *Annals of the American Academy of Political and Social Science* on teenage culture, which I had been asked to edit, they did read and enjoy. In fact, it was one of the least attractive writing assignments I have ever undertaken. As any editor of any volume by different authors can testify, it is harder to get such an anthology through to publication than it is to write the whole thing oneself. I laid out the topics and invited knowledgeable colleagues to write papers on them. Through July and August I kept complaining to Dorothy Lee: several contributors were holding me up, if I didn't get their papers very soon I would have to close shop without their papers; I hoped it wouldn't come to that. A week later the papers were still not all in. "In short, problems, problems, problems, problems." A few days later I was still chewing my nails hoping that all the papers would be in on time. My authors were very promising but to date only half had turned in their papers. Two weeks later I sent off the final papers. What a nuisance that whole job had been! "I had given one paper up for lost and had scurried around to find a substitute when the author called up to tell me I would get his paper yesterday." So now I might have too much material. I had told the *Annals* editor if there was too much material he could cut mine out. Only one promised paper did not show up but I had already discounted it and the author had not threatened to send it so I was letting that one ride. I had also written two long-overdue book reviews and almost felt now that I could breathe again.

I sent several copies of the *Annals* to Dorothy Lee. Had she enjoyed reading it? If she could dispose of more copies I could send her more. She could give them to any of her teachers who would most appreciate having one. (I was running out of the ears with all the copies the publishers had sent me.) There was going to be a little piece based on it in *Newsweek.* The issue had been well received; it was front-page news in Philadelphia; editorials had been written about it. But since I did not see the Philadelphia papers I did not know what had been said. The children found at least two of the papers interesting, Dorothy Lee, the piece on teenage comics and Claude, the one on slang.[19]

Late in the fall of my 1961–1962 sabbatical I was approached by a friend in the Children's Bureau to help her with a project she was planning on out-of-wedlock births. I was to review the research and another woman, a social worker, was to review plans for dealing with them and to make policy reommendations. The work I did was finally used as the seed for a book on marriage and family among blacks. I described the project to Dorothy Lee and added I could hardly wait to get started on it; it sounded fascinating. But I had to wait for a green light from the university for permission to work for pay during a sabbatical. Permission came at the end of January; I did not know what my salary was to be but presumably the same as at the university. I found the work fascinating and became increasingly engrossed in it—thought "about it most of the time." I was studying trends in illegitimacy and trying to interpret them. I wished she were there "to discuss some of the

angles with me." As it now stood, I saw at least three types
of illegitimacy, different according to social class. . . . Then,
remembering who my reader was, I added that I wouldn't
bother her with details unless she was interested. She was
interested. She was seeing quite a bit of Sally Guttmacher,
daughter of Alan Guttmacher, an outstanding leader in the
Planned Parenthood movement. When she had heard about
the new job she had written, "I told Sally that where her
father fails my ma takes over." My work continued interesting, but frustrating. "My hypothesis was that some of
the increase in illegitimacy when marriage rates went down
was due to marriages that never took place even though
the girl had conceived in expectation of marrying."

The book that grew out of this research did not appear
until 1966. I waited patiently for my report to appear
under official auspices. But as the years dragged on I decided to write my own book, expanding and putting it in
sociological perspective. The book was dedicated "to Negro
women, one of the most remarkable phenomena in American history."

With a minimum of preparation, against all but insuperable
odds, these women have borne the major burden of pulling up the Negro population by its bootstraps. They have
been spirited and independent, as well as self-sacrificing. As
wives, they have not taken advantage of their—"unnatural"
—superiority; as mothers, they have worn out countless
washboards earning money to educate their children. They
deserve a place alongside the women who pioneered the
West with their husbands, for the women have pioneered
another frontier—one fraught with no less danger than the
West, against odds no less formidable, and, it is hoped,
with equal, if delayed, success.

Among the most appreciated accolades I have ever received
were the fan letters from black readers who assumed I was
one of them.

A third book was also gestating during that year and the next, namely a book on academic women, which was to prove one of the most influential I had written up to that time. Two of my colleagues—Judith Leventman and Margaret Matson—and I had often held informal discussions on the subject of the position of women in the academic world and we had planned to write the book together. But I was impatient and they procrastinating so, with their permission, I proceeded on my own. I had already begun it by the beginning of the sabbatical. I could hardly wait to get my teeth into it. I was applying for a grant to finance the year after the sabbatical so that I would not have to return to the university to repay the sabbatical. I had a desk at the Library of Congress, "but my record of getting books" was poor, only about one in eight. The other seven were not on the shelves so I had taken to buying them. Fortunately old college records were easily available. I had just done Wellesley which was the critical case, "a school that began with a prejudice in favor rather than against women faculty members. Interesting." I was going to the library every day except when David was sick and plodding away. By the end of November I was trying to whip the data into the form of a research proposal and not enjoying it very much. I had lost a considerable amount of enthusiasm. To Dorothy Lee, I hypothesized:

I paid $25 to have a set of tables run which are awfully interesting. They show that women who receive Ph.D. degrees average considerably higher in testable intelligence than men. The reason is, of course, that they are a much more highly selected group; only a tenth of all doctor's degrees go to women and they are only the very top of the bottle. But my problem is: why, if they have so much ability, do they achieve so much less? Many factors have been proposed and are relevant but the one that interests me most is what I call the "stag factor" or the exclusion of women from places where the best thinking is going on.

Not by design or conspiracy, but just because men feel more free and comfortable without the presence of women when they are at work. That is my hypothesis. I also hypothesize that the quality of thinking is best in one-sex groups. This could be tested experimentally.

The grant request dragged on. As late as June my plans for the fall had not yet matured. I was still hoping that the grant would come through. If it did, fine. But even if it didn't I would remain in Washington anyway. The grant did finally come through and I did stay on in Washington to complete the book on academic women—and worked madly until the spring of the following year:

You are absolutely right to rebuke me for not writing more often. It is explainable but not excusable. I am trying very hard to complete the manuscript for *Academic Women* as soon as possible. I'm tired of it. The most interesting part is over and now it's just a matter of editorial drudgery —checking figures, dates, computations, etc. And, as David can tell you, my materials are in such a mess that I can't locate what I need when I need it. He and I spent hours the other day looking for something which, it turned out, was lying open on my desk. That shows you how far senility has progressed.

There was nothing more in the letters about this book until the following year when I wrote to David in France that the book had not yet appeared. "I have given it up as a dream," I said. "I didn't really write it. I just imagined I did." But it had not been a dream, it was published in 1964.

When in the late '60s *Academic Women* came under criticism from the young feminists, I was faulted for not paying enough attention to the discrimination against women. In fact, in the 1972 reissue of this book I did "recant." I confessed that I had not pushed my analyses far enough; I had not explained all the forces operating to keep the qualified pool of academic women low.

I was faulted also for not writing with enough passion.
There must be depths of rage in me based on my own
experience. I took these charges seriously. I felt obliged
to search my own career, but could not find traces of
discrimination there. It is, of course, impossible to document the vast amount of discrimination that is never
publicized. How would one know how many times one
had been blackballed, voted down, rejected for a job? I
once learned that I had been the subject of what might be
called discrimination by association. Two of my friends,
George A. Lundberg and Read Bain, had recommended me
for membership in a prestigious research association, an ex-
clusive elite group of my fellow sociologists. I was not accepted because it would not do for a woman to be in if her
husband were not and my husband was persona non grata
to the membership. When a friend of mine once looked at
my vita he commented that with a record like that he
could have parlayed it to one of the top positions in the
country. How would I ever know if I had been subjected
to discrimination when candidates for top jobs were being
considered?

My career had been unique. I had been "captured" in
marriage before I had laid out any career plans. I had
worked with and for my husband as I would have worked
with him and for him if he had engaged me as an employee rather than married me. I had been "forced" to
succeed, almost against my will. It was he who had insisted that I get a doctorate. I would need it one day. No
hurry. Take your time. But do not abandon the idea. I
traveled with him to Argentina, to Paris, to all parts of
the country, taking courses wherever he was teaching. And
when the time finally became ripe, I took the degree—
painlessly. Many years later I was suggesting the same slow
pace to Dorothy Lee: "I was a very slow developer. It took
me years to find myself and it was your father who located
me. . . . It's awfully important to know what you want to
do, what you really want, regardless. As I look back over
my own life I find that this is exactly what I did." In my

own case I had, in effect, started at the top. The third or fourth meeting of my professional association that I attended I occupied the presidential suite. My way was made easy, doors were opened for me. When I went to the university in 1947 I was shot up the academic ladder in short order. Salary increases came without turmoil. In 1961 I was writing to Dorothy Lee, for example: "Incidentally, I was surprised—and pleased—to learn yesterday that I had been granted an increase in salary. Convenient and useful." Though I could well empathize with the pain and anguish my young critics were experiencing I could not in all conscience claim that I had had to struggle against great obstacles. If I had not lived a "charmed" professional life, I had lived a facilitated one. All the more reason, I felt, to support their grievances.

The research for *Academic Women* had alerted me to the importance of communication. I had placed a considerable amount of emphasis on the "stag effect" in attempting to explain the handicaps under which academic women labored. My thinking soon went beyond the academic setting and came to center on general communication between the sexes. Not until 1967, however, did any reference to it show up in the letters and by that time the book—*The Sex Game*—was completed and "I was tired of it."

In the late '60s I was in the process of an intellectual shakedown similar to, though far from as traumatic as, the one I had experienced in the late '40s, some twenty years earlier. That one had altered my whole conception of my discipline. The one that came in the late '60s also altered my conception of my discipline, this time in the direction of a feminist conception of it. As an inhabitant of what came derisively to be known as the "sociological ghetto" relagated to women—the study of marriage, family, community—I had spent a considerable amount of time studying women in their several institutional relationships. But I had never seen them from the newly emerging feminist perspective. I had accepted the male-delineated perspective of my colleagues. Although *Academic Women* had dealt with discrimination against women it had not probed deeply enough. It had explained the small proportion of women in the academic world in terms of the size of the qualified pool of candidates. It had not gone far enough in explaining why the pool itself was so small. The book on communication between the sexes, *The Sex Game,* had skirted the salient issues, but had not zeroed in on them.

In June 1969, I wrote to David that I was trying to whip into publishable form a position paper I had written for the White House which, now that Johnson had withdrawn from the political race, was being released. I was going to call it "Women and the Public Interest, An Essay on Policy and Protest." The original manuscript, I supposed, was "locked away in the basement files somewhere or other." Not until I re-worked this material did the new feminist perspective begin to surface in my work. I had first learned about the nascent women's liberation movement from the underground press and felt at once that this was something I as a sociologist had to know more about.

In a 1969 letter to David from Cambridge, where I was visiting Dorothy Lee, I wrote that I was "up to my ears in studying the Female Liberation Movement and I went to the New England Free Press to buy up their literature which I then began to read on Boston Common." I was kept so busy that by April 22, 1970, I was writing that I hardly had time to think—I had just sent off a paper for a women's liberation book—*51 percent*[20]—in which I showed how bad marriage was for women. It had shocked me to discover it myself. I wrote also that in New York at a professional meeting "some of the Radical Women co-opted me and pressed me into some leadership work for them which I vastly enjoyed."

Although the letters included snippets of news about my work from time to time the children themselves showed very little interest in all that writing. In its early stages, though they were co-authors, even this book did not especially engage them. They knew that I was having difficulties, that I could not stay with it for long periods of time, that I could not sustain the emotional effort involved, that I would develop signs of stress and have to put the work aside from time to time, that it proceeded only by spurts and starts, that it never became easy or matter-of-fact. They were sympathetic; they warned me to take care. But it was not until they read the manuscript themselves that they could understand how painful putting this book together had been. For, like the television program of that name some years ago, this was our lives.

chapter fifteen

reprise

I have just finished reading this book for the first time. The original letters on which it is based came to me one by one over a period of time, and thus lost much of their total impact. Only now that I have read them all together in, so to speak, one sitting, am I able to see—I think, for I cannot be certain yet—what they add up to. Not until now have I achieved the distance needed to lend perspective on them. Not in all cases enough distance to ensure the tranquility for recollecting emotion that leads to wisdom as well as poetry, but enough to respond with some objectivity.

Since analyzing data and making sense out of them are the core tasks of my profession, the job of dealing with the letters should have been easy, if not simple. I should have been able to approach them as a cache of data and proceeded to apply the tools of my trade to them. Actually, I could not. It took me a long time just to brace myself even to tackle the job of assembling them, of ordering them, and then, hardest of all, of rereading them. I found I could not stay with the task for long periods of time. I could not sustain the emotional effort involved. I would develop symptoms of stress and have to put the work aside.

It proceeded therefore only by spurts and starts. There were many events that both my co-authors and I preferred not to relive. The years had not wholly expunged the original emotions embedded in many of them. At least the emotions were still subject to recall, to reliving. Some of the letters could still grieve me, even draw tears. This book proved to be the hardest I had ever worked on.

One of the first decisions had to do with format. My original preference was for one that presented the letters intact, with a minimum of editing, as simply a set of self-explanatory documents on "dyadic relationships," a format which Leon Edel has called "woodpile" biography. Even though the "life stuff" in such documents was fascinating, the result could be dull, for there was "usually no integration, no analysis, no style, no insight—simple fact piled upon fact like so many logs, with each reader obliged in the end to write the biography for himself."[1] A chore few are willing to do. The author had to do the work; it could not be put on to the reader. If piles of facts were enough archives alone would be sufficient.

Although I had some say about the format of the book, it seemed to me that the letters themselves would determine the substantive contents. Not so, for the integration, analysis, style, and insight Edel called for meant that I would have to be editor as well as co-author, a role I was reluctant to assume. If one could not simply pile fact on fact it meant one had to pick and choose. There was the rub. There was the chance of bias. Two editors working on the same material could produce two different final products. The same fact in two different contexts could be two different facts. Omissions could emphasize as surely as inclusions. Ellipses could be suspicious. So what criteria to use in the selection?

What, for example, was the most appropriate balance between the children's letters and mine? Since I had written to all of them more than they had written to me or to one another, there were many more letters from me than from them.[2] However, I did not want my co-authors to be

mere "straight men," serving only to give me cues to do
my thing. On the other hand, I was told, "people will read
this book because it is about you, not because it is about
your children."[3] I was advised to include only the letters
that dealt with their relations with me. Many of the letters
would seem, even I could see, frankly boring to outsiders.
How often, after all, can any reader find a child's reports
on school activities interesting? What can a child say about
anything, in fact, that is interesting to nonparents? School
chores? Which team won? Merits and demerits? Who except me would care about a sixteen-year-old's reaction to
Picasso in El Prado? Any more, of course, than, on my side,
about a mother's nagging about money or her homilies?
There would, obviously, have to be some weeding out of
my letters, as well as of theirs.

Still, I was not willing, either as co-author or as editor, to
prune too closely. When one reviewer referred to Plath's
letters to her mother as "tiresome,"[4] I asked myself as
editor if avoiding the "tiresome" was a valid criterion to
use in selection? Can anyone legitimately expect *all* letters
or even most—especially to one's family—to be bright,
vivacious, entertaining, amusing, or profound? True, if one
were not selective enough, the result would be worse than
tiresome. In fact, many of my own, let alone the children's,
were repetitive, symbolic tokens to reassure the recipients
that we were thinking about them but containing no real
news, no message, sent only because we knew they would
want to touch base from time to time. In the end I decided
to lean in the direction of retaining too many letters rather
than run the risk of discarding too many. For if I were too
selective I could well be charged with bias, even censorship.
What did all those ellipses mean? What was being left out?

The ellipses did present problems. For the old cliché—
that context can completely change meaning—kept demonstrating its validity throughout. A harsh rebuke embedded
in a long, tender, loving letter sounded far gentler in that
assuaging context than it did standing starkly, alone, un-
qualified, unmodified. Although not all the letters were,

then, included nor all parts of those that were included, those that were selected appear as they were written.

Whatever the criteria—deliberate or unwitting—none of us were pleased with the way we came through to the reader. We did not recognize ourselves. The images we had of ourselves, built on our own memories, did not tally with the image projected by the authors who wrote the letters. I was, in fact, somewhat shaken by the harsh woman who could lower such a heavy boom. I was dismayed at the mixed signals I beamed at the children, insisting, for example, that grades were not all that important yet making clear that they were, or lecturing endlessly about the importance of being careful about money yet denying them nothing.

Interpretation of the included letters raised problems no less perplexing than did selection itself. As both editor and as co-author I was aware of the hazards involved. The behavior of a woman who voluntarily exposed her selected though uncensored and unexpurgated record as a mother could be interpreted as either bragging or apologizing according to the reader's judgment of her performance. Her record could be viewed as a "what-did-I-do-wrong?" appeal for exculpation or as a "hey-look-how-great-a-job-I-did!" boast. Both exposed her children as well. They were either victims or vindications. A book about oneself could hardly avoid being an *apologia pro vita sua,* and all the *mea culpas* could not erase the implicit plea for the approval they asked for.

I found myself defending myself as co-author to myself as editor. I found myself as co-author, for example, explaining to myself as editor that although Claude may have been right in saying I had become incapable of viewing anything—even my family—from any but a sociological perspective, still it never assuaged the pain to be able to explain it. A "sociological" fact could hurt as much as any other. To see our family as one detail in a large panorama did not dematerialize it or make it any less dear to me. The fact that I had had a sociological concept or category or theory to apply to anything from the simplest family gathering to the most serious family crisis did not seem to me to depersonalize any of it.

As editor I could understand how depersonalizing all those homilies, all those analyses, all the sociologizing may well have seemed to the children. I could understand how the rational mother who took Dorothy Lee's anguish apart in the agonizing spring of 1963 and analyzed it point by point may well have seemed to her to be reducing everything to cold rationality, to be erasing rather than realizing it, to be reducing it, to be making her disappear as a unique human being. Their pains, their hurts, their frustrations were *theirs*. Mine, Dorothy Lee's! Mine, Claude's! Mine, David's! Not "dyadic relationships," not "generation gap," not "sibling rivalry," not. . . . . Just me, my specific, particular, unique self. As editor, I could well see how I must have seemed to be a person of "statistical rules and operations," too old to "examine things on a nonprofessional basis," as Claude had written to Dorothy Lee, too old to be flexible.[5] In neither role—editor or co-author—did I approve. But neither could I interpret it away.

Misgivings waxed as the work got under way. Was this, in spite of my editorial scruples, turning into an apologia? What chance, after all, did a child have against an articulate woman whose profession was writing? I had chosen the medium—the written word—which had added to my advantage as co-author. Further, as editor I had selected the letters. This privilege alone almost automatically tipped the scales in my favor.[6] In addition, as editor I was commenting also, I was interpreting, I was explaining.

There were other caveats. It had been Gordon Allport's obiter dictum that had legitimized the use of the letters for studying the parent-child "dyadic relationship," and as editor I took seriously his warning about "both the artificialities of letter-writing and the effects of distance between writer and recipient."[7] I recognized that the medium itself raised questions; it had an important influence on the message. The relationships mirrored in letters did not truly reflect the total relationships themselves. There was time for pondering before replying. The angry riposte had less chance to explode. (In fact, however, I knew that we had not always availed ourselves of the opportunity to reflect, as when Dorothy Lee became so angry at one of my letters that she returned it, in effect shouting that she never wanted to see it again! Or when David replied hotly to overkill in one of my letters that this was the most obscene letter he had ever seen.) The daily family hassles of parents and children living together were not recorded in the letters. The tears, the hard jaw set are not there; but neither is the tender eye-exchange. The letters left out the walks in the woods, too, and the family reading sessions, the cooking and baking together. These, too, were the essence of family life.

It is a cliché that no two children, even brothers and sisters, are born into the same family. Nor do all children in the same family have the same mother. I was startled to see how different Dorothy Lee's family was from Claude's, and especially from David's; to contrast the ecstatic paeans of joy in the letters to Dorothy Lee before she was born with the desperation preceding David's birth nine years later. Dorothy Lee had a different mother from the boys'. I could understand her bad times, she shared them with me. The boys hid their bad times from me.

Not until the letters had become a book did I see that quite aside from the view of the family itself, they gave a perspective to the times in which they were written. Like the grain of sand William Blake could see a whole world in, if not the wild flower he saw a heaven in. They reflected many of the forces operating in the world in the middle of the twentieth century, forces which found their ultimate impact on families not too different from our own. War and the alarums of war, desegregation, abortion, unprecedented mobility, protest, drugs, changing relations between the sexes, counterculture—all were in the letters.

I had once, in a playfully macabre moment, called

Dorothy Lee my Pearl Harbor baby, Claude my Hiroshima baby, and David my Korean War baby. Macabre the comment certainly was. But it indicated the persistence of the war motif as a backdrop to our lives. For war and the fear of war did, in fact, run like a red thread through the letters. I was surprised to find how much they had intruded in our lives.

Among my papers there is a document signed by President Truman thanking me for my help during World War II in monitoring price controls. War, at that time, however deplorable, had been respectable. Not, as after Hiroshima, utterly intolerable. Even before the escalation of the Vietnam War, I was beginning to "strike for peace." On November 1, 1961, for example, I had written to Dorothy Lee in London that I had "marched with other women in a Women Strike for Peace demonstration—a sort of ban-the-bomb by mothers." About 700 of us had marched from the Washington Monument to the White House. I had volunteered my services locally to the Peace Corps one day a week. Writing to Claude in 1961 about the work camp planned for the next summer in Germany, I had expressed enthusiasm for the idea and added in parentheses, "provided there is a Europe left by that time." Later I was to buck the military bureaucracy in behalf of his assignment to peace work as a conscientious objector, and accommodate the wall-to-wall sleeping bags of the activists he brought home for demonstrations. My 1961 letters to Dorothy Lee in London were filled with references to the possibility of war: "Do people seem afraid of war in Paris?" "We are extremely worried about the possibilities of war in the United States." "I hope you are safe." "I wish Kennedy would come out with a statement that we are not going to resume atmospheric tests; that would restore the moral initiative to us and—I believe—confound if not shame the Russians; it would be a great moral gesture and I think I will send the president a telegram to this effect." "What I am about to say may strike you as almost hysterical and perhaps it is: I am thinking very

seriously of sending all of you to Australia in the spring;
that is when a lot of the atomic debris from the Russian
tests is due to fall in rain and snow in the northern hemisphere. I may begin to stockpile powdered milk. We are
told that by spring milk will be full of strontium 90. What
a world!" Dorothy Lee kept any anxieties she may have
felt to herself and doggedly tried to allay mine. She had
talked to people there about war and they were much
more relaxed and optimistic than Americans seemed to be.
Referring to her anticipated trip to the USSR, she responded with characteristic humor that there was no
reason to worry about her, for they had all "decided that a
detention camp in Outer Siberia will be the safest place in
case of war."

My first glimpse of the drug culture came by way of
news snippets from the children. I had never feared alcohol.
My grandmother had made wine every year and as a child
I had accompanied my father to the basement in the evening to tap the barrel for the dinner table. He himself had
taken a jigger of whiskey neat before dinner until the
doctor forbade it. But the other drugs were frightening,
including even the pills students were beginning to use to
keep awake all night to study—the uppers and the downers.
All—"hard" and "soft"—equally frightening to parents.
Easier for me to accept were the demise of the very idea
of chaperonage, the freedom between young men and
women, the rise of cohabitation among college students,
the incredible mobility of all young people.

The book was also about another trend characteristic
of the middle of the twentieth century, the growing number of employed mothers, a trend that had generated an
almost endless literature of its own on the problems of
integrating the two roles. In the early stages of work on
the letters I read some of them to a group of young
professional women. The reception was less than enthusiastic. The only favorable response—wasn't I brave to
expose myself like that?—was tangentially and tepidly
favorable. I had violated the canon that kept public and

private persona separate, inviolate. This glimpse of the "underside" of my life was not welcome. How could they reconcile their image of me as a benign "mistress of mentors," as I had once been introduced, with the mother in the letters? This was hardly the life of a professional role model.[8] I think they would have preferred to think of me as floating freely in some Empyrean realm, following the male model—described once by de Gaulle as one of aloofness, of something hidden or withheld, of mystery.

I understood. There is no way a woman can come through a day-by-day account of her relations with her children as a heroine. Still, to reveal clay feet is a well-recognized social function. At a moment in time when the integration of the lives of women is a major concern it seemed to me worthwhile to show how one woman wrestled with it. The role model with all the blemishes removed can prove depressing, counter-productive.[9]

More threatening was the caveat from my more experienced and cautious professional *consoeurs.* "Don't do it," one of them said. "There are pieces in the manuscript that may become little classics and be endlessly anthologized," she began, softening me up for the blow to follow. "But it won't do you a bit of good. It will denigrate your status. No one will ever take you seriously again. You will be known not for your insights but as a mother engulfed in banalities." I was not unmoved. Still, I did not wish to be viewed as different from what I was or had been. If clay feet detracted from my work, they should nevertheless be seen.

In the preface I referred to the Twelve Women whose success stories had so appealed to me, and throughout the book I have from time to time called attention to their experiences when they matched, corresponded to, or conflicted with mine. Arlie Hochschild, who participated in the conference where the Twelve Women gave their stories, has made a perceptive analysis of them which is relevant here. She calls our attention to the alienation from the "female culture" they displayed. She describes and illustrates what she calls the "de-feminization" successful women are often subjected to not only by men but also by other—including other successful—women who practice "de-feminization" on themselves. Arlie Hochschild believes, and I concur, that the consequences of such "de-feminization" are harmful. I believe with her that "to buck the pressures to disaffiliate from other women would be . . . the crowning achievement [of successful women], even ironically, the real sign of arrival."[10] I do not believe that a woman must belie the "female culture" of home and family in order to validate her professional identity or pay for one identity by denying the other.

Not all the reactions were negative. Many who read, heard, or heard about the letters were intrigued. They were reminded of family letters of their own in drawers, from which they had learned about their parents' youth or about uncles or grandparents. Or they remarked regretfully that they had not kept letters. They were reminded of their own relations with their mothers or daughters or sisters or brothers. Suddenly they were embedded in a warmly remembered family matrix. They talked excitedly about their own memories. Formal, well-defended professionals melted into daughters and sons, sisters and brothers. The talk swung into a different orbit. They seemed to resonate with the story in the letters but they talked about their own stories. They were on the same wave length. Nothing in the letters seemed strange or unusual to them. They had been there too.

notes

PREFACE

1. See, for example, any current edition of *Who's Who of American Women.*

2. Gwendolyn Safier, *Jessie Bernard: Sociologist.* University of Kansas, 1972.

3. I share with my professional colleagues the frustration over the inadequacies of our vocabulary. There is no adequate term to refer to adult sons and daughters. "Offspring" is not the answer. So, with apologies to all adults with living parents, I resort to the common but inadequate usage, children.

4. In my own discipline, working with such "soft data" does not have the prestige of working with "hard"—read quantitative—data. My own professional training had been primarily in the quantitative tradition.

5. Gerald Clair Wheeler, ed., *Letters to Mother* (Allen & Unwin, 1933), p. 20.

6. Ibid., p. 20.

7. Eva. B. Connor, ed., *Letters to Children* (Macmillan, 1938), pp. 12–13.

8. Ibid., pp. 36–37.

9. Ibid., p. 48.

10. Ibid., pp. 80–81.

11. Ibid., p. 120.

12. Ibid., pp. 138, 140.

13. Ibid., pp. 181, 182. "Mother Clara" had a career as concert

pianist that took her away from her seven children a good deal of the time, as my own did also and, like me, a considerable amount of her mothering was done "by the constant interchange of letters."

14. When I left academia in 1964 it had been assumed that I had retired and I had been urged to write a biography of my husband, including my own autobiography as part of it. I think in some cases a sentimental tale of a working husband-wife team was the idea people had in mind. (A reviewer of one of our joint books had compared it—unfavorably—with the work of Sidney and Beatrice Webb.) Or, perhaps, in the minds of others, an amusing memoir of "great sociologists I have known."

15. When, and only when, it has seemed to me essential for understanding the letters, I have made minor changes in spelling and punctuation. In a few instances, names of people beyond my immediate family have been changed to preserve their privacy.

BEFORE THE LETTERS BEGAN: A FAMILY ALBUM

1. This part of Europe was sometimes under Austrian hegemony, sometimes Russian, sometimes Rumanian. In the time of my children's great-grandparents, Rumanian.

2. As distinguished from the Texas Bernards. Authentic records trace the family back to Peter Bernard, a Hugenot who came to America about 1790 and settled in Virginia. His son married Mary Abney, thus "plugging into" one of the most famous and widely ramifying European families and thus relating them to royalty of all kinds (Ted Bernard, *Bernard "Grandparents" Back to 300 B.C.*, McKinney, Texas, 1977).

3. While I was carrying my first child I wrote letters to—as it turned out—her. In one dated May 16, 1941, nine weeks before she was expected, I wrote: ". . . We have already reconciled ourselves to the fact that you will sooner or later feel ashamed because your parents are old as compared with the parents of your friends and playmates. But there are two sides to that shield. If your parents are old they will not put obstacles in your path when you grow up. A too wide margin of overlapping of the generations may mean a lot of conflict and strain. When children grow up parents have usually served their purpose. There is little more they can do. Whatever contribution I can make to your life I will make while you are young and immature. If I am gone in your maturity there is something to be said for that too." At this point I caught myself and added in parentheses, "it occurs to me how morbid it is for a woman to tell her unborn child such a thing as this!" The children's father did not

live long enough to become ashamed of, and they have all been too kind to express such a sentiment if, indeed, they ever felt it.

4. When my mother completed whatever schooling she was to have—eighth grade, I believe—she became a worker in the garment industry in New York. Her mother allowed her to march in suffrage parades but never to take part in a strike.

5. Of her I once wrote: "My grandmother, a cheerful, industrious, pious soul who had a blessing or a prayer for every event in the day, was the real mistress of our household, and we children recognized her as such. It was to her we applied for permission to do this or that; it was to her we came for moral guidance: was this a sin? or that a blessing? And it was she who disciplined us. She helped with the housework and did the cooking. And it was she who set the Jewish stamp upon our house. She said a prayer as she washed her face and hands in the morning. She said a prayer before and after every meal. She sent us off to school with a blessing and received us back with a blessing when we returned. There was a blessing when we wore new clothes for the first time. She had a prayer or a blessing for almost everything in fact. We children took it as a matter of course that she would be muttering prayers and blessings over us all the time. She was a much more important person than our mother" (Jessie Bernard, "Biculturality: A Study of Social Schizophrenia." in Steuart Henderson Britt and Isacque Graeber, eds., *Jews in a Gentile World*, (Macmillan, 1942), pp. 277–278). Almost as important as God himself. Obviously His wife. She died when I was fourteen.

6. Even their father was dim, except for Dorothy Lee. Visiting a friend in the South when she was seventeen she wrote of him, "I think Daddy was quite southern in many ways though I didn't know him well enough to judge. . . . The farming country reminds me very much of what I can remember of Daddy's family in Kentucky. It's very charming and all that, but I know I couldn't live here. I'm a Yankee girl in spite of it all. . . . I'm not as interested in who my ancestors were . . . as I am in what I'll be and in what I can do."

7. My sister Clara was a strong, courageous, vastly creative child. The world was her oyster. It was she who brought the outside world into our home, who enforced in our household the school's dicta as promulgated by her teachers. Here is how I once described her: "She brought home from school all sorts of new-fangled ideas. . . . She transformed our eating habits, and even our dietary. . . . She also brought home from school strict rules about fresh air, which she went about administering in her customary thorough-going manner. We must have fresh air, and so, though my father protested that we could not heat the whole outdoors, every night she threw open our windows to the bitter Minnesota winters and if there was snow on our bed, we brushed it off and clambered in. . . . If . . . the school

ordered fresh air, she would see to it that we got it." She performed thoroughly and in a workmanlike fashion the traditional role of the first generation in "Americanization." The rest of us—my two brothers and I—were, in effect "second-and-a-half generation." In the half-consciousness between wakeness and sleep, I sometimes confuse my sister and my daughter.

8. I used to say playfully that I attended Harvard because so many of my professors—Pitirim Sorokin, Alvin Hanson, N. S. B. Gras, Karl Lashley—in their prime were teaching me and only later went to Harvard.

9. I resort to the use of the somewhat archaic word *thrall* because *charm, magnetism, enchantment* have become trivialized and no longer evoke the compulsive nature of the relationship. Many years later I described it in more pedestrian terms to Dorothy Lee. In reply to a letter in which she had said, longing for guidance herself, "I think I can understand what someone like Daddy could be for you," I had written: "You sound exactly like me at your age. . . . When I fell in love with your father no one could understand it; everything was against the relationship—age, religious faith, background, etc. But he had exactly the sort of thing you look for in a man—intellectual interests, a sense of humor, understanding, appreciation, and above all, he was vastly my superior. . . . He was the sort of lover and companion that any intellectually inclined girl could want."

10. When I first began working with him he was researching a book which appeared in 1925 as *Instinct: A study in Social Psychology*.

11. Our trip soon after marriage to Buenos Aires—where he was to do work in the university library—was monitored by Interpol on behalf of my family who could only see it as an abduction.

12. Gwendolyn Styrvoky Safier, *Jessie Bernard: Sociologist*. University of Kansas Ph.D., 1972. (Ann Arbor, Mich.: University Microfilms).

13. There was no specification with respect to the number of children. Two was perhaps the taken-for-granted number.

14. The children's father survived the birth of the first child by only nine and a half years, leaving their rearing to me alone.

15. In my letters there seems to have been no bias in favor of either sex. In one of the first, I wrote, "to me the only answer a woman can make to the destructive forces of the world is creation." But the one prenatal letter from LLB was addressed to "My dear Son." And I was well enough aware of the odds to discuss circumcision: "We have had long discussions about you. . . . We agree thoroughly on practically every point. . . . We have decided against circumcision if you are a male-child."

16. When late in the spring I playfully complained to my obste-

trician, a German scientist of the old school, that nine months was too long, he raised his eyebrows in horror: "Madame," he said sternly and rebukingly, "about that I can do nothing."

AUTOBIOGRAPHICAL INTRODUCTION: PART I

1. Egan Schwartz, "An Autobiographical Approach to Literature," *Washington University Magazine*, Spring 1976, p. 33.

2. Still, however, not quite. Only quasi-solo motherhood. For just as during the first two and a half years after the death of the children's other parent Ezra had served as his surrogate, so this year Ralph Lewis did so. Ralph was the cultural officer of the United States Information Office in charge of the local Amerika Haus. He assumed a considerable amount of responsibility for the boys—Dorothy Lee was in school in Geneva—both when I was in Graz and when I was off on trips. He opened his well-equipped modern apartment to us, cooked American style for us, let us use all the hot water we needed for our baths, took us on picnics, and country outings. It was he who hurried David to the hospital in May after an accident while I was off in Scandinavia. I leaned on him as I had on Ezra and appreciated his support as I had appreciated Ezra's. It made the psychological work easier.

CHAPTER ONE: REPORT FROM GRAZ TO GENEVA

1. We had found the Benndorf's through the good offices of Dr. Johann Mokre, a professor at the University of Graz. I had known him when he was teaching at St. Louis University some years earlier. At that time he had invited us to visit his city, a prospect that then seemed remote.

2. For an account of the sibling rivalry between Dorothy Lee and Claude see the autobiographical introduction to Part Two.

3. Olga was Dorothy Lee's roommate at school. She was the daughter of a French diplomat and a Russian noblewoman who modeled Schiaparelli clothes at the opera in Paris, at the races, and wherever else the European haut monde gathered. Several years later she and her sister visited us and there was some vague talk of her spending a year in this country.

4. I was on the research committee of the International Sociological Association that year.

5. I never had nostalgic memories of the year in Graz. The boys, however, did. Thirteen years after our year there, in 1967, Claude reported his recherche du temps perdu: "Graz is completely changed.

The ruins are gone, replaced by new skyscrapers in the European fashion. The streets all look different, and it was as if I had never been in downtown Graz. The suburb where we lived has changed too, but not nearly as much as the rest of the town. We took the same trolley line out to the same stops. First we went to the church, Maria Troste, which still dominates the area. Then on to the stop that led up to the hill where we lived. The general store where I used to get my candy and notebooks had been changed, with new management. There were new houses and apartment buildings all around. But the old farm was still there with the same old farmer. The old Benndorf house is . . . just as it was thirteen years ago. To see if the Benndorfs were still living there I went up and rang. An old lady answered and I asked if the Benndorfs were still living and explained who I was. No recognition. Then all of a sudden she was Tante Frieda. Bernhard had just left for Vienna. We had a nice talk about old times and new. You might just write a letter to them. . . . All in all it was quite nice. . . ." Two years later David was also thinking of revisiting Graz. To refresh his memories I wrote to him at Innsbruck: "Would you recognize the house if you saw it? I believe the same little tram still runs out toward Maria Troste (I believe) church. Claude could tell you more because he was there two years ago. I hope Tante Frieda is still there. She is the grandmother and she hoped to go to the moon some day. When she used to talk like that I used to be patronizing. She was way ahead of me. If she is alive remind her of her talk about the moon and give her my regards." David never quite made it back to Graz and did not seem to want to especially.

CHAPTER TWO: HARD ISSUES, SOFT ANSWERS

1. In the early '50s, Pennsylvania State University had built one of the great first generation computers and the president, an engineer, was urging all of us to visit "Pennstac" and learn how to use it. It occupied a good part of the basement of one of the engineering buildings and the men in charge of it were inordinately proud of it, with the kind of emotional involvement not usually associated with the engineering mentality. I could sense immediately that I was in the presence of at least one wave of the future. Although I never personally came to terms with the computer I rode the IBM wave with considerable monetary reward. When I saw *Think* signs in even the backwaters of Europe during my sabbatical in 1953-1954, I knew IBM and its computer were going places. It was more than the Penn State engineers' delight. I sold the small portfolio I had received at my husband's death, purchased IBM shares and rode the

crest through the '50s, disposing of them only when I left academia and needed to replace a regular salary with regular dividends.

2. Stella Lightner was one of a small army of women who came from the surrounding valleys to work in town. She came to us—herself recently widowed in her middle fifties—soon after I began my solo motherhood and remained with us until we moved to Washington. I still feel gratitude for the enormous help she provided.

3. My own religious background is described in Isacque Graeber and Steuart Henderson Britt, eds., *Jews in a Gentile World* (New York: Macmillan, 1942), pp. 264–293.

CHAPTER THREE: ODYSSEY

1. Walter Clemons, in review of Morris Dickstein, *Gates of Eden: American Culture in the '60s,* in *Newsweek,* March 28, 1977.

2. Erik Erikson, *Identity, Youth and Crisis* (Norton, 1968), p. 265: "The stage of life crucial for the emergence of an integrated female identity is the step from youth to maturity, the stage when the young woman, whatever her work career, relinquishes the care received from the parental family in order to commit herself to the love of a stranger and to the care to be given to his and her offspring."

3. Student quoted by Jessica Mitford Freuhaft, "The Indignant Generation," *The Nation,* May 27, 1961, p. 455.

4. Karel Van Wolferen, *Student Revolutionaries of the Sixties* (The Hague: Interdoc, n.d.), p. 31.

5. Betty Friedan, *The Feminine Mystique* (Norton, 1963).

6. Jessie Bernard, *Academic Women* (Pennsylvania State University Press, 1964), p. 67.

7. Hannah Gavron, *The Captive Wife: Conflicts of Housebound Mothers* (London: Routledge and Kegan Paul, 1966), p. 140.

8. Ibid., p. 140.

9. Esther Rauschenbush, "We Start Chapter Three," a talk given April 21, 1960.

10. Many years later when I asked Dorothy Lee if she had had sexual relations with her driver in Morocco she replied no, she had used the Scheherazade technique on him, charming him with conversation which seemed to satisfy him. A southern belle once noted that one reason her generation had been such fluent talkers was that they had also become proficient in the Scheherazade technique. By December, I must add, two of Dorothy Lee's friends had secured contraceptive pills from the National Health Service in London.

11. Sally Kempton, "Cutting Loose: A Private View of the Wo-

men's Uprising," in Roger J. Porter and H. J. Wolf, eds., *The Voice Within* (Knopf, 1971), pp. 117–118.

12. Sylvia Plath, *Letters Home,* edited by Aurelio Schober Plath (Harper & Row, 1975), p. 496.

13. Edward Butscher expresses the opinion that Plath's dependence on her mother led her to repress any negative feelings she may have had for fear of losing her mother's love (*Method and Madness,* Seabury Press, 1976), p. 13.

14. Shirley S. Angrist and Elizabeth M. Almquist, *Careers and Contingencies* (Dunellen, 1975), p. 40.

15. Plath, *Letters Home,* p. 40.

16. Jane Alpert, "Mother Right: A New Feminist Theory," *Ms.,* August 1973, pp. 52 ff.

17. Lucinda Franks and Thomas Powers, "The Destruction of Diana," *Reader's Digest,* November 1970, pp. 49–58. Diana Oughton made a powerful impression on me. When I once commented to Dorothy Lee that it had, from time to time, crossed my mind that there but for the grace of God she might have walked, she replied, no way. Diana's causes had been Voluntary International Service assignments sponsored by the American Friends' Service Committee. She had been assigned to Guatemala, working in a small village. A Fulbright scholar she met had led her to doubt the value of her reading program there and she had returned to the United States. In Philadelphia she worked in an adult literacy program. In Ann Arbor she met Bill Ayres, who exerted a powerful influence on her. They became extremists in the SDS. Frequently criticized because of her wealthy background, she struggled hard to find her place in the movement and she did, in time, become a leader in her own right. She felt "like part of a vanguard, that we speak of important change to come" (p. 54). She was to be blown to bits in an explosion while making bombs.

18. Some of the young women came in time to free themselves from the oppression of the man and become the nucleus of the women's liberation movement. They achieved their cause independent of men. Some never did. But that is another story.

19. One evening visiting a friend's family near the American Embassy, she and Joan noticed that there was no anti-bomb-testing picket line at the embassy as the plans had called for. At once they went to the police officer to ask where the pickets' signs were. The officer cheerfully turned the signs over to them and they carried on.

20. Not that other activities were curtailed. "I've been going to the Student Union meeting for special action protests against Algeria." She was asked to "canvass for two people running for office at school. They seem to think I can influence the 'American vote'." She felt she had to make a gesture at least.

21. The preoccupation with class among her London friends had never ceased to puzzle Dorothy Lee.

CHAPTER FOUR: A LOSING BATTLE

1. I also read Lawrence Linton's *The Holy Barbarians,* I wrote Dorothy Lee, early in December. It was "a description of the beat pattern of life, especially in Venice, California." Had she seen it?
2. When I was an undergraduate I had been courted by a young reporter. My parents were puzzled. What did a reporter *do* when he grew up? I was courted by an economist. What *was* an economist? and what did he *do*? I was courted by a medical student. That they understood. They knew what doctors did. And by a businessman which, of course, they also understood quite well. I found myself in a similar state of ignorance about some of the young men in Dorothy Lee's life. They did such things as organize ban-the-bomb marches, perform country, western, or blue-grass music, or organize jug bands.
3. My own parents had tried desperately to save me from my own marriage.

AUTOBIOGRAPHICAL INTRODUCTION: PART II

1. The specific details are blurred in my mind. I think it must have been Bruno Bettelheim's "Individualism and Mass Behavior in Extreme Situations," *Journal of Abnormal and Social Psychology,* 38, 1943, reproduced later in *The Informed Heart* (Free Press, 1960).
2. The process of my thinking in those years can be traced in a series of articles published between 1947 and 1950 in which I began to formulate my disillusionment with the social-salvation-through-science creed.
3. For an account of the situation as it related to David, see letter to him on page 251.

CHAPTER SIX: HARD ISSUES, HARD ANSWERS

1. Warren Farrell, *The Liberated Man* (Random House, 1974); Joseph Pleck and Jack Sawyer, eds., *Men and Masculinity* (Prentice-Hall, 1974); Deborah S. David and Robert Brannon, eds., *The Forty-nine Percent Majority: The Male Sex Role* (Addison-Wesley, 1976);

Myron Brenton, *The American Male* (Coward-McCann, 1966). In process: Donald P. Sabo, *Sports and Masculinity*, a "jock" anthology.

2. At twenty-one Claude was still serving as social escort to me: "Next week I go to a conference here . . . and Claude will be my escort at the complementary banquet. It ought to be sort of fun." (to David in Barcelona).

3. Dorothy Lee notes that I had apparently learned from my experience with her. Claude, like her, would in time come to love the school. The first child, she reminded me, trains the parents.

4. The "all this" referred to my last letter to Claude three days earlier, July 27, 1967, in which I had unburdened myself of the anxiety I was experiencing over Dorothy Lee's situation: "I sent DL a check for her birthday and a funny card with graffiti on it including one about something or other that 'Jessie' did, hoping to amuse her. She has not acknowledged either the gift or the card and did not call me on her birthday, last Sunday. I hate to call her if there is any reason why she doesn't call me . . . I can't deny that I am greatly concerned. . . . I know that she hates being dependent on me in any way, shape, or form and I certainly do not want her to be. It is a very sensitive situation. I hope David keeps in touch with her."

5. Perhaps my insistence on autonomy and reluctance to impose my own ambitions on Claude were related to memories of my own older brother who, when confined to bed with a raging fever, nevertheless insisted that he must, absolutely must, deliver his newspapers. It was his obligation—his reponsibility. It was only with great force that he could be restrained. Some "give" in the pressures he was under might have saved him years of traumas. A *Wanderjahr* or two might have given him a chance to find himself. He was not to be allowed to try his hand at newspaper work. He was, instead, to plow his way through medical school. Competent, efficient, but never truly happy in his work.

CHAPTER SEVEN: TWO MAJOR DECISIONS

1. Midge Decter, *Liberal Parents, Radical Children* (Coward-McCann & Geoghagan, 1975), pp. 26–27.

2. Ibid., p. 27.

3. See Steuart Henderson Britt and Isacque Graeber, eds., *Jews in a Gentile World* (Macmillan, 1942), pp. 267–268 for a description of the kind of business ambience here referred to.

4. Decter, *Liberal Parents*, p. 27.

5. Years later I learned that he did write about love, if not girls, in his poetry.

AUTOBIOGRAPHICAL INTRODUCTION: PART III

1. David commented that he liked this paragraph very much.

CHAPTER EIGHT: FAMILY AND FRIENDS

1. When David was fourteen, living with a French family near Limoges, his pleasure in his status as an equal illuminated the down-putting effect of being dealt with so long as just a little brother: "I feel that this summer is the most important in my life. Here I am an independent person, part of a group who is supposed to help each other in their lessons and problems. Though since I am the youngest here by a year, some do treat me as a little brother. But instead of treating me as an inferior thing they help me, listen to my problems, etc. They have told me that when they first heard that I was only fourteen they didn't think I would last the summer. But here I am. I am not a hypochondriac for attention or silent and retiring. Otherwise I am trying to tell you I feel very adult and grown up here."

2. Robert Seidenberg, *Corporate Wives—Corporate Casualties?* (Anchor Books, 1975), p. 61.

3. The year in Graz was not a successful one from David's three-year-old-point of view. I have explained—to my guilt-ridden conscience—though not excused, the seeming rejection implied in my persistence that David attend kindergarten, explained it in terms of my own anguish doing the psychological work of accepting the finality of Ezra's decision not to become part of our family. But at the time David's resistance to kindergarten puzzled me. True, he was only three and perhaps too young; and, true, too, the long hours he was left there when I was in Spain were not right for him. Still, the school itself was a delightful, cheerful place and, for a country just pulling itself out of the aftermath of war, well equipped. It was only toward the end of the year that it occurred to me—reluctantly— that David's name may have been against him in that town. Frau Benndorf, who had suffered along with her husband for anti-Nazi views in the 1930s, once noted casually in passing that in that town anyone with the name of David would automatically be assumed to be Jewish. From the cache of Nazi magazines—especially a complete file of one called *Blut und Bod*—left in an attic closet just off of our room, I gathered that she knew whereof she spoke.

4. I had no idea what was going on in the world of high politics

and was amazed years later to hear charges about the Michigan State University project for helping Saigon organize its police force.

5. My first report to Dorothy Lee reflected my shock at the disarray the Washington schools were in: "The District schools are simply incredible. And now Congress has adjourned without passing enough appropriations, so the schools are going to get worse—short sixty classrooms next year, affecting 2,000 children." And my need for help in planning for David's schooling: "I am going to apply at three private schools for David, but none of them give me any encouragement. . . . David's talents—which, as you know, I consider exceptional—are not the kind that show on ordinary tests. I have thought seriously of the International School at Geneva, but he is too young to be so far from home, although, come to think of it, he probably wouldn't be much farther from here than you were from us in Austria when you were there. If you have any ideas or suggestions, they will be much appreciated."

CHAPTER NINE: LENGTHENING TETHER

1. When first in Washington David had undertaken a history of the city by studying the dates on sewer tops.

2. Project Camelot was a research project with which I was connected. It way my job to organize a conference of the best brains in the world on the subject of social systems—what held them together, what made them fall apart. It was, we would learn later, allegedly funded by the CIA though, of course, the scientific personnel had no knowledge of this at the time.

3. The image of me as a fearsome "ogre" implied by David's fear that I would be angry at him for sending a cable troubled me—as, later, did his surprise when Patty Hearst's parents stood by her in her travails. Did he, I wondered, think I would not?

CHAPTER TEN: WILL THE REAL DAVID PLEASE STAND UP?

1. See Note 1, Chapter Six, for relevant literature. I could have profited from these works a decade earlier.

2. Though challenged by Margaret Mead, who found no evidence for such crises in the South Seas where, however, few of us lived.

3. Not having researched this topic, I have no scientific data to support such a conclusion. I arrived at it on the basis of discussions with my friends whose sons or nephews were showing similar kinds of malaise.

4. To this day David, who was one of that cohort, finds assassina-

tion a major preoccupation that he cannot exorcise. "*Now* did I believe in a conspiracy?" he could ask as recently as the surfacing of wrongdoing by the CIA.

5. I was reminded of this comment when a guideline by HEW forbidding father-son banquets under Title 7 as discriminatory against girls aroused a great brouhaha and was immediately rescinded. Supporters of the guideline reminded hostile critics that not only all girls but also fatherless sons were discriminated against in such events—all told, not an inconsiderable proportion—14 percent—of all school-age children.

6. Many years after that shattering entry was made in his journal I learned that suicide had, in fact, actually been a recurring theme in his life. That even in Austria he had stood at the window debating whether or not to jump. I can well believe it but I cannot believe it a meaningful suicidal impulse in a three-year-old. I had myself as a child jumped from high barn windows at six or seven and children make outrageous jumps all the time. I do not believe that David at three knew the possible consequences of such a jump.

7. This was not the first such advance. At the age of eleven he had come home to tell me of a driver who had invited him to ride with him.

8. It may have been David's efforts to protect me by hiding his unhappiness that made me so insistent on reassurances that he really was happy. I undoubtedly got the latent message.

9. The next year he was looking forward to seeing me on Parents' Day.

10. Sally Quinn, "Old Pols, New Pols, The Generation Gap," *Washington Post,* June 5, 1976.

11. Joseph D. Whitaker, "Reasons Sought for Adolescent Suicide Increase," *Washington Post,* June 4, 1976.

12. Some years later, when he had learned of the search for an abortion, he found it hard to change the image of a father he had cherished so long. He was defensive of that man. "I am a bit confused that he would want it [the abortion] so much. The confusion is genuine." He was inclined to trace the search for an abortion to my own ambivalences, not to the father he so admired.

CHAPTER ELEVEN: GIRLS AND JOBS

1. As I wrote to David, the bride, Marilyn Bratton, wrote to me "such a glowing letter about you that I wonder which boy she is in love with, you or your 'brother'?"

2. It was in Vicki's matriarchal family—all extremely fond of David and he of them—that David became attracted to Judaism. With no educational background whatsoever he became strongly attached to the religious forms and thereafter fasted and meditated on Yom Kippur, though he had no formal affiliation.

3. In college, feelers were out to see if he would care to model for advertisements. In reply I wrote: "I casually mentioned to DL about posing in New York and she said all the men in that profession were homosexuals. She said she had told you that but that Claude had sort of undone the effect by saying that some were probably not. I also mentioned it to Catherine Chilman and she said exactly the same thing. I know you have been approached by homosexuals in the past so I suppose you are the kind of beautiful young man they are attracted to. Just another decision."

4. *Instinct, A Study in Social Psychology* by L. L. Bernard (Holt, 1924) was one of the great classics of the day when it was published.

5. David was also taking a field-work course in sociology, observing anti-war demonstrations. Of one, he wrote: "It was a little funny at one demonstration where there were only 8 protesters against the IRS. There were treasury agents, the protesters, the police, t.v. cameramen, and us three observers with our pads. No one could figure out what we were doing there and people would approach us as if we were either police or protesters."

CHAPTER TWELVE: WOMAN'S WORK

1. Art Buchwald, *Washington Post,* March 31, 1977.

2. Ruth B. Kundsin, ed., *Women & Success* (Morrow, 1974).

3. I lost thousands of dollars because of my reluctance to devote attention to money management. To Dorothy Lee, for example, I had written in connection with inefficient services by a stock broker: "I hate to hurt anyone's feelings, so lose money in the process."

4. See Chapter 4 above for the emotional setting for this letter.

5. Elise Boulding, "The Human Services Component of Non-market Productivity in Ten Colorado Households," paper prepared for Round Table, Reyaumont, France, 1977.

6. Ellen Goodman, "Naturally, It Was the Working Mother's Fault," *Washington Post,* December 20, 1976.

7. I became a psychological casualty when I was 18 years old. My father was driving—an enormous Nash—when we ran over a small boy. It was a shocking experience. Fortunately the boy was not seriously injured.

CHAPTER THIRTEEN: WHAT IS MOTHER DOING?

1. In *Academic Women* I referred to some of these forces, including increased tension between faculties and administrations; there was demand for more administrative functions as student bodies grew and curricula expanded; fundamental decisions in regard to maintenance, classroom scheduling, food services, parking, use of equipment, contractual provisions had serious repercussions on the academic program itself.

2. The identification of the individual with his or her work became increasingly clear when I left the university. Who in the world was I with no organizational affiliation? Conscientious chairpersons fidgeted in their introductions. How should they introduce me? Editors of anthologies wanted to know how they should identify me? At the inspired suggestion of a colleague, Dr. Fred Matson, I had been awarded the honorific title of Research Scholar Honoris Causa, a cut or two above Emerita. It proved a bit cumbersome. When asked to identify myself I say simply that I am a sociologist-at-large.

3. It also dealt with phenomena that were less amenable to the prestigious mathematical analyses so congenial to, let us say, the economists. My training and early work had been in the quantitative "denomination." I was gung-ho about measuring; both of my graduate dissertations had relied on it. But I am one who also professes faith in the humanistic or "soft" side of my discipline, a basically optimistic faith in human ability to deal with, if not "solve," the ineffable challenges every age poses. I never professed a belief in final solutions; I never professed a belief in the "discovery" of universal laws which, once we had found them, would lead to some ultimate utopia. Though I had learned about "original sin" from Jonathan Edwards, I had come to terms with it. It did not overshadow "original goodness." I saw both all around me all the time. Some sociologists have professed a hands-off faith; they were *not,* repeat, *not* do-gooders. Others have seen the justification for the discipline in terms of its ability to help deal with our human problems. I am one of them. I might add as an afterthought that my professions have not always been invited. In a letter to David I wrote: "I just got back last night from Dorothy Lee's where I had the best time ever in Cambridge. Her boss invited me to sit in on a committee meeting at the Joint Center and that was fun and though I was only a visitor I ended by telling them what to do and how to do it. They were very tolerant, though, and no one said Jessie go home."

4. About half of all medical research, we are told, for example,

is in the minds of the scientists doing it, not yet available in either journals or official reports, certainly not in textbooks.

5. I came in time to reject even nomination in my professional societies. In 1961 I told Dorothy Lee, "I have been given a rather serious assignment by the Society for the Study of Social Problems; I have repeatedly turned down nomination for presidency of this Society because I didn't want to do so much work. I accepted the vice-presidency because until now it has not required any work. Now all of a sudden they make the vice-president coordinator of all the committees, the most-work job of all." I later asked my professional association not to nominate me for the presidency.

6. The Twelve Women were more relaxed. Said one of them: "They [her children] have also been . . . saddled with a mother who could never be 'Room Mother,' who could not always attend the school Christmas Play, who never made cookies for the bake sale, but does any of this matter in the long run?" Ruth B. Kundsin, ed., *Woman and Success* (Morrow, 1974), p. 74.

7. Jessie Bernard, Helen E. Buchanan, and William M. Smith, Jr., *Dating, Mating, and Marriage: A Documentary Approach* (Cleveland: Howard Allen, 1958), pp. 350–351.

8. *Washington Post,* May 21, 1974.

9. The thought of marriage had crossed my mind. There had been several suitable possibilities and one might have succeeded if he had not been so timid. Only several years later did I learn of his interest from a mutual friend, but by that time the children were older and the idea of marriage no longer appealed to me. I wrote to one prospect to explain—as much to myself as to him—why I could not marry him, but I never sent the letter. Rereading it later, I destroyed it. It spelled out in detail how jealous I was of my time and how demanding my work was. I could say things to a grown man that I could not to my children. I reproduce the letter from memory; the accuracy of the thought, if not of the wording, I can vouch for:

I think I owe you an explanation of the reason I declined your proposal. I would not want to hurt you. I would give the same answer to anyone who made the same proposal. You are asking for my life. At least for large parts of it. You would want time that I would prefer to use other ways. You would want companionship that would involve effort on my part. I would prefer to expend my time other ways. You would want me to spend a lot of time listening to you, building you up, sharing your doubts, anxieties, uncertainties. I do not fault you for this. It is a right husbands are accorded and which most women are happy to grant. A certain amount of this I could gladly offer. But my own life is so interesting, so exciting, so stimulating that I would resent having to give much of it up.

CHAPTER FOURTEEN: THE OTHER CHILD

1. I wrote my first novel in the first grade. I was first "published" in elementary school. The *Minneapolis Journal* ran a weekly "Journal Junior" for schoolchildren, the two best contributions winning a picture for their school. Two of my pieces won pictures for the Horace Mann School and were carried from room to room by my best friend, Mona Emslie, and me to receive the proper kudos.

2. Anne Morrow Lindberg, *Locked Rooms and Open Doors* (Harcourt Brace Jovanovich, 1974).

3. Fortunately, publishing was no more serious a problem for me than writing. One of my former graduate professors, F. S. Chapin, was editor of a series for Harper's and he was delighted to sponsor my first book. Later I was taken under the wing of Stanley Burnshaw, a Renaissance man of publishing himself—poet and businessman—then making quite a splash in the publishing world with his Dryden Press. At Ezra's suggestion he invited me to submit *American Community Behavior,* a rather unconventional book which I doubt if more timid publishers would have accepted. Stanley Burnshaw liked it. Later he asked for the book on remarriage and on social problems before he sold his firm to Holt, Rinehart and Winston. A book on the sociology of community was also a solicited book, as were *The Future of Marriage* and *The Future of Motherhood.*

4. One of the Twelve Women suffered a breakdown when her need to pursue her career conflicted with the ideals her father had insisted on for her.

5. As was the work of the Twelve Women. "I had a need . . . for fulfillment"; "I love my work intensely; I really work for love"; "I do research and management for fun."

6. I raced against budgets also. My frugality was another kind of race. If I allowed myself $100 I tried to do with $99. I might lose or give away the edge I gained but that was beside the point. I had tried to better my plan.

7. I never succeeded in keeping a notebook on my person as, reportedly, Emerson did. I was, however, always recommending to my students that they should.

8. My style of writing contrasted with LLB's. He could make an outline, sit down, follow it, and produce a finished paper. He, in brief, imposed an outline on his ideas. I discovered the outline in mine. C. H. Cooley, a distinguished sociologist, and LLB once had some correspondence on this interesting difference. Herbert Spencer was an outline man; Cooley was suspicious of this approach. Apparently his style, like mine, was the "discovered outline" kind rather than the "imposed outline" kind. His own books seem to validate this inference, consisting of series of a sometimes fragmentary nature.

9. David Park, "Math Production," review of S. M. Ulam, *Adventures of a Mathematician* (Scribner's, 1976) in the *Washington Post*, May 23, 1976.

10. Ruth B. Kundson, ed., *Women and Success, The Anatomy of Achievement* (Morrow, 1974), pp. 64, 71.

11. R. F. Bales, *Interaction Process Analysis: A Method for the Study of Small Groups* (Addison-Wesley, 1950).

12. Eric Berne, *Games People Play* (Grove Press, 1964).

13. Jessie Bernard, *Women and the Public Interest, An Essay on Policy and Protest* (Aldine, 1971).

14. I felt—and still do—a violent revulsion against that premature rat race. Children had to work too hard for too little psychic reward.

15. Occasionally, to be sure, I did bare my fangs. In some of the letters that make me cringe as I reread them even now, I lowered the boom. This despite the fact that I had learned long ago to control the verbal cruelty I was capable of. I had, for example, written a bruising review of a book only to learn later that before the review appeared the author had dedicated his next book to my husband. After that, so far as I know, I never used my talent for intellectual cruelty on anyone, making it a point to do the opposite. Indeed, my own letters and statements in behalf of candidates and applicants all but lost their credibility. "She always accentuates the positive," the recipient of such a letter of recommendation once said. "You'll learn all the assets and none of the liabilities. She'll tell you what a prospect can do, never what he [increasingly she] can't." Even in my reviews: "The reader has to find the defects himself."

16. This book, *Origins of American Sociology* (Crowell, 1942), appeared under co-authorship with L. L. Bernard. He contributed twenty-seven chapters, I contributed thirty-three. He had published some work on the history of sociology and I had brought it up to date in 1927 ("History and Prospects of Sociology" in George A. Lundberg and Read Bain, eds., *Trends in American Sociology* (Harper, 1927). The first of these books was reissued by Russell & Russell.

17. This book—*American Family Behavior* (Harper, 1942)—brought together the relevant research, as I saw it, as of the first three decades of the century. It dealt with many of the topics still engaging the attention of researchers and scholars. While I was then strongly under the influence of the measurement approach, there was a considerable amount of attention devoted to "rules of nonconformity," "the nature of housework"—including reports on what research there was on the effects of isolation on the housewife—the influence of the home on social stratification, among other topics of continuing concern. This book was also reissued by Russell & Russell in 1973.

18. But not article productivity.

19. The children were in college before they had an inkling of what all my writing was about. References to it in their letters were few and far between, and usually in a humorous vein. Thus David, as a freshman: "Dear Mother, I just happened to have been leafing through a copy of *Playboy* when I came across your name [in a letter solicited by the editor]. Imagine, one of the last places I would expect to. I read your letter and the reply and I just couldn't help write this fan letter to my favorite radical. To me your letter and its criticism of the . . . article seemed so tame and reasonable that I couldn't imagine that a social anarchist had been behind such a nefarious plot. Obviously, if you concede an inch to these women they will bury you. Seriously, I thought your letter was very reasonable and I found myself agreeing completely with what you said (how unusual). . . . Of course what struck me was not the label radical . . . pinned on you, but the type of . . . radical that you had become—heckler, tearer of helpless infants from the breasts of their mothers, etc. Knowing that you are a radical, but one with much more sophisticated tactics . . . I couldn't help but laugh. Your fan, David Bernard." Marketing with a friend one day, he saw flaming headlines about marriage in a national tabloid: "Good God, it must be about Mother!" he said to his friend and, indeed, it was.

20. The book referred to appeared not under the title *51 Percent* but as *Woman in Sexist Society* (Basic Books, 1971). It was edited by Vivian Gornick and Barbara Moran.

CHAPTER FIFTEEN: REPRISE

1. Leon Edel, "Biography Is . . ." *Today's Education*, December, 1972, p. 18.

2. It was only when I began to assemble the letters that a whole cache of letters the children had written to one another came to my attention. Many of them were "don't-tell-Mother" or covert letters. In a way the children conspired to protect one another—and me— against the generational differences between them and me. Since I never saw them I did not know what was going on between and among them. Most of the "covert" letters were between Claude and David. Only through them did I learn of the world they shared, a world I had had no way of knowing. Everything about it was different from the world of the "overt" letters—vocabulary, ambience, implicit understandings. I did not share it. There was a pervasive, male, freewheeling ambience of shared experience. They wrote man-to-man letters about, for example, their riotous drinking behavior; or they might write about girls; or about their financial dilemmas. The letters between Dorothy Lee and Claude traced the relationship

from one of patronizing big sister and humble little brother to one of solicitous big brother and appreciative older sister. The early letters between David and Dorothy Lee consisted to a large extent of adoring letters from David to a loving but casual sister who deigned from time to time to express her affection. Later, like all of us, David suffered from the trauma of Dorothy Lee's marriage. He telephoned her from time to time because he just couldn't allow himself to lose so much contact. (The "covert" letters are available in a document, "Sister and Brothers," in the archives of Pattee Library, the Pennsylvania State University.)

3. One reader said: "I enjoy visiting the Blanks—but only after the kids are put to bed." This statement expressed the feelings of more than one friend of the Blanks. The friends wanted to talk with the adult Blanks and not be distracted by the intrusion of the children demanding attention. They did not share the parents' indulgences which encouraged the children to be not only seen but heard, loud and clear, but also talked to, listened to, smiled at, reacted to.

4. Larry McMurty, *Washington Post,* November 24, 1975.

5. When young women tell me I am a role model for them I resist the intended accolade. A model is one who, presumably, shows how it can be done—a sort of Horatio Alger account of how to overcome obstacles. My life had not followed that pattern.

6. Claude felt I leaned over backwards in their behalf.

7. Gordon W. Allport, *The Use of Personal Documents in Psychological Science* (New York: Social Science Research Council, 1942), pp. 108–109.

8. When young women tell me I am a role model for them I resist the intended accolade. A model is one who, presumably, shows how it can be done—a sort of Horatio Alger account of how to overcome obstacles. My life had not followed that pattern.

9. Sylvia Berliner, for example, shows the depressing effect a successful role model can have on women in her lament: "Every time I come across one of these . . . articles about the successful woman of today, I am beset by feelings of self-contempt, loathing, and failure. . . . For us, the superwomen who unite marriage, career, and motherhood into a satisfying life without dropping a stitch is as oppressive a role model as the airbrushed Bunny. . . . The superwoman image is a symbol of the corruption of feminist politics. It places emphasis on a false ideal of individual success. . . . The superwoman image ignores the reality of the average working woman or housewife. It elevates an elite of upper-class women. . . . In the end . . . all it does is give women like me a sense of inferiority" ("How the Superwoman Myth Puts Women Down," *The Village Voice,* May 24, 1976.

10. Arlie Hochschild, "Making It: Marginality and Obstacles to

Minority Conscienceousness," in Rush B. Kundsin, ed., *Women and Success, The Anatomy of Achievement* (Morrow, 1974, pp. 199–100. Hochschild is one who practices what she preaches, integrating her life as a professor with her life as a mother. When her children were infants she took them to the campus with her and nursed them in her office.